WITHDRAWN

Tricksterism in Turn-of-the-Century American Literature

Tricksterism in Turn-of-the-Century American Literature

A MULTICULTURAL PERSPECTIVE

 Edited by

ELIZABETH AMMONS

ANNETTE WHITE-PARKS

TUFTS UNIVERSITY

Published by University Press of New England / Hanover and London

CALVIN T. RYAN LIBRARY
U. OF NEBRASKA AT KEARNEY

TUFTS UNIVERSITY
Published by University Press of New England, Hanover, NH 03755
© 1994 by the Trustees of Tufts University
All rights reserved
Printed in the United States of America 5 4 3 2 1
CIP data appear at the end of the book

Contents

ELIZABETH AMMONS

Introduction

Trickster disrupts.

This disruption is normal. It is part of what we know is there. Making trouble—messing up the order—is part of the order. It fits within the pattern. Referring to a description offered by Henry Louis Gates, Jr., Paula Gunn Allen explains that trickster is the presence "who is male and female, many-tongued, changeable, changing and who contains all the meanings possible within her or his consciousness."[1]

Like trickster, the purpose of this book is disruption. Most scholarship about turn-of-the-century United States literature defines the period in terms of the literary paradigms of realism, naturalism, and modernism. This volume, in contrast, places trickster at the definitional center, a concept not privileged by Eurocentric notions of the real, natural, or modern. In doing so, it suggests a significantly different perspective on late nineteenth- and early twentieth-century United States literature. Multicultural in origin, the concept of trickster offers a way of thinking about the turn of the century that brings into view authors, texts, and traditions ignored until very recently or, if mentioned, denigrated, dismissed, or misunderstood.

Perhaps the most obvious problem with the usual academic construction of turn-of-the-century American literature is its narrowness. The terms realism, naturalism, and modernism admit only a very small set of writers—as is intended, of course. Henry James and William Dean Howells, along with heirs such as Edith Wharton, Theodore Dreiser, Frank Norris, and Willa Cather, find easy access. The same cannot be said of most writers of color. It is hard, for example, to define Pauline Hopkins as a realist or naturalist, or, given her penchant for exploiting the strategies of the sentimental novel, a modernist, at least in any conventional sense. And what about Sui Sin Far? Or Alice Dunbar-Nelson? W. E. B. Du Bois? Zitkala Ša? If James and Howells (or even their forebears Harriet Beecher Stowe and Rebecca Harding Davis) determine the paradigms, then the paradigms—not surprisingly, given the homogeneity of these figures—exclude many writers.

The exclusion is not ideologically innocent. As Frederic Jameson argues, it is important for us as readers and critics to "foreground the interpretive categories or codes through which we read and receive the text in question." Articulating a position that has now become commonplace, Jameson reasons "that we never really confront a text immediately, in all its freshness as a thing-in-itself. Rather, texts come before us as the always-already read; we apprehend them through sedimented layers of previous interpretations, or—if the text is brand-new—through the sedimented reading habits and categories developed by those inherited interpretive traditions." Guiding and shaping how we read is a culturally constructed "metacommentary," a set of interpretive presuppositions that tell us how to make sense of what we take in. In particular, the standard critical question "'What does it mean?' constitutes something like an allegorical operation in which a text is systematically *rewritten* in terms of some fundamental master code." Such master codes, Jameson argues, always operate in the service of a political agenda.[2]

The master codes at work within the literary-critical terms realism, naturalism, and modernism really comprise one code. Further, the political agenda to which that code is committed is in many respects quite simple: the preservation and maintenance of elite white male power in the United States, which at the turn of the century (as is still true at this turn of the century) had everything to do with empire, dominance of others. The thought-systems shaping realists', naturalists', and modernists' perspectives consisted of many elements. But certainly paramount among those influences were the advent of contemporary western psychology, including the new theories of human sexuality and an intense focus on individual consciousness; the vigorous emergence of commodity culture capitalist economics; the impact of Social Darwinism on the new social sciences of sociology and anthropology to create, among other things, supposedly scientific bases for the alleged racial and cultural superiority of Anglo-Saxons; and the increasing power of the United States globally as an imperial ruler.

The master narrative that these forces gave rise to—that is, the fundamental, shared plot of realists, naturalists, and modernists—simply worked a variation on previous dominant culture narrative designs. Like its nineteenth-century predecessor, the typical turn-of-the-century high culture plot is privatized and individualistic. The unique experience of a unique individual (rather than the shared experience of the community) plus that unique individual's private, innermost responses to his or her experience typically constitute the prized plot of elite, modern western literature. The familiar shape this plot takes is the pitting of the individual against society, a binary opposition within a win/lose framework. The desires of the individual go up against the power of the system, and the system wins; the master plot performs the victory of state authority. A protagonist/antagonist relationship governs the battle between the rebellious, unruly desires of an individual and the coercive, controlling power of the corporate system or state, which is hierarchically organized to force the individual into obedience. This master plot inspires classic texts of American realism from James's *Portrait of a Lady* (1881) to Chopin's *The Awakening* (1899) to Cather's *The Professor's House* (1925); works of American naturalists from Crane's *Maggie* (1893) to Johnson's *Autobiography of an Ex-Coloured Man* (1912); and masterpieces of American modernism from Stein's *Three Lives* (1905–1906) to Faulkner's *Sound and the Fury* (1929). Finding ways to complicate this basic individual-against-society plot—disguising and altering its fundamental repetitions—often represents the major narrative challenge. But the skeleton remains intact. Regardless of the particulars of the individual's resistance to hierarchical authority, that resistance ends with the individual overpowered, brought into line, controlled by the superior authority of the state/system/group. Whether for texts or for authors, in their individual lives and careers, the plot articulates a binary opposition wherein there is no inhabitable territory outside white, patriarchal, hegemonic authority. One conforms, goes mad, or dies. In any case one fits in, or is cast out. Vertical power based on authority and submission stands at the heart of the master plot.

Trickster offers a different plot. As the essays in this book suggest, embodied in trickster and trickster energy is a principle of human rebellion and resistance that exists both within a protagonist/antagonist framework *and* within a totally different context, one in which the disruly—the transgressive—is accepted as part of the community's life. Individual desire and group authority cohabit within a network or web of relations; the dynamic is one of interaction rather than dominance and submission.

The essays in this volume consider many different tricksters, manifestations of trickster energy, and strategies of tricksterism. Included are discussions of diverse writers: Sui Sin Far, Zitkala Ša, María Cristina Mena, Frances Ellen Harper, Charles Chesnutt, Winnifred Eaton (who used the pen name Onoto Watanna), Alex Posey (who published under the name Chinnubbie Harjo), Frank Norris, Mourning Dove, L. V. McWhorter, and several unnamed Native American tellers of traditional tales recorded by white listeners. Likewise, the United States literary traditions treated are various: Asian American, African American, Mexican American, European American, and Native American. This heterogeneity of texts, writers, and traditions precludes simplistic generalizing, which is part of our point.

Another part of our point, however, is the shared ground that emerges across cultures and among many women writers in the United States when trickster becomes the focus. The concept changes significantly depending on context, culture, author, and text. Esu, Coyote, Rabbit, Monkey, La Malinche, Mrs. Spring Fragrance, Uncle Julius—and the list continues; each differs from the other. Inspiring almost all of the discussions in this volume, though, are certain fundamental questions. What are the possibilities and strategies for self-assertion, self-definition, and voice for the writer who is a person of color in a racist, imperial context? How does a writer occupying a liminal position—as does trickster—survive? How does one negotiate the power relations between group and individual desires? How especially does a woman do this? Perhaps most urgent, how is it possible even to conceptualize multiculturality and the preservation of vital, self-empowering cultural differences (as opposed to museumification) within a political environment committed, at the least, to racial and ethnic discrimination and, at the most, genocide?

Although not the only such concept, tricksterism is especially useful for analysis that seeks to cross cultural boundaries without relying on dominant culture maps. David M. Abrams and Brian Sutton-Smith discuss the importance of cross-cultural differences among tricksters, pointing out, for example, how African tricksters contrast with their African American counterparts "in being greedy and mercenary rather than promiscuous and obscene, and the clever Afro-American trickster is rarely portrayed as the clumsy, self-defeating clown of some of the Indian tales." Then they observe: "For this reason, perhaps, Levi-Strauss sees the trickster as reflecting a more logically sophisticated level of culture that can create a mediating character in response to the perception of contradictions in a belief system."[3] This function of complex mediation between and among conflicting value systems plays a major role in the appeal—indeed, the necessity—of tricksterism and trickster tales for many of the authors discussed in this volume. Living and writing between worlds, in the phrase of Amy Ling,[4] they are constantly challenged to resist ghettoization and silencing and find ways to write from borderland territories of cultural connection and clash. Indeed, for a majority, John W. Roberts's analysis of trickster tales' psychological and political utility for slaves provides an analogue. Roberts theorizes that "despite their importance as models of behavior, the animal trickster tales of enslaved Africans were not intended to provide a literal guide for actions in everyday life, but rather served as an expressive mechanism for transmitting a perception of cleverness, guile, and wit as the most advantageous behavioral options for dealing with the power of the slavemasters in certain generic situations."[5]

The complex relationship between trickster strategies, tales, and energies on the one hand and hegemonic white patriarchal power in the United

States on the other defines a recurrent theme in this book. It is not simply a matter of trickster strategies being subversive, a perspective that, as Paula Gunn Allen and Henry Louis Gates, Jr., argue, merely reinscribes white power at the center of discourse. If subversion is the sole purpose of a narrative or of an author's choices, then the whole project of that narrative or author remains totally defined in terms of the dominant culture's power and presence. As Paula Gunn Allen explains, "to my Indian eyes it is plain that subversion cannot be the purpose or goal for women of color who write, though it likely is a side effect of our creating, our transforming, our rite. . . . Subversion, diffidence, and acceptance of self as marginal are processes that maim our art and deflect us from our purpose. They are enterprises that support and maintain the master, feeding his household on our energy, our attention, and our strength."[6] Trickster strategies are not just a way to get "in" or "back at" the dominant culture. Tricksters and trickster energy articulate a whole other, independent, cultural reality and positive way of negotiating multiple cultural systems.

Because trickster won't be contained, trickster strategies and tales provide a way of pulling together conflicting world views and sets of values into coherent, new identity. This identity is turbulent, shape-changing, contradictory, "bad," culturally central, liminal, powerful, power-interrogating. It is a place to be in and of itself, and for itself—an authentic, age-old location that is not western-dominated, where the artist, especially the artist who is a person of color or a white woman, can envision and maneuver. It is a place located and constantly reinventable in cultural borderlands or even in a space totally outside white patriarchal authority. This is probably why so many women writers are represented in this book. Freedom to see and speak is the issue.

In approaching and defining tricksters and tricksterism variously, some essays in this volume function relatively familiarly, analyzing ways in which well-known traditional tricksters such as Coyote, Iktomi, or African American conjurers operate in particular literary texts. Others self-consciously depart from convention by providing new readings of figures such as La Llorona and La Malinche or investigating African American folk characters' covert expression of trickster themes. Still others approach the concept of trickster completely innovatively, interpreting a range of authorial strategies of cultural intervention and survival as manifestations of trickster energy. One goal of this volume is to suggest and demonstrate a flexibility and adventuresomeness—neither being alien to trickster, of course—in approach, method, and style.

At the same time, all of the writers in this volume ground their discussions in particular, named, cultural practices, histories, and values. Tricksterism is not proposed as a culturally indiscriminate concept. It is always attached to specific, identified group realities and traditions, no matter how flexibly deployed or surprisingly redefined. To do otherwise is to dilute beyond usefulness or recognition a paradigm that the contributors to this volume all agree must be rooted in culturally specific analysis. Tricksterism is not simply one brand of ethnic chic, to be ripped out (off) of particular cultural contexts and applied willy-nilly, regardless of an author's heritage or political context, to any and every text one wishes. Respect for cultural origins and differences and acknowledgment of crucial power relations such as those institutionalized in racism and sexism are imperative. Equally problematic, however, are attempts at trickster purism, arguments claiming that only traditional, conventional definitions and usages are admissible. The essence of tricksterism is change, contradiction, adaptation, surprise. Between the extremes of irresponsible aculturality on the one hand and fossilizing purism on the other lies a territory, examined in this book, we hope, in which traditional tricksters and contemporary, innovative concepts of tricksterism can meet to illuminate certain kinds of cultural productions. We are concerned here with turn-of-the-century writers and texts that have too often or for too long been neglected.

Of certain Indian trickster tales Andrew Wiget points out: "Many stories suggest that the very attempt to impose order and structure on human experience is laughably presumptuous." As Wiget goes on to explain, "Trickster functions not so much to call cultural categories into question as to demonstrate the artificiality of culture itself. Thus he makes available for discussion the very basis of social order, individual and communal identity."[7] Participating in trickster—which means drawing on various diverse cultural traditions *and* inventing new ones out of the intersections of their own lives—the authors discussed in the following pages and the authors discussing those authors, the contributors to this volume, invite us into just such a discussion of the bases of culture and the constitution of individual and communal identity in the United States.

Notes

1. Paula Gunn Allen, "'Border' Studies: The Intersection of Gender and Color," *Introduction to Scholarship in Modern Languages and Literature,* ed. Joseph Gibaldi (New York: Modern Language Association of America, 1992), p. 307. Allen refers to Gates's discussion of the Yoruba trickster Esu in *The Signifying Monkey: A Theory of African-American Literary Criticism* (New York: Oxford University Press, 1988).

2. Frederic Jameson, *The Political Unconscious: Narrative as a Socially Symbolic Act* (Ithaca, N.Y.: Cornell University Press, 1981), pp. 9, 58, 20.

3. "The Development of the Trickster in Children's Narrative," *Journal of American Folklore* 90 (Oct.–Dec. 1977): 30.

4. Amy Ling, *Between Worlds: Women Writers of Chinese Ancestry* (New York: Pergamon Press, 1990).

5. John W. Roberts, *From Trickster to Badman: The Black Folk Hero in Slavery and Freedom* (Philadelphia: University of Pennsylvania Press, 1989), pp. 37–38.

6. Allen, pp. 311, 312. See also Gates, "Ethnic and Minority Studies," *Introduction to Scholarship*, pp. 298–300.

7. "His Life in His Tail: The Native American Trickster and the Literature of Possibility," *Redefining American Literary History*, eds. A. LaVonne Brown Ruoff and Jerry W. Ward, Jr. (New York: Modern Language Association of America, 1990), pp. 91, 94.

Tricksterism in Turn-of-the-Century American Literature

ANNETTE WHITE-PARKS

"We Wear the Mask": Sui Sin Far as One Example of Trickster Authorship[1]

In his poem "We Wear the Mask" (1896),[2] Paul Laurence Dunbar evokes the image of disguise, deceit, and ambiguity implied in masking to describe a strategy African Americans of the late nineteenth century used to survive under oppressive Jim Crow conditions. At the same time, Dunbar metaphorically reveals the process of his own poetry and highlights trickster strategies that writers, especially those whom society persecutes and excludes, have used across time to endure both in life and as artists: "We wear the mask that grins and lies/It hides our cheeks and shades our eyes." For such writers this business of tricksterism, or wearing a mask, signifies vastly more than just literary antics or aesthetic techniques. As Dunbar well knew, what is revealed to a given audience makes the difference in whether or not one survives.

Among these writers, and publishing contemporarily with Dunbar, was a woman of Chinese-English parentage, christened Edith Maude Eaton but known by her family and in the stories she signed between 1896 and 1913 as Sui Sin Far.[3] From my first acquaintance with Sui Sin Far's work, especially in efforts to get it reprinted, I encountered the question that Jane Tompkins has framed: "But Is It Any Good?" (pp. 186–187). Because Sui Sin Far was, inasmuch as is known, the first Asian American to write from an inside perspective in North America, and because she opened windows into the world of Chinese American families, especially women and children, otherwise sealed under the stereotype of "bachelor society," this question astonished me. Wasn't the mere fact of this writer's existence enough? Researching the implications here led to a further perplexity: How had Sui Sin Far, a woman of Chinese descent who used her writings to defend Chinese North Americans during an era of severe abuse and exclusion of people of Chinese descent throughout Canada and the United States where she worked, managed to get published originally? The examination of both questions demanded close work with style and led me into a whole world of trickster figures and strategies, leading in turn to the hypothesis that Sui Sin Far devised certain strategies to write against the dominant racial and cultural ideologies of her time, strategies fully dependent on tricksterism. This essay illustrates some of my findings from selected Sui Sin Far works. More broadly, I suggest that Sui Sin Far is not alone in these strategies, that she shares the trickster manipulation of style—Dunbar's "masking"—with other women and ethnic minority men who were writing and finding print in publishing houses and magazines at the turn from the nineteenth to the twentieth century.

Some attention to historical grounding illuminates trickster concepts in context. Referring to the trickster as "originating in the most psychologically primitive strata of the human mind," as Paul Rodin argues, and citing Carl Jung, who sees the trickster as "an archetypal psychic structure of extreme antiquity," William Bright describes the figure Coyote as "extremely archaic," and, though most commonly recognized in American Indian legend, as "the archetypal trickster known from literature all over the world" (p. 375). By linking the "trickster's constant quest for food" under the faminelike conditions of Africa to trickster quests portrayed in African American folk tales under the starvation conditions of slavery, John W. Roberts offers one example of the roots tricksters in North American literature tap globally (p. 25). From the time when Coyote is said to have preserved speech for the animals, tricksterism has been connected with language, particularly with the power to create or deceive by the word.

Although Bright claims that Coyote is "always male" (p. 342), in his study of Native American tricksters Andrew Wiget argues that such an assumption may result from "a peculiar bias in the collection of . . . stories"—males usually did the collecting and talked to male storytellers—that "stories [feature] both male and female tricksters . . ." and that "Trickster can be imagined as either sex" (p. 89). That women are deft at the arts of playing tricks for survival is dramatically illustrated in an example closely related to Sui Sin Far as a woman of Chinese descent: "Nushu," a secret language traced legendarily to the Song Dynasty in China (960–1279 A.D.). Nushu is said to have originated when a girl who was taken as a concubine to the Imperial Palace devised "a secret code to communicate to her sister back home without the messenger or the Emperor's spies being able to read what she wrote" (Li Hui, p. 11).[4] Remaining alive through the centuries, Nushu contains about 800 words and has been passed down from mother to daughter orally, in books, or on cloth embroidery. Described by Li Hui as "a system of writing created for and used exclusively by some rural women in a few mountain villages in China," Nushu was used by women both to enter a world of story-communication they were denied by formal education and to express emotional ties among women who became "sworn sisters." Thus, the practice of Nushu illustrates how tricksterism can become a survival strategy through which oppressed groups or individuals may attain a certain degree of personal and political autonomy within the restrictions of an oppressive dominant system.

Similarly, the modern trickster figure can be said to grow out of a political system that oppresses certain cultures and—for purposes here—out of the exclusion and persecution of women and ethnic minority male writers in Canada and the United States, in particular. In this sense, American tricksterism becomes a style unique to a culture, conceived and developed by the makers of literature from the earliest oral pieces[5] forward, as a means of achieving voice and visibility in a context of oppression, even of overturning the established hegemony—and without those in power being the wiser.[6] In this sense, trickster stylistics testify to the irony that Mary Dearborn suggests, that the trickster "can, through language, assert the ultimate authority of language against authorities that forbid it" (p. 28). As a writer pushed to the social margins in terms of race, class, and gender, who had to survive in a world of contradictions and find strategies to get published, Sui Sin Far was a natural for trickster methods.

Born in 1865 in Macclesfield, England, of a Chinese mother and English father, Sui Sin Far entered the world between two warring cultures and learned at an early age to survive by the "myriad subtleties" to which Dunbar refers. It may have been at a children's party in England, when the writer recalls being "called from my play by the hostess for purposes of inspection," that she first learned the need to sort aspects of herself into various compartments. The adult author remembers a "white haired old man" adjusting his eyeglasses and exclaiming, "Ah, indeed! . . . now I see the difference between her and other children"—at which point she hid herself "behind a hall door until it was time to go home" ("Leaves," p. 126). When, as a schoolgirl, Sui Sin Far migrated with her family to New York, hiding her Chinese ancestry became armor against physical violence. That Lotus Blossom, the Chinese mother, was usually kept out of sight is implied when Sui Sin Far and her brother are beat up by another boy on the New York streets, and Sui Sin Far offers this chilling reason: he "lives near us and has seen my mother" ("Leaves," p. 126).

The young girl's first decision to consciously "mask" or subdivide her personality is recalled by the adult author as having occurred in Montréal, where the family eventually settled and where Sui Sin Far, with her siblings, was forced to leave school at age eleven to help "earn my living." In defense against the drudgery, humiliation, and recalled dangers of "tramping around" Montréal streets to sell her father's paintings and the lace she designed and crocheted herself, Sui Sin Far describes dividing her life into two perspectives:

I, now in my 11th year, entered into two lives, one devoted entirely to family concerns; the other, a withdrawn life of thought and musing. This withdrawn life of thought probably took the place of ordinary education with me. I had six keys to it; one, a great capacity for feeling; another, the key of imagination; third, the key of physical pain; fourth, the key of sympathy; fifth, the sense of being differentiated from the ordinary by the fact that I was an Eurasian; sixth, the impulse to create. ("Sui Sin Far," p. 6)

This division of personalities, explicitly outlined in the writer's consciousness at age eleven, laid the dual vision that would underlie Sui Sin Far's approach to both life and art. Revealing selected portions of truth and camouflaging the rest served her in everything from playing games to relieve boredom—as a legislative reporter in Jamaica, the writer reveals that she "used to look down from the press gallery upon the heads of the honorable members and think a great many things which I refrained from putting into my report" (*Globe,* p. 6)—to crossing international borders in an age when a $500 Head Tax was charged to all Chinese immigrants who wished to enter Canada, while the United States, with a few exceptions, excluded Chinese entirely.[7] As a woman of Chinese descent who traveled broadly in countries that practiced indenture—a grand-niece of Sui Sin Far states that Lotus Blossom warned her children not to tell anyone they were Chinese lest they be sold into "coolie labor" (Eileen Lewis interview)—Sui Sin Far knew that masks were more than a game; they spelled basic survival. As a woman of English descent who looked European, shifting disguises (which was "the mask" and which "the real thing"?) were readily accessible and part of her training.

From the earliest located pieces—journalism, essays, and fiction—trickster skills define Sui Sin Far's literature. "The Origin of a Broken Nose," published in 1899 in the *Canadian Dominion Illustrated,* bylined "Edith Eaton" and preceding her Chinese emphasis by half a decade, caricatures a young English Canadian who, acting on advice to "gallant youths" from the evening newspaper, stations himself at an icy street corner, looking for an "unfortunate maiden" whom he can "rescue." When a girl happens along who fits his dream image, the narrator "sprang toward her"—only to slip and break his nose, while she gets "past the perilous place in safety"—then turns and rescues him (p. 302). Using a technique that will become a hallmark in her Chinese North American fictions—setting up images she sees as false (that men perform heroic deeds, while women wait helplessly), then bowling them over—Sui Sin Far overturns the romantic rhetoric of her era to show that popularized sex roles are in practice ridiculous.

The skills at reversing unjust but socially accepted images that aided Sui Sin Far in her fictional battle with stereotypes appear also in her journalism—where she frequently plays at what I call "hiding out in the open." An unsigned newspaper article that came out during the years when Sui Sin Far was, in her words, "fighting the battles of the Chinese in the papers" ("Leaves," p. 129) from her Montréal office directly addressed a subject we know to have been central to her life and sense of identity: the children of Chinese-white parentage whom society labeled "Eurasian." Entitled "Half-Chinese Children: Those of American Mothers and Chinese Fathers," the article appeared in the *Montreal Daily Star* in 1895. Both content and style suggest Sui Sin Far as its writer. The article tells of the children of Chinese-white parentage in New York, where "the white people with whom they come in contact . . . jibe and jeer at the poor little things continually, and their pure and unadulterated Chinese cousins look down on them as being neither Chinese nor white." Both language and attitudes foreshadow the ambiguous racial traits that Sui Sin Far would claim, in her autobiographical "Leaves from the Mental Portfolio of an Eurasian" fourteen years later, that people saw in the faces of herself and her siblings: "There is occasionally to be seen a half Chinese child with bright complexion and fair hair . . . but a person who has been informed of the child's parentage notices at once a peculiar cast about the face . . ." ("Half-Chinese Children," p. 4). As with the Eaton siblings, in the news story the children's "peculiar cast" calls forth "mocking cries of 'Chinese' 'Chinese' " and gives rise to street fights waged by "white" children with whom they come into contact.

Further evidence that Sui Sin Far authored the news story comes from a comparison between the story and the fiction "Sweet Sin," published by Sui Sin Far in 1898. Scenes in both highlight the Eurasian children's reactions to white people who patronize them. Here is the dialogue as it appears in the news story:

> "Mamma, I'm not going to see Mrs. G— today."
>
> "Why not?" said the mother, "she is always so kind to you and gives you more toys than you know what to do with."
>
> "Yes," said the child, "but I don't care for the toys. It is just because I'm Chinese that she likes to have me there. When I'm in her parlor she whispers to some people about me, and then they try to make me talk and pick up all that I say, and I hear them whisper 'her father's a Chinese' 'Did you know' 'Isn't it curious' and they examine me from head to toe as if I was a wild animal—and just because father is a Chinese. I'd rather be dead than a show." (p. 4)[8]

Here is the dialogue as it appears in "Sweet Sin," after the child tells her mother she does not want to go to "Mrs. Goodwin's party tonight":

> "Why not?" queried the mother. "I'm surprised, she is so kind to you."
>
> "I do not think so," replied Sweet Sin, "and I don't want her toys and candies. It's just because I'm half Chinese and a sort of curiosity that she likes to have me

there. When I'm in her parlor, she examines me from head to toe as if I were a wild animal—I'd rather be dead than be a show." (p. 224)

A clue to the origin of both pieces may be found in Sui Sin Far's recollection in "Leaves" of a visit to her office by "a Chinese scholar," the graduate of "an American College," who has "an American wife and several children": "I am very much interested in these children, and when I meet them my heart throbs in sympathetic tune with the tales they relate of their experiences as Eurasians. 'Why did papa and mamma born us?' asks one. 'Why?'" (p. 128). Only the quotation marks offer guidance to where the voice of these children leaves off and Sui Sin Far's voice begins—albeit reversing the roles of "American" mother and "Chinese" father and setting the anecdote not in Montréal but New York. For children of Chinese-white parentage, the reporter implies, which side of the border one lives on makes little difference.

By thus disguising—or masking—her own life in her work, Sui Sin Far was able to abstract the experience of herself and her siblings to Eurasians in general, to communicate their situation to the public, and to insert an empathetic tone into news publications that ran counter to the prevailing attitudes of her era. A year previous to this article, in 1894, the *Montreal Daily Star* headlined an interview with two wives of Chinese Montréal merchants and one "girl slave," together described as "the only three [Chinese] females in Montreal." The piece was bylined simply, "a lady reporter." Combining the content and tone of these articles with knowledge of Sui Sin Far's life at this moment again leads to the conclusion that Sui Sin Far was the writer. First, the articles give sympathetic and humanizing accounts of Chinese Montréalers—in contrast to the stereotypical and abusive accounts from other reporters that filled the papers. Second, the articles coincide with the dates, from 1894 to 1897, when Sui Sin Far had her own office as a free-lance journalist. Third, they offer examples of the "Chinese reporting" she was receiving from Montréal newspapers and "the battles" she describes "fighting . . . [for] the Chinese in the papers" ("Leaves," p. 128).

Because in the nineteenth century a career in journalism for women was considered, in the words of Susan Crean, "quite as improper as going on the stage" (*Newsworthy*, p. 16) and unknown writers of either gender were not allowed bylines, disguise was a natural, a discreet bit of camouflage reinforced by a media where fact and fiction, as they concerned persecuted and exotically depicted Chinese minorities, were barely distinguishable. That Sui Sin Far recognized the smudging of fact–fiction lines allowed her to play tongue in cheek with the knowledge that, had her reading audience known about her, her mother, and her eight sisters, "the only three

[Chinese] females in Montreal" cited in "Only Two Women from the Flowery Land in Town" would have taken a quick leap to ten. In addition, because statistics for persecuted immigrants cannot be relied on, a fact even more true for females than males, we really have no idea how many Chinese women were in Montréal at the dates Sui Sin Far was writing.[9]

Such "myriad subtleties," in which Sui Sin Far shuffles "facts" between stories and enters or exits at will, show up in her writings much as Alfred Hitchcock shows up in his movies—anonymously, in masquerade as a character, and invisible to an audience that does not know the difference. They form a common thread among journalism, essays, and short stories across her career. One of her first signed essays, "The Chinese Woman in America" (1897), was published in the southern California magazine *Land of Sunshine*—for a California audience, with the implication that it was about Chinese women in California. What gives this piece added interest is that Sui Sin Far signed it from Montréal, and many of its details parallel details of the 1894 interview with the Montréal merchants' wives.[10] Were her subjects, perhaps, the same women who were interviewed for the earlier article? In the sense that, as far as is known, Sui Sin Far had neither lived in the United States nor visited the West Coast prior to 1897 when "The Chinese Woman in America" was published, the piece is a tour de force. Yet, whatever the extent of her acquaintance with Chinese immigrant women in any part of North America during this period, Sui Sin Far was able to identify with them in her writing because, at certain key junctures, she shared their experience. If she could not speak as an immigrant woman from China, she could speak as the daughter of a woman who had immigrated into the western world in an era when it was said—in both England and Canada—that no Chinese women were there, and she could speak as a woman of Chinese descent who had migrated from England to North America at a time when Chinese North Americans were being most cruelly maligned. Certainly she knew that white North Americans made no geographical distinctions when it came to racist laws and practices against Chinese North Americans. Regardless of her infidelity to facts on the outside, the trickster carries a truth of her own.

In their study "The Feminist Voice: Strategies of Coding in Folklore and Literature," Joan Rodner and Susan Lanser talk about coding: "a system of signals . . . that protects the creator . . . in the context of complex audiences, in situations where some of the audience may be competent to decode the message, but others . . . are not" (p. 414). These critics cite Susan Glaspell's "A Jury of Her Peers" as exemplary: After a woman is arrested for murder, two other women are able to "decode" the message in the quilt blocks in her basket, while the men present, including the sheriff and district attorney, overlook such evidence as insignificant. Sui Sin Far uses such coding—partly, as Bright describes for Coyote, "out of impulse, or appetite, or for the pure joy of trickery" (p. 349), but also as a means to survive under the mask of an English woman, while still becoming a voice for the Chinese North Americans with whom she identifies at an integral level.

Sui Sin Far's ongoing pattern of transmitting the voice of current experiences in her life through situations and characters in her writings shows itself with playful subterfuge in a series of articles entitled "Wing Sing of Los Angeles and His Travels." In this series, "Wing Sing" is identified as "the pen name of a well-known Americanized merchant . . . [who] recently left Los Angeles to . . . visit his old home in China, going by way of Montreal." Wing Sing takes the reader on this indirect route (the same Sui Sin Far used herself), going by steamship and rail to San Francisco and Vancouver, then by the "one big train name Canadian Pacific . . . to railway station, Montreal." Upon Wing Sing's arrival in Montréal the visitor observes: "The Chinese lily, the Chinaman call the Sui Sin Far, it bloom in the house of the Chinese at this time and its fragrance greet me like a friend." Furthermore, as a Chinese American tourist, Wing Sing goes to "pay my respects to the Gambling Cash Tiger"—a "god" repeatedly referred to in Sui Sin Far's fiction, but for which I have found no source anywhere else.[11] The series appeared in the *Los Angeles Express* from February 4 to March 9, 1904—dates after Sui Sin Far had worked for the *Express,* and spanning the time period when she claimed to be writing a "series of articles" for the Los Angeles paper from Montréal, during a visit back to see her family. Added to the fact that no other articles have been found in the *Express* with Sui Sin Far's byline between these dates, these clues almost certainly mark the coy path of the trickster, and lead me to believe that Sui Sin Far and Wing Sing are the same writer.

"Wing Sing" is a striking example of how essential it is to have some knowledge of context when trying to uncover the trickster's numerous masks—only an audience familiar with the author's travel patterns, earlier literature, and the subtleties of her nomenclature could spot the landmarks above. Using her own byline, but following a similar pattern, the previous year Sui Sin Far had introduced "Chinatown Boys and Girls," one in a series of articles she was writing about Los Angeles Chinatown for the *Express,* with this preface: "A Chinese mother says the following verses are her daughter's":

Hast thou forgotten fairyland,
The maze of golden light
The flower-gemmed bowers,
The crystal founts,
The skies forever bright—

Save when the evening shadows crept
Athwart the roseal blue,
And the pale moon whispered to the sun,
"Say to the earth, Adieu!"

While it is not stated explicitly, the implication is that this "daughter" belongs to a Chinatown family in Los Angeles in 1903. Only the reader familiar with Sui Sin Far throughout her career would recognize that, thirteen years earlier (in 1890), "Edith Eaton" had published these same lines in the *Canadian Dominion Illustrated* in an essay entitled "In Fairyland." By reading both pieces, we are made aware that Sui Sin Far was the "daughter" to whom the *Express* article referred as composing these verses, implying that Sui Sin Far's mother, Lotus Blossom, was the described "Chinese mother."

Such word play, again, may be for mischief or for fun or for the "pure joy of trickery." Simultaneously, though, I would argue that trickster methods allowed Sui Sin Far—a child of four countries who felt always on the borderland between national and racial identities, and whose sense of exile equaled that of the Chinese North American community about whom she wrote—under the mask of her art, to code herself as a member of that community.[12] In another article for the *Express,* "Leung Ki Chu and His Wife," Sui Sin Far features a woman in literal exile, the wife of the Chinese reformer who, for the sake of her physical safety, has been sent to live in Japan. Envisioning this woman's plight, Sui Sin Far imagines her voice: "Those who believe in ideals and hero-worship may picture her—when her children are in bed and her husband over the sea—stretching her arms Chinaward and crying:

'Oh, China, misguided country!
What would I not sacrifice
to see thee uphold thyself,
among the nations?'"

In this apostrophe summoned from over the ocean, Sui Sin Far creates a double, another woman with whom she may share the dream of restoration for a lost homeland. Interestingly, the identical words reappear nine years later in a 1912 Sui Sin Far short fiction, "Chen Hen Yen, Chinese Student," as part of an essay promoting his homeland written by the Chinese student Chen Hen Yen (p. 464).

The journalistic pieces examined here reveal a trickster stance in Sui Sin Far's writings that evolves in complexity when interacting with fictional plots. "The Story of Tin-a" was published in 1899, the year of Sui Sin Far's first trip to southern California, and the narrator who reports Tin-a's tale is described as a southern California traveler: "I had been riding many miles; and feeling tired and hungry, I dismounted and knocked at the cottage door" (p. 101). The traveler is invited into a room from which her or his eyes "stray over the garden" and spot the recently immigrated Chinese woman, Tin-a, bending over a large bush of scented geranium. With the questions "Who was she? Why was she living here?" the traveler invites Tin-a to share breakfast and describes drawing "her out to talk of herself, and here gives the story as she related it." Because of the reader's conditioned responses to gender roles and fictional formulas, it is easy to suppose that this traveler is male. But neither distinguishing pronouns nor evidence support this assumption. Because Sui Sin Far's first trip to California is dated at 1898, the author herself could easily have been the "traveler" who narrates the story—and who is giving us an inside, playful glimpse of the storyteller at work. Tin-a's liberated spirit and the intense bond of friendship between Tin-a and a friend back in China are pivotal themes of the story. The young woman has fled from her father in China with a troupe of traveling actors, to escape the arranged marriage that would make her second wife to the husband of her best friend. In an era of Yellow Peril literature, when most writers of the western world portrayed Chinese women as passive victims, the character of Tin-a emerges as an exception, reflecting the ingenuity, perseverance, and courage that will become hallmarks of Sui Sin Far's female characters—and indeed of the author herself.

Such play with audience expectations intertwines with motifs of disguise and deceit to overturn socially assigned reality at every level in Sui Sin Far's fiction; it raises the question, "Which is the mask?" We see this question raised in "The Story of Tin-a," when the troupe of actors overturns such verities as female and male, youth and age: "The female characters were taken by boys, and an old man was represented by a youth wearing a false beard; another youth with a shrill voice played the part of an old woman" (p. 102). We see it raised in "Lin John," when the story's main character saves $300 to "rescue" his sister from prostitution, only to have the money stolen by someone who approaches with "stealthy step," and slips the bag of gold from Lin John's sleeve. The reader only learns later that the thief is Lin John's own sister—who likes her life as a prostitute better than what her brother has planned for her—an arranged marriage. We see it in "A Chinese Boy-Girl," when the naive reader is trapped along with the mission teacher Miss Mason into believing the son a Chinese American father sends to school in disguise is really a girl—a misconception we get caught in largely because of our gender- and culture-bound expectations for boy and girl modes of behavior; that is, to "run wild on the streets" is acceptable for a boy, but not for a girl (p. 829). We see it in "The Smuggling of Tie Co," with the confusion of the Chinese Canadian men in a Montréal laundry who cannot understand how a body "found with Tie Co's face and dressed in Tie Co's clothes" could belong to "a girl—a woman" (p. 104).

At this point we realize what has been long suspected: In Sui Sin Far's imaginative vision, tricksterism and masking are not stylistic details; they are central to the world of her plots. This integration of trickster methods with the structure and themes of a story is well illustrated in a short fiction of 1898, "The Sing-Song Woman," which presents two Chinese American women with opposing views about their national and racial preferences: Mag-gee, a "half-white girl" who wants to marry an Irish American and stay in the United States but whose father arranges for her to marry "a Chinaman" who will take her to China; and Lae Choo, "a despised actress in an American Chinatown" who feels stuck in the United States and dreams of returning to her life as "a fisherman's daughter on the Chinese Sea." As the "fair head and dark head" are depicted drawing "near together" plotting "a play," the doubling between the two characters is visually symbolized. The motif of disguise is as central to plot as it was to the author's life every time she crossed borders. However, whereas Sui Sin Far as a "Eurasian" must masquerade as "white," the Eurasian Mag-gee is forced by her father to masquerade as "Chinese." To this end, Mag-gee is portrayed in the costume of "red paint, white powder and carmine lip salve" with which Chinese women were stereotyped at the turn-of-the-century. The narrator looks at Mag-gee's mask, though, askance; it is described as "besmeared over a naturally pretty face," over which, when Mag-gee cries, the paint runs "in little red rivers." Lae Choo joins the masquerade by disguising herself as the bride and going through the wedding ceremony as a stand-in for Mag-gee, who escapes with her Irish lover. "It is but a play like the play I shall act here tomorrow," Lae Choo tells Le Keang, the groom—who, when the veil is lifted, discovers he has wed the wrong woman. Masks disappear and all tricks are resolved when Mag-gee stays in America eating "potatoes and beef" with the "white man" she loves, while Le Keang returns with Lae Choo to China, assuring the actress "Hush! . . . you shall act no more." In the fictional context, masks, commonly seen as "unreal," are used to break through to a more desirable reality for the individuals involved. Moreover, for Lae Choo and Mag-gee, "masking" becomes a means of exchanging the expectations of the patriarchy—that women marry the men whom men choose and behave as men want—for their own choices over their lives. Appropriately, then, and contrary to conventional assumptions that males corner the market on tricksterism, Sui Sin Far's tricksters are usually female—and very skillful at turning the tables on men in all aspects of life.

Throughout Sui Sin Far's corpus, the pattern repeats itself: The author teases us by presenting situations and characters that appear to fit stereotypes, then does a flip that we miss if we are not reading closely. And it is usually in that undefinable space between where a word departs and lands that political matters are addressed, for they are rarely explicit. Consequently, just as a South African mother may compose revolutionary songs in the guise of love ballads, the most ideologically radical themes slip by unnoticed. In Sui Sin Far's mature fiction the playful style mixes with scathing ambiguities, as the author juxtaposes a sugary simplicity against some of the day's most potent racial injustices. Among the many examples that illustrate this is "Pat and Pan," a short story whose most clever masking may be that it was placed in the children's section of Sui Sin Far's book-length collection, *Mrs. Spring Fragrance*. For while its major subjects are children, the themes of knowledge and innocence explored here are not limited to a child audience, but probe the depths of adult-created intercultural nightmares.

Nothing could be sweeter than the portrait with which this story opens, as the two children—Pat, a "white boy," age five, and Pan, a "Chinese girl," age three—are framed in the entry to a Chinatown joss house: "Her tiny face . . . hidden upon his bosom, and his white upturned chin rest[ing] upon her black, rosetted head." Painted in the language of fairy tales, this is a cameo of races in harmony, but the narrator does not let it last long. For—in the third sentence—it is exactly "that white chin that caused the passing Mission woman to pause and look again at the little pair." Amazed, she questions a lichi vendor—a Chinese girl and white boy intimately positioned together? It cannot be happening—and learns, as do we, the audience, that Pat's dying white mother gave him as a baby to her Chinese friends, the Lum Yooks, to raise. Edenic motifs continue as the Mission woman—with a name as virginally white as Alicia's blonde hair, Anna Harrison—purchases lichis, which she offers as a lure to the children. Pan is smarter than Eve, though. Not eating directly, she feeds her companion until he is full, "Whereupon the little girl tasted herself of the fruit." Implications of danger intensify as the Chinese mother, Ah Ma (perhaps having experienced Mission women before, or knowing their wiles through her neighbors), runs out and calls in her children. Described as a "sleek-haired, kindly-faced matron in dark blue pantalettes and tunic," the mother receives affectionate obedience from her eldest, as demonstrated when Pat "jumped up with a merry laugh" and ran toward her.

The Mission woman will not give up, though; this we know, not only from having read other Sui Sin Far stories in which she is stockly "the snake," but because we have heard her protest to the lichi vendor: "But he is white!" We have seen her shock as the children wake and chat in the private language tricksters are famous for ("Ho'm Ho?" "Ho! ho!"). We have had our eyes guided by hers toward the entrance of the joss house, to imagine the unseen "heathen" rituals practiced inside. And somewhere in the space between image and idea, form and content, what alarms Mrs. Lum Yook alarms us. Anna Harrison is after her children. This, of course, is the established job of a Mission woman. But in the case of Pat and Pan, there arises a further complexity. Anna Harrison's task is not only to win the soul of a child who is Chinese, but to reclaim that of a child who is white.

Thus when, in scene two, Anna Harrison opens "her school for White and Chinese children in Chinatown," it is with the determination that Pat shall "learn to speak his mother tongue." And when Mr. Lum Yook agrees that his son should "learn the speech of his ancestors," contrary attitudes between English- and non-English-speaking American cultures toward language are clearly expressed. Having no interest in Pan except as a decoy, Anna Harrison seats the little girl in "a little red chair" with "a number of baby toys," when Pat will not attend school without her. For "Pan was not supposed to learn, only to play." Further exposure of the Mission woman's insincerity and lack of genuine interest in Chinese culture is conveyed through omniscient comments: "It had not been very difficult for her to pick up a few Chinese phrases"—and through access to the character's inner mind. Anna Harrison describes seeing Pat "with a number of *Chinese urchins*," and at "*some kind of* Chinese holiday," and feels that for the boy "to grow up as a Chinese was *unthinkable*" (italics mine). The trickster's reversal of perceived expectations turns on the simple sentence: "But Pan did learn"—to recite verses, sing hymns, and pronounce a wide English vocabulary—while Pat, "poor little fellow, was unable to memorize even a sentence." As precocious a trickster figure as her cleft-hoofed namesake, Pan is also the "originator of most of the mischief which Pat carried out with such spirit." This includes cutting classes and being punished by caning.

The ambiguity of the value of knowledge is further entangled, then, as, against the image of Pan singing "Yesu love me"—words Pat cannot learn—the little boy mutters, "I hate you, Pan." At this point we recognize that the Mission woman (ostensibly in the name of Christian love) has introduced violence, competition, and hate into the garden. That such as Anna Harrison—recurrently the assimilationist, or destroyer of Chinese culture, in Sui Sin Far's aesthetic vision—has the power to dissolve bonds of human love is revealed through the step-by-step process with which she is seen to dissolve Pat's bonds with the Lum Yook family. As three years pass, Ah Ma's heart moves from happiness to hang "heavy as the blackest of heavens" in response to the "many tongues wagging because [Pat] lives under our roof." In Sui Sin Far's understated style, news of the actual arrival of the "comfortably off American and wife who were to have the boy and raise him as an American boy should be raised" is delivered by an omniscient narrator and so subtly tucked between lines that if we blink we could miss it. Narration is followed, however, by a climactic scene of parting between the Lum Yooks and Pat: "You are a white boy and Pan is Chinese," Mr. Lum Yook explains to Pat's protest, "I will not leave my Pan!" Set against his previous choice to ignore racial differences and raise Pat as his son, the father's present surrender to race as justification for the severance of family indicates the extremes of the pressures of Anna Harrison's world. "I am Chinese too!" insists Pat. "He Chinese! He Chinese!" the voice of Pan reinforces. "But," the narrator moves in to say, "Pat was driven away." By whom? or for what? The change to passive voice leaves us to wonder. As with Sui Sin Far and her siblings in England, the children in "Pat and Pan" have no awareness of racism until adults teach them. "Yes, him white, but all same, China boy," the lichi vendor had answered to Anna Harrison's beginning astonishment, shrugging off her socially contrived racial barrier with, "Lady, you want to buy lichi?" Of what significance are white chins or black heads in the arena of human justice and love? the narrator seems to be asking. The question is as incomprehensible as the entire process in this mad racist reasoning where, as Mrs. Lum Yook considers, if it had not been for her, "there would have been no white boy for others to 'raise.'"

"Pat and Pan" is a simple story, published in 1912 as part of the book-length collection *Mrs. Spring Fragrance* and placed under the heading "Tales of Chinese Children." Yet immense things are happening, as blinders are pulled off the eyes of society's most powerful taboos—miscegenation, incest, cultural genocide. For, as the Mission woman sees the two children "asleep in each others arms" in what, if we did not know their ages, could be the pose of adults after lovemaking; as Pat sits stoically through his own caning but shakes his fist at the teacher, shouting "in a voice hoarse with passion: 'You hurt my Pan again!'" when Anna Harrison begins to slap Pan; as the narrator explicitly divulges: "They were not always lovers—those two," we, as readers, recognize what Anna Harrison must. In this girl and boy from different and conflicting races lies the potential for sexual relations, childbearing, and marriage. This is the deepest trick, the fear of which no one dares speak, and the reason, implicitly, why the Mission woman believes she must save Pat for "white" culture.[13]

The irony in her attempt reveals itself when the children are brought together for two final meetings, both of which depict Pan encountering Pat with "white" schoolmates and calling a new woman "mother." In the first, Pat's boast to Pan that he is learning "lots of things that you don't know anything about," juxtaposed against Pan's lament, "Pat, you have forgot to remember" when the little boy cannot recall A-Toy, "the big gray meow," measures the acquisition of knowledge in one cultural world with its loss in another. Subsequently, such gains and losses move from the material arena into the deepest realms of the human spirit. At Pat and Pan's last meeting, Pat's new "white" friends taunt, "Hear the China kid!" in response to Pan's "ah, Pat! . . . I find you!" Counterpointing the scene where Pat "was driven away," he now drives Pan away, shouting, "Get away from me!" The last line, though, is Pan's, as she runs away and calls back, "Poor Pat . . . He Chinese no more. . . ."

Thus, even though Pan is the one left to shake her head "sorrowfully," it is Pat for whom the reader is left to feel the most pity. Pan knows who her mother is and, even brokenhearted, can run home to find her. Contrarily, the implications for Pat are of losing more than a sister, a family, a culture. Between images, ideas, and the placement of words on the page, ripples spread outward lamenting, no less than Eden, the loss of a soul. Again, trickster tables are turned, as he who appears to gain loses, and she who is perceived as insignificant, "only to play," carries the author's thematic intentions.

Did the editors of "Pat and Pan" really see this as a "children's story," with all the implications of simplicity that suggests? Or does the preposition "of" in "Tales of Chinese Children" connote not *for* but *about,* or perhaps *coming from?* In this case, we see Sui Sin Far's skills with tricksterism at their cleverest. Through children (the mouths of babes) an adult audience naively accepts what it could not if spoken by its peers. Moreover, in depicting a Mission woman (heroine of the Progressive Era) as villainous and a Chinese American family as heroic, in "Pat and Pan" Sui Sin Far upsets conventional ideas of "Other-ness" and displays instead the humanist, politically unpopular vision she extends to readers in "Leaves": "Only when the whole world becomes as one family will human beings be able to see clearly and hear distinctly" (p. 129).

Altogether, examining Sui Sin Far's writings from her early journalism through her mature fiction convinces me that tricksterism describes her style most effectively because she was able to present the popular formulas that a turn-of-the-century marketplace and a reading audience of European descent demanded for public acceptance, and at the same time to overturn the stereotypes embedded in those formulas as she pursued her own personal and ideological themes. In her experiments with such strategies, Sui Sin Far was not alone. Her writings share techniques with those of other women and ethnic minority male writers who were publishing from similarly precarious situations during the late nineteenth to early twentieth century time period. "This debt we pay to human guile," the narrator of Dunbar's poem admits in true trickster fashion. If our reading audience wants to be fooled, these writers might say, why not let them?

The challenge for contemporary readers is to listen closely when reading works by authors whose cultures were excluded and persecuted at the turn of the century, recalling the conditions under which they were writing and the miracle that their stories reached print at all,[14] asking when we read phrases such as "quaint little thing" (Anna Harrison's description of Pan): Whose voice is our witness? We need to remember that beneath the pen of a trickster, perspectives may interchange within a line or a sentence. Otherwise these writers will be misunderstood, considered "not good," not through any lack of ability on their parts, but through our own inabilities to perceive trickster methods. The result, ironically, will be that the very styles—frequently "flowery" and "simple" on a superficial level—that got these writers published in the 1890s could keep them from getting republished in the 1990s. Paul Lauter's reminder is crucial here: "One must ask, then, not how to apply a given and persisting set of standards, but where standards come from, whose values they embed, and whose interests they serve" (1992, p. 104).

Like many turn-of-the-century writers, for Sui Sin Far finding a style in which to write and get published required accommodating the monolithic, racist views of white America. For writers committed to their own people, it also required breaking through them. Such a transaction could only be handled covertly, or by finding strategies to negotiate with a dual audience. From these circumstances, I suggest, a writer's stance defined by Dunbar in "I Wear the Mask," a stance that may be translated as "tricksterism," emerged.

Notes

1. This essay is a revised version of a paper I presented at the 1992 Modern Language Association Convention in New York City. I would like to thank my students in Multicultural Literature of the United States at the University of Wisconsin–La Crosse for working with me to explore trickster methods in many literatures. For a book-length study of Sui Sin Far and reprints of the works under discussion here, my critical biography, *Sui Sin Far: The Beginnings of Chinese North American Literature*, and *Selected Works of Sui Sin Far*, co-edited by Amy Ling and me, are forthcoming from University of Illinois Press. For earlier critical work on this writer, see S. E. Solberg, "Sui Sin Far/Edith Eaton: First Chinese-American Fictionist," *MELUS* 8, no. 1 (1981): 27–40; Amy Ling, "Edith Eaton: Pioneer Chinamerican Writer and Feminist," *American Literary Realism, 1870–1910* 16, no. 2 (1983): 287–298; Lorraine Dong and Marlon K. Hom, "Defiance or Perpetuation: An Analysis of Characters in *Mrs. Spring Fragrance*," in *Chinese America: History and Perspectives*, eds. Him Mark Lai, Ruthanne Lum McCunn, and Judy Yung (San Francisco: Chinese Historical Society of America, 1987), pp. 139–168; Amy Ling, "Pioneers and Paradigms: The Eaton Sisters," in *Between Worlds: Women Writers of Chinese Ancestry* (New York: Pergamon Press, 1990), pp. 21–55; Xiao-Huang Yin, "Between the East and West: Sui Sin Far—The First

Chinese American Woman Writer," *Arizona Quarterly* 7 (Winter 1991): 49–84; Annette White-Parks, "Sui Sin Far: Writer on the Chinese-Anglo Borders of North America," Ph.D. diss., Washington State University (1991); and Elizabeth Ammons, "Audacious Words: Sui Sin Far's *Mrs. Spring Fragrance*" in *Conflicting Stories: American Women Writers at the Turn into the Twentieth Century* (New York: Oxford University Press, 1991), pp. 105–120.

2. The full text of Dunbar's poem reads:

We wear the mask that grins and lies.

It hides our cheeks and shades our eyes.—
This debt we pay to human guile;
With torn and bleeding hearts we smile,
And mouth with myriad subtleties.

Why should the world be over-wise
In counting all our tears and sighs?
Nay, let them only see us while
We wear the mask.

We smile, but, O great Christ, our cries
To thee from tortured souls arise.
We sing, but oh the clay is vile
Beneath our feet, and long the mile;
But let the world dream otherwise,
We wear the mask!

3. Although the writer was cited on her birth certificate as "Edith Maude Eaton," the name "Sui Sin Far" does not seem a pseudonym, but is rather a term of address her family identified her by from early childhood. In the autobiographical "Leaves from the Mental Portfolio of an Eurasian," she recalls being called "Sui" as a toddler. In my work, I purposefully use "Sui Sin Far" to underline the personal choice this writer made to distinguish herself from the English-Canadian identity that most of her family maintained and to help bring to visibility the Chinese heritage for which she fought through her lifetime. The family name comes first in Chinese, but in Sui Sin Far's case, the syllables, translating roughly in English as "the Chinese Lily,' cannot be separated into "Far, Sui Sin" or simply "Far," as is the convention. Meaning depends upon sequence "Sui Sin Far" and does not work if the sequence is broken.

4. See also Cathy Silber, "A 1,000-Year-Old Secret," *Ms.* 3, no. 2 (September–October 1992): 58–60.

5. Examples we especially noticed in multicultural literature classes were the African American slave songs or folktales (slaves "tricking" slaveholders), and Hispanic folktales (Indians "tricking" Spanish priests and the church), as collected in *The Heath Anthology of American Literature,* Paul Lauter et al., eds. (New York: Heath and Co., 1990).

6. In *Literary Democracy,* a study limited to male writers of the white middle and upper classes, Larzer Ziff seeks an aesthetic unique to the United States, one made possible by factors that began on the North American continent after the arrival of Europeans and that was developed by the writers Ziff covers. I would suggest that writers excluded by race and gender who conceived methods of tricksterism were also creating aesthetics unique to North America and essential to our ongoing quest for what American literature is about.

7. Canada raised the head tax against Chinese to $500 in 1904, the same year that the United States extended the Chinese Exclusion Act, initiated in 1882, indefinitely. For both nations, the Chinese were the first immigrant group to be so taxed and excluded.

8. Compare this passage from "Leaves," regarding people's responses to Sui Sin Far and her siblings: "older persons pause and gaze upon us, very much in the same way that I have seen people gaze upon strange animals in a menagerie" (p. 127).

9. In advance of doing this research, I was repeatedly told that there were no Chinese women in Montréal in the nineteenth century.

10. Compare, for example, these two descriptions of the women's living environments: "the walls were hung from top to bottom with long bamboo panels covered with paper, on which were printed Chinese characters, signifying good luck" (1894 interview); "Chinese ornaments decorate the tables and walls . . . long bamboo panels covered with paper or silk on which are painted Chinese good luck characters" (1897 essay).

11. As located by Alexander Hammond, dates for this series are February 4, 5, 6, 10, and 24; and March 9, 1904. Each is on page 6 of that issue of the *Express*.

12. As a Chinese-English immigrant to North America herself, Sui Sin Far was technically, of course, already a member of the Chinese North American community. Yet, because the ocean she crossed had not been the Pacific, her appearance was not Chinese, and she occupied a household that passed as English in many ways, she relates feeling a perpetual outsider from both cultures. This is illustrated in her reluctance to confide in either her mother or father: "They would not understand. How could they? He is English, she is Chinese. I am different to both of them—a stranger, tho their own child" ("Leaves," p. 128). It is also reinforced by her early experiences of trying to enter the Chinese San Francisco community: "The Americanized Chinamen actually laugh in my face when I tell them that I am of their race" ("Leaves," p. 131). For a book-length study of the "between worlds" enigma of which Sui Sin Far was a part, see Amy Ling, *Between Worlds: Women Writers of Chinese Ancestry* (New York: Pergamon Press, 1990). Sui Sin Far healed the breach through her writing.

13. Subversive meanings in "Pat and Pan" are enhanced by the knowledge that in 1880 the California State Legislature extended previous laws prohibiting marriage between "whites" and "Negros or mullatos" to include "Mongolians," and in 1905 the law declared such marriages illegal and void.

14. Elizabeth Ammons' words concerning Sui Sin Far are exemplary: "That Sui Sin Far invented herself—created her own voice—out of such deep silencing and systematic racist repression was one of the triumphs of American literature at the turn of the century" (*Conflicting Stories,* p. 105).

Works Cited

Ammons, Elizabeth. *Conflicting Stories: American Women Writers at the Turn into the Twentieth Century.* New York: Oxford University Press, 1991.

Bright, William. "The Natural History of Old Man Coyote." In *Recovering the Word: Essays on Native American Literature,* eds. Brian Swann and Arnold Krupat. Berkeley: University of California Press, 1987, pp. 339–387.

Crean, Susan. *Newsworthy: The Lives of Media Women*. Toronto: Stoddart Publishing, 1985.

Dearborn, Mary. *Pocahontas's Daughters: Gender and Ethnicity in American Culture*. New York: Oxford University Press, 1986.

Dunbar, Paul Laurence. *Lyrics of Lowly Life*. New York: Dodd, Mead and Co., 1906.

Lauter, Paul. *Canons and Contexts*. New York: Oxford University Press, 1992.

Lauter, Paul, et al., eds. *The Heath Anthology of American Literature*. New York: Heath and Co., 1990.

Lewis, Eileen. Interview by the author, 20 September 1990.

Li Hui. "Nushu: A Written Language for Women Only." *Anima: The Journal of Human Experience* 16, no. 2 (The Spring Equinox, 1990): 10–110.

Ling, Amy. *Between Worlds: Women Writers of Chinese Ancestry*. New York: Pergamon Press, 1990.

Roberts, John W. *From Trickster to Badman: The Black Folk Hero in Slavery and Freedom*. Philadelphia: University of Pennsylvania Press, 1989.

Rodner, Joan N., and Susan S. Lanser. "The Feminist Voice: Strategies of Coding in Folklore and Literature." *Journal of American Folklore* 100 (October–December 1987): 412–425.

Sui Sin Far/Edith Eaton. "Chen Hen Yen, Chinese Student." *New England Magazine* 45 (January 1912): 462–466.

———. "Chinatown Boys and Girls." *Los Angeles Express* (22 October 1903): 4.

———. "A Chinese Boy-Girl." *Century* 67 (April 1904): 828–831.

———. "The Chinese Woman in America." *Land of Sunshine* 6 (January 1897): 60–65.

———. "Girl Slave in Montreal: Our Chinese Colony Cleverly Described. Only Two Women from the Flowery Land in Town." *Montreal Daily Star* (1 May 1894), n.p.

———. "Half Chinese Children: Those of American Mothers and Chinese Fathers." *Montreal Daily Star* (20 April 1895): 3–5.

———. "In Fairyland." *Canadian Dominion Illustrated* 5 (18 October 1890): 270.

———. "Leaves from the Mental Portfolio of an Eurasian." *Independent* 66 (21 January 1909): 125–132.

———. "Leung Ki Chu and His Wife." *Los Angeles Express* (22 October 1903), n.p.

———. "Lin John." *Land of Sunshine* 10 (January 1899): 76–77.

———. "The Origin of a Broken Nose." *Canadian Dominion Illustrated* 2 (11 May 1889): 302.

———. *Mrs. Spring Fragrance*. Chicago: A. C. McClurg & Co., 1912.

———. "The Sing-Song Woman." *Land of Sunshine* 9 (October 1898): 225–228.

———. "The Smuggling of Tie Co." *Land of Sunshine* 13 (July 1900): 100–104.

———. "The Story of Tin-a." *Land of Sunshine* 12 (December 1899): 101–103.

———. "Sui Sin Far: The Half Chinese Writer Tells of Her Career." *Boston Globe* (5 May 1912): 6.

———. "Sweet Sin." *Land of Sunshine* 8 (April 1898): 223–226.

———. "Wing Sing of Los Angeles and His Travels." *Los Angeles Express* (4 February–9 March 1904): 6.

Tompkins, Jane. *Sensational Designs: The Cultural Work of American Fiction, 1790–1860*. New York: Oxford University Press, 1985.

Wiget, Andrew. "His Life in His Tail: The Native American Trickster and the Literature of Possibility." In *Redefining American Literary History*, eds. A. La-Vonne Brown Ruoff and Jerry W. Ward, Jr. New York: Modern Language Association, 1990, pp. 83–96.

Ziff, Larzer. *Literary Democracy: The Declaration of Cultural Independence in America*. New York: The Viking Press, 1981.

TIFFANY ANA LÓPEZ

María Cristina Mena: Turn-of-the-Century La Malinche, and Other Tales of Cultural (Re)Construction

Maybe it's because I went to Catholic school; maybe it's because I am the defiant oldest daughter of a very oppressive man; maybe it's because as an undergraduate English major all the stories I ever read in the first person seemed to be about English men from an era and culture not mine; maybe it's for these and other reasons that I find trickster tales and what I would term trickster discourses liberating and fascinating, providing hope that there is a space for acts of resistance within hegemonic modes of cultural production.

Trickster tales take many shapes and forms—songs, tales, language play. They are a part of the literature, oral and written, of almost all cultures. They are a means by which the underrepresented engage in a politics of visibility by asserting—if only to their own cultural group—the significance of their culture, its interpretations of history, its methods of survival outside of the hegemonic systems that seek to contain them. The points of mediation, the trickster's methods of cultural translation, are her tricks, the turn of her story, the twist of her tale, the skeleton key for the cultural insider. She is multilingual and double-voiced, a speaker of many languages. Henry Louis Gates, Jr.'s example of this is embodied by the trickster figure of Esu as "the ingenious black metaphor for the literary critic" linked in Gates's readings to Hermes, messenger to the gods from whose name we get hermeneutics, the "study of the methodological principles of interpretation of a text."[1] Trickster tales are defined by their function in the interpretation of culture. We can't define a story as a trickster tale until we describe how that tale "demonstrate[s] the artificiality of culture itself."[2] Thus, trickster tales make "available for discussion the very basis of social order, individual and community identity."[3] In essence, they delineate cultural survival in a world that threatens one's very existence as an individual and as a communal being.

In John W. Roberts's critical analysis of African American trickster figures, he makes clear that one must understand how interpretation functions and, most importantly, for whom. He writes,

When confronted with the animal trickster tale, which portrayed the hero as a small animal whose cunning and wit could explode into acts of brutality and violence, scholars evaluated the tradition in terms of the duality that governed their own thinking about African people. Most could readily equate the character and actions of the animal trickster with those of Africans on the continent; however, they could not so easily accept them as an accurate reflection of black identity or behavior, actual or potential, in America. Consequently, early scholars clung tenaciously to the African-origins thesis and suggested that animal trickster tales in their more brutal aspects reflected their development in Africa. Nevertheless, Africans enslaved in America continued to perform trickster tales because they could identify with the witty creature to whom nature had assigned an inferior position in the animal kingdom, a position not unlike that of African people in the human order.[4]

Those fully invested in a definition of western folklore lacking the ability to envision other cultural perspectives narrowly saw these trickster tales according to the reading codes they had been taught about black people and culture. Andrew Wiget, in his essay concerning Native American trickster figures, also discusses how "in any storytelling situation the audience and the storyteller do not always form a homogeneous group."[5] Just as readers absorb reading codes concerning race, they also absorb codes concerning gender. Wiget explains that a "peculiar bias" can arise in reading trickster stories. That bias is a male bias. Though trickster stories purportedly speak for the "community," often they have spoken primarily for the male members, because the tales have been told primarily by the male storytellers to the designated future storytellers and cultural historians—who are the males chosen by the elder males. Wiget sheds light on this "peculiar bias" by providing the example of "male ethnographers of the Boasian school [who] expected elder males to be the repository of traditional knowledge and [therefore] seldom sought out women storytellers."[6]

I cite these issues because in reading a Mexican American woman writer's work as participating in the construction of a Chicana trickster tradition, it is important to consider the kind of western bias that occurred for readers and promoters of her work; furthermore, it is also important to understand the kind of gender bias that occurs in the act of passing on trickster tales, both orally and through media. I want to set up the more in-depth reading of the La Llorona and La Malinche figures I will provide later in this essay by stating at this point that both are figures of horror within Mexicano/Chicano folklore. They function in the ways that other cultures' trickster tales do in that their primary purpose is to teach the terms of cultural survival. It is certainly erroneous to say that there is such a thing as a "universal" or "generic" trickster narrative; however, there are definitely shared traits among various cultures' trickster narratives, number one being that trickster narratives develop when the existence of a culture is threatened.

For example, Br'er Rabbit and Br'er Fox teach cultural survival in the face of slavery. Coyote is involved in tales that often instruct on the reality of invading peoples. Similarly, in Mexicano and Chicano folklore La Malinche stories are meant to instruct about colonial oppression. La Llorona stories are told in order to teach the importance of thinking about *la familia* (familial survival) *y comunidad* (and community). However, these horrific female figures *alone* are attributed the responsibility of bringing about the downfall of the family and, by extension, the entire culture. The exclusion of the feminine thus becomes the very basis for the social contract, with cultural negotiation taking place through the sacrifice of women. In this essay, I want to analyze the significance of race and gender in a reading of the creation of deliberately female trickster figures by a Mexican American woman writer (whom I read as a precursor to Chicana literature) who signifies on the La Malinche and La Llorona myths in order to pass on to readers new kinds of tales of cultural survival that take into account the importance of women's roles in the survival of culture and community.

María Herrera-Sobek, in her analysis of the significance of oral traditions and Chicana/o writers, sees the trickster figure as the resisting voice of the colonized in direct response to very specific historical circumstances. In an unpublished essay, she writes that Américo Paredes

> has posited a theoretical construct for the analysis and comprehension of Mexican American folklore. This theoretical construct views much of Chicano/a folklore as arising from a specific socio-historical political situation: clash of cultures between the Catholic, Latino native populations of the American Southwest and the Protestant English-speaking Anglo-Saxon colonizers who invaded and acquired through the Mexican American War (1846–1848) Mexico's northernmost territories. Many of the oral and literary texts extant during that period and subsequent eras can be viewed within the parameters of resistance literature. That is to say, the defeated populations . . . developed through . . . genres of popular culture . . . a corpus of literary productions whose underlying theme was a critique of the political and social oppression of the Mexican American population living in the Southwest. Thus many of the *corridos* (ballads), folksongs, folktales, folk humor, essays, novels, and poems critique the social structure, institutions, and laws in the United States and the economic disparity between Mexican Americans and the Anglo-Saxon population among other issues. . . . The figure of the trickster, important in oral tradition, underscores the position of the subaltern in a conquered society.[7]

Mexican/Mexican American/Chicana/o writers signify a history of conquest throughout their literatures, as is made clear in Sobek's readings of these writers and their oral tradition. One such writer to emerge from the historical conditions described above is María Cristina Mena, one of the first Mexican-American women to write fiction in English and to be published in the mainstream popular press.[8]

Mena's stories appeared in *Century Magazine* from 1913 to 1916. They follow a very clear trajectory, beginning with colorful narratives about a quite pious, devoted, and hard-working Mexican people and then developing into works that can be read as allegories for the political tensions of the period between the United States and Mexico. If one rereads Mena's works considering her subject position as a cultural translator between Mexican and American cultures, it becomes increasingly clear that her work stands in dialogue with the historical events that influenced her as a Mexican woman whose family had sent her to live in the United States due to the escalating political tensions in Mexico preceding the Mexican revolution. Mena was affected, no doubt, by her subject position in regard to the Mexican revolution. An increasingly colonial stance and controlling "open door" policy by the United States toward Pan-Americanism was seeking to take more Mexican territory (as well as other Latin American territories) than acquired through the Treaty of Guadalupe Hidalgo, the Monroe Doctrine, and the Platt Amendment, among other political pacts, all of which had been designed to expand U.S. business into an easily controllable and highly profitable foreign trade. For political reasons Mena found herself in the United States, yet culturally her Mexicanness was always with her, as most clearly exemplified in her stories, which always centered on Mexican culture and people.

There is extremely little biographical information readily available about this writer. Therefore, my reading of the significance of her work heavily relies on piecing together what little biographical information there is with the markers of Mexicano folklore evident in her stories, along with relevant historical information from the time of her writing. In this essay I will examine Mena's work in the context of the need to read history as part of reading trickster narratives. I also want to explore how she, as a cultural insider, portrays images of Mexicans, as opposed to how members of the dominant culture see Mexicans in the stories, sociopolitical essays, and advertisements that appear in the same and bracketing years as Mena's work in *Century Magazine*. Most importantly, I want to do so with an emphasis on gender and on analysis of the "peculiar bias" put forth by *Century* that undoubtedly influenced how Mena's work was and wasn't read. I will examine trickster discourses as part of a politics of visibility in terms of the political potential of popular cultural production, as well as discuss how media create systems of images that simultaneously threaten and enable acts of resistance such as those found within trickster narratives, all of which very much depend upon theories of reception that include race, class, gender, and sexual biases. The systems of images concerning Mexicans put forth by the Anglo male writers of *Century Magazine* are quite different from those posited by Mena. In a reading of these works and tricksterism, I want to question what these images do and for whom.

❧

Mena was born in Mexico City, April 3, 1893, and from the age of fourteen lived in the United States. *Century Magazine* published her first story in 1913 and later contracted with her to produce a series of stories on Mexican life. These appeared every three or four months for about five years, with the majority of her writing produced from 1913 to 1916. She was the daughter of a Spanish mother and Yucatan father of European descent, a politically powerful and socially prominent businessman during the last two decades of the rule of Porfirio Diaz. She was raised privileged and upper-class, educated at the convent and later an English boarding school. She began writing poetry at the age of ten. At fourteen, she was sent to live with family friends in New York City because of the political turmoil in Mexico, which led up to the Mexican revolution that would begin in 1910. In New York she continued her studies and writing; her first two short stories were published in November 1913, one in *Century Magazine,* "John of God, the Water-Carrier," and the other in *American Magazine,* "The Gold Vanity Set."[9]

In 1916 Mena married the Australian playwright and journalist Henry Kellett Chambers. Both moved in literary circles that included writers such as D. H. Lawrence and Aldous Huxley. Her husband died in 1935 and she is said to have become a "virtual shut in." When she did leave her home, it was to participate in regular meetings of the Catholic Library Association and the Authors Guild of New York, which enabled her to maintain contact with the literati. Mena continued to write children's novels, which are said to be reworkings of her short stories, most notably her first published work "John of God." Descriptions of these works suggest that their subject matter is in keeping with the trickster discourse begun in the short stories: "she touched on the lives of the religious and the sacrilegious, the faithful and the hypocritical, the industrious and the lazy, the wise and the gullible."[10] As with her stories, she continued to write works that examined in detail the social structure of Mexico. Mena died in Brooklyn on August 3, 1965.

The trajectory of Mena's writing follows three stages. Her first move was to introduce readers to images of Mexicans that were not politically threatening. The characters in "John of God" are lower-class and humble; those in "The Emotions of María Concepción" are upper-class and the scene of the story is a bullfight, which plays into a romanticized image of Spanish culture that readers would most likely recognize and be comfortable with. "The Education of Popo" features an English couple's encounter with a Mexican boy who has his first crush on the English woman eleven years his senior; it is a tale of first love that also addresses language and cultural differences in a way that would not, I argue, threaten readers, and it is an immature relationship in which the white subjects of the story can be read positively while at the same time sympathy is evoked for the adolescent Mexican male through the universal emotion of love. Mena's images of Mexicans here do not conform to stereotypes, but they do present images that are assuring for white readers, images of Mexicans that allow for identification with the status of the Other through imagined mutual suffering.

Once her audience was established, Mena began to signify upon Mexican folklore, which formed the second stage in her work. It is a stage in her writing that indicates her working to assert a politics of visibility in terms of "positive" portrayals of Mexicans, and through affirming Mexican literary history. Also, it demonstrates her assertion of Mexican female characters as powerful figures in the community, as matriarchs, storytellers, and heroines. "Doña Rita's Rivals" concerns a Mexican upper-class woman's obsession with class status at the expense of her son's happiness and life. "The Birth of the God of War" centers entirely on the storytelling introduced to the narrator as a young girl by her *mamagrande,* who shares with us her store of "Aztec mythology" in the story of Huitzilopochtli ("Weet-zee-lo-potch-tlee"), the god of war. Both of these stories tap into the two strands of the La Llorona trickster tale. Strand one is based in Spanish-influenced storytelling: La Llorona, the wailing woman, is engaged to be married to a man higher in class than she. They have children together (out of wedlock?). One day she sees him ride through town with a woman of his own class. In anger, she throws her children in the river and drowns them. Later she repents and spends eternity wandering the banks, searching for her children. Strand two is rooted in Aztec mythology: La Llorona is an extension of an Aztec myth concerning an Aztec mother who, knowing of the Spanish conquest, kills her children rather than see them live a life of domination. In both strands of the tale, the murder is an act of resistance, and La Llorona a tactician who operates within a delineated space as a model of adaptive behavior. Her power is contained within the sphere of male prerogative; hence, she must work outside the law.[11]

The third stage in Mena's trajectory is what I would label direct signification in relation to the political tensions of the time. By this point in her writing for *Century Magazine* Mena had gained recognition and status as, in the words of the magazine, "Author of 'The Education of Popo,' 'Doña Rita's Rivals,' etc.," and, it would follow, had gained an audience as well. It should also be kept in mind that Mena was commissioned by *Century* specifically to write stories about Mexican life. This information leads me to read her writing as having a very important and strategic function in terms of the cultural work performed by the magazine at this time. For example, following xenophobic essays like those of Edward Alsworth Ross[12] or essays such as W. Morgan Shuster's "The Mexican Menace," Mena's stories would have assured readers that Mexicans are not threatening, are not savages. Quite to the contrary, in Mena's stories they are noble, distinct, and most importantly light-skinned. The "code" of her stories in this reading I would compare to the codes always embedded in trickster narratives for their cultural insiders, such as slave narratives that led masters to believe slaves were singing spirituals, like "Follow the Drinking Gourd," while they were carefully planning the road to their freedom. Again, I want to emphasize the role reception plays in such readings, for example in terms of the hoped-for reception by the editors who asked Mena to write stories specifically about Mexico in a period of American history in which there were great tensions between the United States and Mexico.

The stories I will focus upon in this part of my analysis are "The Vine Leaf" and "The Sorcerer and General Bisco," both published from 1914 to 1915. In my readings of these works, I will discuss the surrounding articles by Anglo writers in *Century* that focus upon Mexicans, women, and people of color. I will do so in order to facilitate discussion of the trickster elements in Mena's work and to expose the constructed systems of images concerning race and gender present in *Century*, that is, the systems in which Mena had to work.

An advertisement for the Santa Fe Railway in the November 1912 *Century* pictures an Anglo woman looking out of a train at blanket-bundled Southwestern natives. The distinctively Southwestern adobe pueblito is in the background. Part of the caption reads, "a delightful journey through the Southwest Land of Enchantment to winterless California where you can motor and play golf under sunny skies." Obviously this ad is targeted toward the leisure class; the gaze is a colonial one in which the southwestern subjects are there as part of the landscape, props to pleasure the viewer, whose perspective is that of the outsider looking in, the moving subject to the isolated object. Pierre Liflan, in his analysis of images of Chicano/Mexicanos in photography, places images like those just described in a framework that examines how such images work and what they say about the people producing and receiving them. He writes:

> In the case of the Chicano/Mexicano each news and advertising image becomes an exchange between an Anglo idea of "Mexicanicity" and Anglo culture itself. The images represent the desire of the dominant culture for a silent, subservient, productive minority whose only wish is to provide their nature and their culture as gifts. The body of the Other is there to give pleasure and/or power to the Anglo within the frame and to the Anglo viewing the image. The Chicano/Mexicano in

advertising is presented as being "at your service," so that his/her body itself becomes a signifier meaning service. . . . The Mexican people are depicted as awaiting your arrival. Even the art is there to serve you. . . . It is interesting not within itself, but for what it holds for the viewer.[13]

Like the art Liflan mentions, the image of the Mexicano as "at your service" is clear in the testimony that provides the leader for the Santa Fe ad: "I unhesitatingly recommend these two California trains to travelers who wish ideal service." The notion of service is not only connected to what the Santa Fe Railroad can provide, but also to what the Mexicano will *naturally* provide in connection with the image of the Mexicanos outside of the window as part of the journey's destination, as part of the service to be received. Mena herself was implicated in this system of service for the pleasure of Anglo viewers in her role as a commissioned "authentic" Mexican voice. Significantly, she was asked to write stories that translated Mexican culture for the same audience that would be buying their tickets for Santa Fe based on images of the Southwest like those in the preceding ad.[14]

The depiction of people of color as servants becomes part of a system of images associated with darker skin color and Otherness, particularly emphasized in narratives concerning travel. This association with skin color could be one reason why Mena depicts all of her characters as light skinned. Again, it is important to note that none of Mena's stories is about Mexicans in the United States. All of her stories take place on foreign ground, thereby playing into a type of travel narrative, that is, a fantasy of people and places. In the April 1914 volume of *Century,* Julian Miller's "We Find the Island of Servants" includes illustrations that make visually clear to the reader the relationship or equation between "servant" and skin color. This is done through a mimetic connection of blackness to servility through "portraits" of the cook, the garden boy, and the borrowed maid as black-skinned, big-lipped natives with excessively large hands and feet. The opening illustration above the title of this story features a kind of Christopher Columbus character leaning on his sword, while wild-looking, long-haired island natives (all males) are on their hands and knees, one of them reaching out to the figure of the conquistador. This travel narrative provides an example of how people of color are turned into a vacation commodity fetish:

The British, when they moved into the island [of Jamaica], found it one of the best-filled white man's burdens in the world, and it is getting fuller all the time, owing to an enthusiastic avoidance of race suicide.

Before eager housekeepers or speculators rush to the steamship offices to lay down their forty-five dollars with the intention of returning to the States with a ship-load of servants, they must take warning. They can get the ship-load. They need merely announce their desire from the deck on arrival in Jamaica, and the ship-load will deliver itself so impetuously that the entire royal constabulary will be needed to save the ship from being submerged below its Plimsoll's mark. . . .

This list sounds so much like *Sinbad* at his worst that I hardly dare venture on my next statement, which is that in Jamaica a hostess can invite as many guests as she pleases for as long a time as she pleases, and never has to wonder if her servants will stand it. They not only will stand it, but they will be pleased!

The person of color satisfies the white travelers' needs—with a big "please!" no less. Such accounts send out clear messages that domination is natural, that it is desired by people of color.[15] These images play an important role in the construction of the readers' world view.

Along these lines, one is led to ask what role did (and does) Mena's work play in the imaginary of the white audience? Conditioned to read the Other as existing for white service, readers would have coded Mena's works within that system of images, because she was herself a Mexican woman serving a white audience. This would obscure the possibility that she would be read by that audience as writing in resistance. The effect of such a system of images puts writers of color in a double bind: They want and need a way to assert a politics of visibility; however, at the same time, by virtue of the system they are rendered invisible. Their writing is appropriated into the existing system of images rather than read against it.[16] A trickster discourse is not naturally read; one has to be trained to read it. What is naturalized is the culturally constructed system of dominating images.

In addition to these images being racialized, they are also gendered. The fetishization of the woman of color has always been part of the colonial mentality, most violently asserted in the acts of rape that accompany colonial occupation. Trickster traditions provide commentary on such realities in the life of the dominated. For example, one reading of the Aztec version of La Llorona is that the Aztec mother killed her (girl) children to save them from the rape that would have accompanied Cortés's attack. *Century,* as well as constructing systems of images concerning race, constructed systems of images concerning gender, and they are always racialized. Hugh Johnson's "Race" (*Century,* August 1914) addresses the possibility of an interracial marriage between a white soldier in the Philippines and a Filipino/Spanish woman. The woman becomes part of the setting of the war in the Philippine islands following the U.S. invasion in the late 1890s and early twentieth century, an invasion staged for the purposes of seizing the fertile lands and the potential profits from the rich resources of rice, coffee, sugar, coconut, hemp, and tobacco. The woman of color becomes part of the landscape, and like the resources, is there at the soldier's service:

> He was standing there one morning when something softly pressed aside two elephant-ear palm-leaves on the water's-edge, as a butler pushes aside portieres, and through the aperture silently slipped a black prow. Standing, one bare foot on the gunwale, head thrown back, hair flowing free, was what might have been a Naiad of the marshland, if Naiads wore print trade-color skirts. . . . The Naiad looked at him thoughtfully and spoke. . . . "You are most magnificently wet, Señor."[17]

The woman of color is placed both under a colonial gaze, in the ways that Liflan discusses, and under a male gaze. In a double bind, she shares a position with other women; yet she also does not share a position with all women in that she is seen as both a female and a racialized body.

Whiteness occurs here as being un-raced, as what is naturalized. This can be seen by contrasting the exoticized image of the woman of color quoted above to that of the elegant white woman in *Century* who is not in the jungle, but in her home. Her role is not to emerge gracefully from the depths of the jungle, but to stay home looking fresh and radiant. In this case, beauty equates with whiteness, as prescribed by an advertisement for Pond's Vanishing Cream: "A protecting cream has become *an absolute necessity*. . . . An application of Vanishing Cream gives your skin an exquisite finish, a milky tone like a baby's skin. *Any* skin responds to it quickly . . ." (emphasis mine).[18] The assumed universal norm is whiteness, while darker skin is Othered and given a specific cultural role, as Homi Bhabha points out in an essay on the stereotype and colonial discourse:

> Not itself the object of desire but its setting, not an ascription of prior identities but their production in the syntax of the scenario of racist discourse, colonial fantasy plays a crucial part in those everyday scenes of subjectification in a colonial society.[19]

It is this setting of "colonial fantasy" as communicated through a system of images such as the examples I have cited (among many others) that Mena worked within. As a featured writer, she would certainly have read the magazine, as her stories reflect a high sense of social consciousness; also, the patterns of the later years of her life suggest that she was a politically and socially aware individual. In the belief that Mena was influenced by her environment, both literary and social, I want to turn to her story "The Vine-Leaf" as a trickster tale that provides commentary on those "everyday scenes of subjectification in a colonial society."

"The Vine-Leaf" is about a large painting of a beautiful woman who is looking into a mirror, her back to the viewer. The intrigue surrounding the painting concerns the obliterated face of the woman looking in the mirror and the identificatory vine-leaf birthmark hastily added to the back of the female subject by the artist, who is said to have been murdered while finishing the piece. The painting is taken by the marqués who is purported to have been negotiating for it with the artist so he could give the picture as a "betrothal gift."

It is the marqués who finds the artist's murdered body. The story is told to the reader by the surgeon who carries the secret identity of the woman who possessed the vine-leaf birthmark, for he has removed the marking. In Mena's tale, it is the woman who decides to remove the birthmark from her own body. This removal of the "wine-red vine-leaf" from her back does not kill her; quite the opposite, it saves her life. The story points to one reading that indicates she murdered the painter of her portrait; but before he died, he implicated her in the murder by placing a birthmark onto the canvas in order to identify his murderer. If the police were to discover her as the murderer, she would be delivered to the "hands of the public executioner." Removing the birthmark unmarks her by her own volition.

The story, however, also points to a second, more sinister reading. The marqués, the woman's husband, is the one who discovers the murdered artist and who takes the painting to add to his collection: "I wished to make it a betrothal gift to the beautiful Señorita Lisarda Monte Alegre, who had then accepted the offer of my hand, and who is now the *marquesa*. When I have a desire, Doctor, it bites me, and I make it bite others. That poor Andrade [the artist], I gave him no peace." This part of the story suggests that the marqués killed the artist and painted the vine-leaf as the mark of Alegre's (body) on the body of the canvas. In keeping with this reading, it could be deduced that she was possibly having an affair with the artist and was in love with him; the marqués discovered this, killed her lover, and painted the birthmark in order to blackmail her into marrying him.

The ending of the story, which brings these readings together, states:

> With one look from her beautiful and devout eyes she thanked me [the surgeon] for that prudence . . . and then she sighed and said:
>
> "Can you blame me for not loving this questionable lady of the vine-leaf, of whom my husband is such a gallant accomplice?"
>
> "Not for a moment," I replied, "for I am persuaded, *Marquesa,* that a lady of rare qualities may have power to bewitch an unfortunate man without showing him the light of her face."

If we read this as a trickster tale—whether she had the birthmark removed because she murdered the artist or she was being blackmailed by her politically and economically powerful husband—the marquesa is using her wit to outsmart her oppressors; he/they want to identify her through her body as marked; she uses the means at her disposal to escape that status as marked, female, outlawed body. Peggy Phelan writes of this marking of the female body:

> As Lacanian psychoanalysis and Derridean deconstruction have demonstrated, the epistemological, psychic, and political binaries of Western metaphysics create distinctions and evaluations across two terms. One term of the binary is marked with value, the other is unmarked. The male is marked with value; the female is un-

> marked, lacking measured value and meaning. Within this psychophilosophical frame, cultural reproduction takes she who is unmarked and remarks her, rhetorically and imagistically, while he who is marked with value is left unremarked, in discursive paradigms and visual fields. He is the norm and therefore unremarkable: as the Other, it is she whom he marks.[20]

Alegre marks herself in order to remove that status as Other. Whether or not this move is successful is not as important as the significance of the gesture to create a politics of visibility for the subject in question. This is also true in that Mena's stories in *Century* indicate a great effort on her behalf to remove cultural stigma concerning Mexicanness as the marked status of an undesirable Other. Her writing of these stories, like Alegre's removal of her birthmark, is a gesture to create a politics of visibility in which she is marked with value and, by association, her *familia,* her *raza* are valued as well.

In the history of marking of the female body, advertisements and cultural myths function to enforce such codes. Advertisements in *Century* primarily promote travel packages, beauty products, and cooking products. The beauty myth in these ads equates domestic success with, for example, good baking skills (i.e., ads for Gold Medal Flour); and by extension, the successful homemaker is a beautiful woman, and a beautiful woman is a valued, a *re*markable, woman. This beauty is equated with whiteness: the domestic beauty is found in what the white flour can provide, just as the physical/racialized beauty is found in the whiteness of the cream that Pond's Vanishing Cream can provide: "just a dainty touch of powder and you will have that *natural* smooth, transparent complexion, *which glows from within,* and which is the envy of *every* woman. There is no better base for powder than Pond's Vanishing Cream" (emphasis mine).[21]

Throughout "The Vine-Leaf" emphasis is placed on the whiteness of the back of the woman in the painting and on the whiteness of the back of Alegre, as when she visits the surgeon: "this delicate, wine-red vine-leaf, staining a surface as pure as the petal of any magnolia." The mark contrasting with the whiteness is what must be removed, is what makes it so she cannot pass as unrecognizable from the image in the painting. If we read this in the context of Mena's work, in which the majority of her characters are portrayed as fair-skinned Mexicanos, this fear of racial marking has much larger meaning. It is the fear that the fair-skinned Mexican, s/he who has historically been more readily accepted by Anglo society (as seen in gestures to de-Mexicanize individuals by referring to them as Spanish, Hispanic, etc.), will have her/his (im)poster status revealed. Such fears are culturally constructed and very much linked to cultural systems of images, such as those in *Century* equating dark skin with servitude and those in Mexico (and elsewhere) equating light skin with class status. These two systems come together in the image of the marked woman in "The Vine-Leaf," for she is both light-skinned and racially marked, both high in class status as wife of the marqués and in servitude to him who holds the secret over her. Like the figure of the trickster, Alegre is simultaneously visible and invisible, her actions taken strictly for survival. In this story, Mena exposes the multiple layers of the positionality of the woman of color as trickster, as subverter of the patriarchal system she is contained within. Alegre is of the ruling class, but her gender ultimately contains her within a "marked" body, as in Phelan's use of the term.

Historically, dark bodies have been hypersexualized and marked as excessive. As Fanon writes of the black male body, "the Negro is eclipsed. He is turned into a penis. He *is* a penis."[22] Similarly, the natural wine-red birthmark marks Alegre as a woman and attracts the male gaze to her as such ("But it seems to me a blessed stigma. . . . With permission, I should say that the god of Bacchus himself painted it here in the arch of this chaste back, where only the eyes of Cupid could find it . . ."). She *is* her white back. The vine-leaf marks her as sexually excessive and sexual outlaw, both of which are the status of the trickster. Because she is a woman of color (in the case of the painting, literally a colored woman contained within the frame of the portrait), her body becomes a site for subversion and/or change within the system for survival purposes. The body—in this case especially in terms of the Mexican female body as depicted in the La Malinche narrative I discuss later—has been historically taken. Yet, for Mena, female sexuality becomes a source of power rather than a marker of colonization. In this way, Alegre's reclamation of her body is a reclamation of boundaries.

I want to connect this reading of "The Vine-Leaf" to another of Mena's stories by further developing an analysis of a distinctly female trickster discourse. Mena's works demonstrate that as a bilingual, bicultural, woman writer she worked through a large network of cultural mythology—from the tale of Huitzilopochtli to the beauty myth of her time to La Malinche. The story of La Malinche is that of Doña Marina, who, according to folklore, slept with Cortés, begot his children, and contributed to the oppression and eventual demise of the indigenous people at the hands of Cortés. She is said to be a traitor to her race for having been a translator between Cortés and the indigenous people. Mother of the first mestizo, Mexico's first mixed-blood child, she is known in folklore as La Malinche, the fucked one (*la chingada*). Consistently, male tricksters are allowed sexual power; yet a female trickster figure who wields her sexual power is designated as the fucked one.

There are clearly gendered differences in the various Chicano/Mexicano trickster figures. The pachuco figure, for example, is an undoubtedly male figure, whose flamboyant dress and oversized zoot suit mark him as large and powerful, the suit working to mark him as male, his style marking him as Chicano. His multilingualism, based in English, Spanish, and barrio slang (caló), also marks his status as a powerful spokesperson, the underdog fighting the invading peoples who threaten his very cultural existence. He is flagged by rucas (women) who, ironically, signify his autonomy in that he doesn't really "need" these women; they are merely part of his *estilo*. The ability to create emotional distance is crucial to el pachuco's ability to survive the pain of racism, the witnessing of the rape of his women, and colonization. His pride and defiance are the very basis of his status as a trickster hero.

The La Llorona and La Malinche figures, however, do not share the same access to power, nor are they perceived (in traditional readings) as (s)heroes. La Llorona is a woman who was scorned by a lover and destroyed her children in her anger and grief. She is portrayed as passive, having waited so long for her lover's return. Her angry actions, unlike those of the pachuco, are not seen as bold or defiant; they are seen as gestures for attention by an irrational and hysterical woman. The pachuco's outlaw status makes him a cultural hero; in contrast, La Llorona's outlaw status makes her a cultural betrayer. Many Chicana critics have provided revisionist readings of La Malinche which focus on what it means for women to possess an outlaw status. For example, Herrera-Sobek re-envisions La Malinche as "the founder of a new people, the Latin American/Mexican/Chicano people. And this is a creative act, not a destructive one."[23] Likewise, in her work, Mena revises the La Malinche reading to depict women as sexually assertive and communally productive—rather than destructive—individuals.

Such potential tricksters as La Malinche are traditionally depicted as women who betrayed their race and, more importantly, their male masters. From such tales women are supposed to learn the limits of their behavior—for example, the danger of talking too much and of taking too much power into their own hands. Gloria Anzaldúa writes of this, "*Hocicona, repelona, chismosa,* having a big mouth, questioning, carrying tales are all signs of being *mal criada*. In my culture they are all words that are derogatory if applied to women—I've never heard them applied to men."[24] Additionally, women of color are always put in the precarious position of having to choose between alliances with their race and alliances with their gender, as seen through the La Llorona narrative in which the female figure is pitted against another woman of her race in a system of compulsory heterosexuality designed to keep racial (and class) purity. In the Aztec version of the story, La Llorona kills her children as a gesture to her race. Most La Malinche narratives take an act of a woman's asserting her voice and status as a translator and turn it into a tale of cultural betrayal. Having lived in Mexico until the age of fourteen, Mena would most likely have been familiar with La Malinche tales, along with other myths prescribing extreme role models in the form of La Virgin and La Puta/The Whore. This is especially probable given her story "The Birth of the God of War," in which she writes of her grandmother telling her numerous tales of "Aztec mythology."

In trickster narratives from various cultures, the uncontrolled sexual prowess demonstrated by such figures as La Llorona and La Malinche is precisely a mark of the trickster. The African trickster figure of Esu, the sole messenger of the gods who interprets the will of the gods to man and the desires of man to the gods, is "characterized as an inveterate copulator possessed by his enormous penis."[25] In one version of a Winnebago trickster tale, Trickster "awakes to find his enormous, erect penis—one must imagine it several yards long—raising like a flag the blanket that had been covering him."[26] This figure keeps his "life principle in a box" that he wears on his back. Both of these figures are kinds of culturally valorized "fuckers." However, the (lack of) status and power of La Malinche depend upon her being "the fucked one."

In a revisionary reading, it is important that La Malinche be read as "La Chingóna," *the one who fucks*; in this role she joins the ranks of her numerous trickster cousins. Alicia Arrizón defines the chingóna figure as a female figure who is "aggressive, angry, passionate, fierce, vibrant, ambivalent, erotic, assertive, dynamic."[27] These are characteristics traditionally associated with male tricksters. However, La Chingóna turns the tradition around. She is the woman who makes use of her anger and does not fear the wrath of the males who assert their authority over her, the kind of assertion displayed in Mena's story by Alegre—whose name in Spanish means glad, joyful, reckless, wanton—and who says, when the surgeon balks at her directions, "For Favor, good surgeon, your knife!"—and by the character Carmelita in "The Sorcerer and General Bisco."

In this story, Mena addresses issues of land expansion, capitalist exploitation, and woman as cultural translator and critic. The plot concerns a wealthy, avaricious landowner, Don Baltazar Rascón, and General Bisco, a type of Mexican Robin Hood. Rascón masters the art of hypnosis as a means of assuring that the local "peons" will cooperate with his land laws and taxes:

> It was known that by devious means he had become possessed of a large part of the inheritance of her [his wife's] younger brother, Aquiles de la Vega, of whom the law had appointed him guardian. Indeed, at the time of the arrival of the rebel army

the peons had been whispering over the disappearance of Don Aquiles since the previous night, and now that their tyrant had fallen, they were eager to accuse him of having murdered that most amiable young man.

Mena also brings in the issue of sexual violence as part of colonial land expansion in regards to the character of Rascón:

Doña Carmelita, too,—the saintly Doña Carmelita, his second wife, young daughter of a family *muy distinguida* which had been despoiled by Rascón and compelled to give him its cherished lamb in marriage,—where was she? Search was being made for the bodies of those two in order that as many crimes as possible might be brought home to the oppressor before the eyes of the noble and just General Bisco.

Bisco works the countryside, taking from the rich and giving to the poor. He is a local hero whose methods are violent, and his primary focus is on raising the standard of living for the underclass.

Carmelita and Aquiles are the two lovers who are fleeing from Rascón. It is thought that Rascón has murdered them and consequently he has been captured and turned over to General Bisco. Carmelita and Aquiles are soon thereafter found in the woods and taken to the general as well. They arrive in his quarters to find General Bisco and Rascón together. At this point in the story Carmelita emerges as a trickster figure. Mena shows the reader that gender does make a difference in regards to the political efficacy of the trickster figure in her very different treatment of what are seemingly the story's two trickster figures: Rascón and Carmelita.

When the general is ready to shoot Rascón, Rascón makes the request to hold the crystal paperweight that adorns Bisco's desk. However, Bisco seizes the crystal and begins to gaze into it. Rascón resorts to a pernicious form of tricksterism that on the surface seems to use wit in an effort to escape from his captor; but Rascón is a capitalist/hypnotist preying on those who are economically oppressed. His targets are the men who wish to overthrow him and the woman, Carmelita, who is working in solidarity with their movement. As a landowner, Rascón understands precisely what hypnosis is all about: the seduction of the consumer and the creation of the dependent subject. The act of hypnotism in this story serves as a metaphor for images of colonial conquest:

He was drawing upon his own experiences to hasten the passing of his subject into the deeper stages of suggestibility. . . . When he had found his voice he went on to dictate such visions of battle, victory, plunder, political triumph, coarse pleasures, and popular adulation as might be expected to tickle the aspirations of such a man as he conceived El Bisco to be; and always in the background of the picture lurked the figure of Don Baltazar Rascón, faithful, beneficent, indispensable, a modest custodian of wisdom and conjurer of fortune. . . .[28]

In my reading, I discount Rascón as a trickster figure because hypnotism is not an act of wit; it is simply a further demonstration of oppression, a metaphor for the way that capitalism works: a seduction of the mind and a general taking over of the will. Hypnosis and the techniques of advertising, propaganda, and brainwashing employ tactics to disorient the subject through sensory overload, which facilitates submission and encourages suggestibility.[29]

At the time Mena's story appeared, a very paternalistic United States government sought to turn American attention away from domestic problems, which took the form of monopolies, workers' strikes, and growing dissatisfaction with labor conditions nationwide; the government used international conflict to create a safety valve for explosive domestic class conflict. Once foreign markets were seen as important to prosperity and "American safety," expansionist policies, even war, were projected to have wide appeal. The hypnotic package disguised colonial expansion as "good will" and a sharing of American democracy with the rest of the world. That this sentiment was, indeed, sold to the American public is evident in such political commentary as Lincoln G. Valentine's "Meddling with Our Neighbors," in *Century* in 1915.[30]

> Nicaragua is entitled to manage its own affairs, choose its own President, and work out its own business. Instead of having imposed upon them a trembling figurehead executive, the people have the right to free elections and to the recognition of the successful candidate. As proof of their honest intention, the people of Nicaragua are quite willing to have such elections impartially supervised by the United States. . . .
>
> Let us show the world that the germ of "right by might" has not contaminated our hemisphere of freedom and justice, that we do not wish to rule by force, but collaborate in sympathy! Let us, then, give our weaker sisters what made us great—liberty and union!

This passage further emphasizes the gendered positions of two figures: United States/Mexico, Rascón/Carmelita, as I will discuss below.

In trickster traditions such as the African American and Native American, there are always tales that tell of what happens when a cultural insider forgets his subjectivity is linked to that of Others, his community. In *From Trickster to Bad Man,* John W. Roberts writes:

> As the story of the trickster and the tar baby reveals, one of the easiest traps that an enslaved African could get caught up in was that of accepting illusion for reality, especially the illusion of shared identity that the masters were all too capable to creating. However, as the actions of the trickster revealed, the solution to the dilemmas created by existence in a socio-cultural environment in which trickster and dupe could suddenly reverse their roles was to always remember one's cultural roots. By embracing their roots, enslaved Africans found in their cultural heritage

and their tradition of animal trickster tale creation, if not a solution to slavery as an institution, a system of values guiding action which greatly minimized its impact on their lives.[31]

When one places issues of the self over the community, dire consequences ensue. In the Mexicana/o and Chicana/o traditions, in La Llorona tales the woman is punished forever for putting her "selfish needs" as an individual woman over her more communal role as mother. In Mena's narrative, however, it is the men who risk such punishment. When Bisco puts aside community interest, if only for a moment, he is immediately subjected to discipline. El Bisco responds to Rascón's bid that "I can reward your Excellency in coin more precious than gold. I can show him his own august future, as I have seen it myself," with the reply "Show me of what you are capable, but move quickly." Subsequently, there is a price to pay for his having placed his own interests first: He risks losing important community allies and being thrown into the imprisonment of Rascón's hypnotic gaze.

Aquiles and Carmelita are summoned to appear before General Bisco. They do not fear him. Carmelita has a vision of their meeting: "We are to see Don Baltazar. I do not understand clearly yet. Be resolute for all that God may permit to happen." Carmelita is the only figure in this story to have a true vision of the future. Additionally, having experienced and fought the hypnotic gaze of Rascón, she is the only person who can reveal his tricks to others. Carmelita then becomes the voice of resistance and the cultural critic, calling for Bisco to examine the abuses of capitalist power:

> It is *he* [Rascón] who mocks you . . . it is *his* voice that you speak with. . . . While you looked into the crystal he made himself your master, as he is master of many others as he was of me until I freed myself and learned to use his own arts to spy upon him—I, little and weak as you see me, with no power but love.

As in "The Vine-Leaf," the woman's marked body—here Carmelita's cataleptic seizures as part of her clairvoyance—simultaneously frees her (from Rascón's gaze) and enslaves her (under the protection of both Bisco and Aquiles). Significantly, the word "master" becomes the key, for Bisco replies:

> "My master?"
>
> He tried to look at Don Baltazar, but his eyes dropped to the floor.
>
> "My friend," began Don Baltazar.
>
> "I am your friend, eh?"
>
> "My more than friend, brother, companion of my future, illustrious conqueror and savior of the constitution, in whose service God has commanded me to spend the remaining years of my life—"
>
> "Wait a moment," stammered the general. "Fewer words and more explications. . . ."

Again, the role of gender becomes significant to the story's power dynamics and to the trickster figure's ability to explicate those imbalances. Carmelita's relationship to patriarchy makes more than clear the "master"/servant roles Rascón works to enforce. Carmelita then provides a reading of what happened when Bisco stared into the crystal. She decodes Rascón's methodology—that is, his voice hypnotically demanding that peons submit to his capitalist agenda for land expansion. If we carry this reading further, she then explicates the desire of *Century*'s advertisers that readers submit to seductive advertising messages; and if we extend this even further, she ultimately explicates the desire of the American government that Mexicans and other Central Americans submit to the colonizing presence of American soldiers in their lands. In each of these cases, her status as Other, as Mexican, as Woman, empowers the clarity of her commentary on cultural institutions and various socioeconomic and cultural powers.

The more Carmelita insists that Bisco examine how Rascón has made himself master, the more fervently Rascón demands that she be put to death. The female trickster, and the voice of the female cultural critic, is seen as overwhelmingly threatening. In the La Llorona and La Malinche stories, the woman's voice offers important cultural readings of abusive socioeconomic relationships. But always her gender and sexuality are immediately "blamed" as the cause of her challenge to male power figures. For example, Rascón cries, "It is the guilty woman. She is possessed, and has tried to bewitch your Excellency. . . . Death for the woman!" When her voice cannot be contained by her male oppressor, it is immediately connected to an uncontrolled sexual prowess. It is a very common strategy for men to contain women by sexualizing them, as illustrated in the phrase, "You're really sexy when you're angry," or through the enforcement of cultural myths, such as the beauty myth and those of La Llorona and La Malinche, that say women's anger is inappropriate or marks a woman as a cultural betrayer. The angry woman leaving her lover, yelling no when she really means yes, or leaving enraged as a ploy to sexually arouse him, is a recurring theme in cultural productions, which only serves to contribute to a climate of rape culture and to feed a system of images that says there is something *inherently evil* in women that needs to be *controlled*. This is the message Rascón exploits when he says, "She is possessed, and has tried to bewitch your Excellency. . . ." Yet, as demonstrated in my reading of "The Vine-Leaf," uncontrolled sexual prowess is precisely a mark of the trickster. And this is empowering in teaching ourselves to be resisting readers.

It is significant that the male figures in Mena's story cannot theorize—which is one of the most important parts of successful political action. When General Bisco finally understands the import of Carmelita's explications, he escapes the hypnotic bond: "I am no longer El Bisco . . . I am nothing. I am less than that tarantula there." (Perhaps here she is like Arachne, who vividly painted in her tapestry, in picture after picture, the crimes of the Olympian gods against women?) Rascón hears of the tarantula's presence: "A tarantula! Fear and antipathy stung Don Baltazar into swift movement, and he wheeled to face the loathed invader of his library." When Rascón's back is turned from Bisco, the hypnotic gaze is severed, and the general at this point "did not theorize on a method for liberating a personality from external control. He merely became a practical man with a magazine pistol."

However, one cannot analyze power by looking at one's oppressor's back. In order to change existing systems of oppression, one must be able to conceptualize how power works. Mena's work features women as active and vital parts of cultural and political change; they have the ability to examine how power works as a result of their subject positions as women in patriarchal societies. As Anzaldúa sets forth in *Borderlands*:

> The new *mestiza* copes by developing a tolerance for contradictions, a tolerance for ambiguity. She learns to be Indian in Mexican culture, to be Mexican from an Anglo point of view. She learns to juggle cultures. She has a plural personality, she operates in a pluralistic mode—nothing is thrust out, the good, the bad and the ugly, nothing rejected, nothing abandoned. Not only does she sustain contradictions, she turns the ambivalence into something else.[32]

This turning "ambivalence into something else" is what Diana Taylor has referred to as "transculturation,"[33] which is what happens when Third World artists influenced by First World approaches to cultural production appropriate First World methods to produce something entirely different, an end product that has been translated across cultures. This is precisely what is taking place in Mena's works and what takes place in (re)constructing a mythic tradition that makes women central to cultural production: a movement across a culture that is set up to limit woman, and toward a location of empowerment. This is what defines the mode of the feminist trickster.

It is significant that Mena's story ends with Carmelita as the voice of analysis. Mena revises the story to make room for the Mexican woman as trickster, La Chingóna. It is the woman who demystifies the uses and abuses of power. And by extension, Mena as Mexican American author is a trickster herself, duping the editors of *Century* who would invite her to publish her stories in the same volume where they would place Edward Alsworth Ross's racist tracts, colonial advertising, and anti-Mexican stories and essays, among other aggressively xenophobic and arguably misogynist writings.

❧

There are, of course, limitations to trickster discourses. We can reread these literatures and discuss them as subversive and resistant. The works *are* political, but they do not incite political action in and of themselves. And this is where theories of reception become important. Readers must also want to change the system, must be ready to receive the trickster discourse and to do something with it, to respond in the performative. Writing alone has limited impact, especially if the audience receiving the images continues to contain the discourses. Readers must be active readers. Becoming an active reader is, as you know, a hard-won skill. We live in a culture whose political systems do not promote the power of the people. All civil rights movements have been grassroots movements. Advocates of any kind—of race, class, gender, sexual rights—are actively made, not born.

I think of the first trickster tale I ever read. It was in a Chicano literature course. I went to a small state college whose English department was fortunate enough to have a Chicana scholar among their faculty. Having felt much missing from her own education and seeing a great need among the Chicana/o students on that campus, Professor Olivia Castellano created a Chicana/o literature course. It was only brought into official being, that is, as a course for which students could get credit, after students protested and called attention to the matter by calling a press conference. I remember hearing a professor say, "Chicano literature? Those people can write?"

While reading Sandra Cisneros's "Woman Hollering Creek," those La Chingóna elements came into full force with the vivid image of the *grito* yelled by the truck-driving mujer over that story's Tex-Mex bridge. I was reminded of my undergraduate epiphany: It was in my first Chicano literature class that I read for the first time—near the very end of my bachelor's degree—a trickster narrative. It was also the first time in my life that I saw my cultural background described in a book assigned for a class. It was electrifying, but at the same time it was terribly sad. It had taken me twenty years to find that integral part of myself in literature. For twenty years I had gone along with the system—had been the good girl for my parents, had been the straight A student, had never questioned authority or brought up politics because everyone knows that's so impolite. I had been that "silent, subservient, productive minority" because no one showed me an alternative. And I don't think it was until then that I was ready to see myself in such a light, either. Until that class.

The power of the trickster tale was in *me* because it showed me my own potential to challenge the system. I didn't have to be La Llorona or La

Malinche. I could be, and often these days am, La Chingóna. Maybe it's because I went to Catholic school; maybe it's because I am the defiant oldest daughter of a very oppressive man; maybe it's because as an undergraduate English major all the stories I ever read in the first person seemed to be about English men from an era and culture not mine; maybe it's for these and other reasons I find trickster tales and what I would term trickster discourses liberating and fascinating, providing hope that there is a space for acts of resistance within hegemonic modes of cultural production. . . .

Notes

This essay is a composite of papers given at the 1992 Modern Language Association and the 1993 National Association of Chicana/o Studies conferences. I am indebted to Elizabeth Ammons for having introduced me to the works of Mena and having supported this project and the larger project of minority literatures in American literary studies.

As ideas do not exist in a vacuum, I would also like to thank the following people for their conversations, which significantly contributed to the formative thinking presented here: my colleague Darryl Carr, with whom I team taught an interdisciplinary summer research seminar on pranksters and tricksters (University of California at Santa Barbara, 1992); our student Laura Jiménez, who brought to my attention treacherous woman serpent tales and charritas coloradas; the participants of the first Chicano graduate student seminar with Antonia Casteñeda at the University of California at Santa Barbara (spring 1993) for their critical comments on drafts; and Pierre Liflan and María Herrera-Sobek for permissions to use their unpublished works.

1. Henry Louis Gates, Jr., *The Signifying Monkey* (New York: Oxford University Press, 1988), pp. 8–9.

2. Andrew Wiget, "His Life in His Tail: The Native American Trickster and the Literature of Possibility," *Redefining American Literary History,* eds. A. LaVonne Brown Ruoff and Jerry W. Ward (New York: Modern Language Association, 1990), p. 94.

3. Ibid.

4. John W. Roberts, "The African American Animal Trickster as Hero," *Redefining American Literary History,* p. 100.

5. Wiget, p. 92.

6. Ibid., p. 89.

7. María Herrera-Sobek. Paper given at the University of California at Santa Barbara, 21 May 1993, "Oral Traditions and Chicano/a Writers: A Gramscian Analysis." Used here with permission of the author.

8. María Amparo Ruiz de Burton is said to be the first Mexican woman to write fiction in English. Like Mena, she was married to an Anglo, a military man. She, too, went to the East. See *The Squatter and the Don,* edited and introduced by Rosaura Sánchez and Beatrice Pita (Houston: Arte Publico Press, 1992).

9. The only biographical sources I have found on Mena are in Matthew Hoehn, ed., *Catholic Authors* (Newark: St. Mary's Abbey, 1948), pp. 118–119, and Edward Simmen, ed., *North of the Rio Grande* (New York: Penguin, 1992), pp. 39–40.

10. Simmen, p. 40.

11. There are numerous versions of this story; I have provided only a few. For

further reading see Norma Alarcón's essay "Traddutora, Traditora: A Paradigmatic Figure of Chicana Feminism," *Cultural Critique* (Fall 1989): 57–87; Sandra Messinger Cypess's *La Malinche in Mexican Literature* (Austin: University of Texas, 1991); and Monica Palacios's "La Llorona Loca: The Other Side," in Carla Trujillo, ed., *Latina Lesbians: The Girls Our Mothers Warned Us About* (Berkeley: Third Woman, 1991), pp. 49–51, which addresses the issues of compulsory heterosexuality and mandated motherhood embedded in the traditional tale.

12. Edward Alsworth Ross's series in *Century Magazine* on immigrant groups in America includes such titles as "The Old World in the New: Economic Consequences of Immigration" (November 1913); "Immigrants in Politics: The Political Consequences of Immigration" (January 1914); "Racial Consequences of Immigration" (February 1914); "Origins of the American People" (March 1914); "South of Panama: Western Columbia and Ecuador" (November 1914); "The Native Races" (January 1915); and "Chile and Argentina" (February 1915). This "series" was legitimized by Ross's title of "Professor of Sociology, University of Wisconsin," and his position papers on Latin America were introduced by John Barrett, "Director-General of the Pan-American Union; former Minister to Siam, Argentina, Columbia, and Panama." These titles give authority to the writer as a political scientist. His articles make claims such as:

> It is fair to say that the blood now being injected into the veins of our people is 'sub-common.' To one accustomed to the aspect of the normal American population, the Caliban type shows up with a frequency that is startling. Observe immigrants not as they come travelwan up the gang-plank, nor as they issue toil-begrimed from pit's mouth or mill gate, but in their gatherings, washed, combed, and in their Sunday best. You are struck by the fact that from ten to twenty per cent are hirsute, low-browed, big-faced persons of obviously low mentality. Not that they suggest evil. They simply look out of place in black clothes and stiff collar, since clearly they belong in skins, in wattled huts at the close of the great ice age. These oxlike men are descendants of those *who always stayed behind*. Those in whom the soul burns with the dull, smoky flame of the pineknot stuck to the soil, are now thick in the sluiceways of immigration. ("Racial Consequences of Immigration," February 1914.)

All of his articles depict as scientific fact a social structure in which immigrants are burdensome, unwanted, dirty, "sub-common," economically and racially threatening, hostile foreigners, among other pernicious interpretations of diverse cultures and peoples. I call attention to Ross's writings not to single him out so much, for there is a multitude of other like articles to be found in *Century* and other magazines of the era. I call attention to Ross's work to expose how such articles create a particular cultural climate and to suggest that it is this climate in which Mena wrote.

In an editorial column, "Topics of the Time" (November 1913), a reader responds to Ross's writings:

> There is no other so ably equipped to study this subject impartially and to present it in true perspective to American citizens. Professor Ross, during his seven years in the chair of sociology at the University of Wisconsin, has made a worldwide reputation. Before that he was connected with the University of Indiana, Cornell, Leland Stanford, and the University of Nebraska, and has been special lecturer at Harvard and the University of Chicago. He is the author of seven books on sociological subjects, several of which are text-books in wide use. He has traveled in search of first-hand information. His analysis, in this and succeeding papers, of the voluminous and complicated reports of the Immigration Commission, place the results of this vast work within the grasp and use of busy Americans.

What I find frightening about this writer is that he is prolific, he is a university professor, he writes textbooks, and his work becomes the ten-minute information sheet—much like the same sheet Reagan demanded?—for readers' report of world events. Again, this example calls attention to the role cultural production plays in shaping systems of images concerning race, class, gender, and sexuality.

13. Pierre Liflan, from his unpublished essay "Bandidos y Mojados: (Un)Popular Images of Chicanos," part of his M.A. thesis, Department of Art History, University of California at Santa Barbara, 1993. Used with permission of the author.

14. See also Ramón Gutiérrez, "Aztlán, Montezuma, and New Mexico: The Political Uses of American Indian Mythology," *Aztlán: Essays on the Chicano Homeland* (Albuquerque: Academia/El Norte Publications, 1989), pp. 172–190.

15. One such analysis of how media constructs naturalized images of the Other (in terms of gender) is in Sut Jhally's controversial video *Dreamworlds: Sex, Desire and Power in Rock and Roll Video on MTV.* Jhally analyzes how systems of images in rock and roll video naturalize roles of women in society as those of the nymphomaniac, the dancer/stripper, the tease, the all-night partier, among others. He then juxtaposes these images with scenes from the film *The Accused* in order to illustrate that when consumers of popular culture are trained to read through such systems of images that naturalize behaviors, there are very specific consequences. His thesis is that viewers of MTV are trained to see women within very narrow systems of images that reinforce male domination and that these images desensitize viewers to issues such as date rape; consequently, viewers come to believe the images given to them through the television fantasy dream world. Images such as the nymphomaniac or the woman on the prowl for a good party with anybody she can find reinforce culturally destructive beliefs connected to these images, such as "she was wearing a short skirt, therefore she asked for it," or "she was dressed seductively so she really wanted me to."

16. There is always a risk that trickster discourses and other narratives of resistance will be appropriated, and thus contained, by the hegemony and reconfigured into a dominant system of images. Examples of such moves include the current cultural vogue of jazz music as the new classical music/commodity fetish of the upper-class and/or the sign of the truly cultured consumer; the move to label minority discourses as "Post-Modern" in a way that depoliticizes the role of race and gender in the literatures and privileges, for example, the role of pastiche or cultural deterritorialization without likewise privileging race, gender, sexuality, and the sociocultural and historical reasons behind demonstrated feelings of a fractured identity; the current vogue of "Queer Theory" as the mark of the academic "hypourgeoisie," in which psychoanalysis is privileged over identity-politics (rather than, say, the two seen as equally important voices within the discourse) in a move to legitimate queer studies that also functions as a move that in many cases depoliticizes the activist role played by the many writers, academics, and students who have contributed to the visibility of such a body of literature within academia. These are simply my own observations as to how I see what I would call subversive discourses, changes and challenges to the system kept in check by larger hegemonic forces, such as capitalism, the politics of who gets what accepted to which conferences, what kind of work by whom is legitimated in tenure reviews in which kinds of departments at which universities, etc.

17. I want briefly to call attention here to the explicit sexual imagery of her placing her foot on the gunwale of the (phallic) ship, her (sexually) wild look, her sexual gaze to him—all of which I read as the projected male gaze and how this

male writer wants to be seen and see. This fits into the fantasy of the colonial subject as one who is there to please the colonial visitor, particularly in regard to (sexual) service. It also links into the system of images discussed by Jhally in his film, that is, the fantasy that it is really women who objectify men. The male fantasy dream world is rooted in an adolescent male dream that all women are sexually available to him and under his control, ready to serve his every sexual whim.

18. *Century* (November 1912).

19. Homi K. Bhabha, "The Other Question: Homi K. Bhabha Reconsiders the Stereotype and Colonial Discourse," *Screen* (November–December 1983): 18–36.

20. Peggy Phelan, *Unmarked: The Politics of Performance* (New York: Routledge, 1993), p. 5.

21. *Century* (November 1913).

22. Frantz Fanon, *Black Skin White Masks* (London: Paladin, 1970), p. 120, as quoted in Richard Fung, "Looking for My Penis: The Eroticized Asian in Gay Video Porn," *How Do I Look?: Queer Film and Video,* ed. Bad Object-Choices (Seattle: Bay Press, 1991), pp. 145–168.

23. Herrera-Sobek, op. cit.

24. Gloria Anzaldúa, *Borderlands/La Frontera* (San Francisco: Spinsters/aunt lute, 1987), p. 54.

25. Gates, *The Signifying Monkey,* p. 6.

26. Wiget, p. 91.

27. Alicia Arrizón, "Chingóna Subjectivity," paper delivered at "Unnatural Acts: The Conference—Theorizing the Performance," University of California at Riverside, 12–14 February 1993.

28. A theory of reception is extremely important here. This story could be and probably was read as a metaphor for political struggles in Mexico. Bisco would represent Pancho Villa, the Mexican revolutionary who joined the rebels and fought vigorously for President Madero (and later against General Huerta and President Carranza). Madero eventually failed to implement notable reforms. Revolts broke out, and Huerta imprisoned Madero. However, as president, Madero was a champion of democracy and social reform who led the revolution and overthrew the Diaz regime. Diaz was a dictator who ruled Mexico for 35 years in the interest of the few and at the expense of the peons. He promoted prosperity by encouraging foreign investments. Growing popular discontent culminated in the 1910 revolution led by Madero. Diaz fled and died in exile. Huerta overthrew Madero and set up a dictatorship marked by corruption and violence. Numerous revolts forced him to resign as president (1914) and to flee into exile. Carranza became president in 1914 after fighting in the Mexican revolution and helping to overthrow Huerta. In this reading, Rascón would represent Diaz. However, the figure of Rascón can also be read as a stand-in for that of the United States in regard to current political tensions at the time, with the figure of Bisco representing Mexico trying to unite a divided Central America.

29. See also Naomi Wolf, "Religion," *The Beauty Myth* (New York: Doubleday, 1991), pp. 86–130.

30. *Century* (October 1915).

31. John W. Roberts, *From Trickster to Bad Man: The Black Folk Hero in Slavery and Freedom* (Philadelphia: University of Pennsylvania Press, 1989), p. 42.

32. Anzaldúa, p. 79.

33. Diana Taylor, "Transculturating Transculturation," *Interculturalism and Performance* (New York: PAJ Publications, 1991), pp. 60–74.

JEANNE SMITH

"A Second Tongue": The Trickster's Voice in the Works of Zitkala-Ša

Iktomi, Lakota trickster, takes his name from the spider, a creature that travels seemingly anywhere: through air, on water, underground, on land.[1] As William K. Powers notes, the spider's ability to fly, swim, and walk on six legs makes the creature "impossible to classify along traditional Lakota lines," and thus allows it a freedom and power not accorded to most earthly creatures, who are restricted to one element (W. Powers, p. 229). The trickster Iktomi enjoys the same freedom and power, frequently changing forms, donning disguises, breaking cultural taboos and natural laws, defying even death.

Iktomi is a vital part of Lakota tradition. A cluster of Iktomi tales appears in nearly every collection of Lakota legends, and Iktomi's comic displays of human frailty and ingenuity make the stories popular, funny, and even morally edifying for those who choose to find a lesson in trickster's negative example.[2] It is not surprising, then, that as a young, educated Lakota woman writing at the turn of the century, Zitkala-Ša would launch her literary career with *Old Indian Legends* (1901), a collection of mostly trickster tales.[3] Yet several things about Zitkala-Ša's career make her position in relation to the trickster exceptional.

Like the spider who travels through many spatial planes, Zitkala-Ša moved in many cultural worlds, belonging fully to none. She was one of the first Native Americans to tell her own story and the stories of her culture in English, without the aid of a translator or editor. Politically active throughout most of her life both in Lakota and pan-Indian affairs, Zitkala-Ša recognized the critical juncture at which so many Native American cultures had arrived at the beginning of the twentieth century. The Lakota people were quickly losing their land and their traditional way of life to the land allotment policies, the new reservation system, and the acculturationist thrust of Indian schools. As Zitkala-Ša's descriptions of her missionary boarding school education indicate, turn-of-the-century assimilationist education policies created a generation particularly drawn to and reliant on tricksterism, cultural "marginals" speaking English and Lakota, poised between western and traditional Native American cultures. Tricksters figure prominently throughout Zitkala-Ša's writing, from *Old Indian Legends* (1901; hereafter, *OIL*) to the contemporary short stories and autobiographical sketches collected in *American Indian Stories* (1921; hereafter *AIS*). By transplanting trickster tales into written English, telling contemporary trickster stories, and describing her own experience of living between two cultural worlds, Zitkala-Ša explores both the enabling and the destructive potential of the trickster for the future of her culture.

In Lakota tradition, as in many Native American traditions, the trickster is both a hero and a scapegoat. Iktomi named all creatures, invented language and culture, saved his people from the insatiable Iya; yet he is deceitful, greedy, selfish, and amoral.[4] Barbara Babcock-Abrahams notes the cultural implications of the trickster's paradoxical nature: "While trickster's power endows his group with vitality and other boons, it also carries the threat and the possibility of chaos" (p. 154). Iktomi's paradoxical position outside the traditional boundaries of Lakota culture, then, makes his power as well as his position ambiguous: He can potentially save or destroy his culture.

One of Iktomi's greatest skills is his ability to smooth-talk listeners into unwittingly cooperating with him; and in her preface to *Old Indian Legends,* Zitkala-Ša plays the part of a skilled trickster herself, duping her readers into an acknowledgment of an inherently valuable and living Lakota culture. While she presents her collection conventionally as children's stories, Zitkala-Ša's insistence on the ongoing viability of these stories contrasts strongly with the more conciliatory tone of other collections of its kind.[5] In her preface, she adopts the persona of a cultural liaison and a careful gardener "transplanting" the tales into English. "These old legends of America belong quite as much to the blue-eyed little patriot as to the black-haired aborigine," she says (*OIL,* p. vi). While this generous diplomacy suggests that she writes to link all the children of "our country," her highly metaphorical language reveals other aims as well (*OIL,* p. v). Under the guise of tactful diplomacy, Zitkala-Ša's preface to *Old Indian Legends* reminds the reader of the primacy of Native Americans on American soil and reaffirms the validity of Native American culture, thereby redefining its relationship to the dominant culture. She introduces the legends as "relics of our country's once virgin soil," to which the "little black-haired aborigine" listened around the campfire—long, she implies, before the forefathers of the "little blue-eyed patriot" ever arrived to despoil it (*OIL,* p. v). Reinforcing this thought, she explains: "Now I have tried to transplant the native spirit of these tales—root and all—into the English language, since America in the last few centuries has acquired a second tongue" (*OIL,* p. vi). The English language is not only a "second tongue" to Zitkala-Ša; she reminds her readers that it is indeed America's second tongue, superimposed, as is Anglo-American culture, on a rich body of languages and traditions that had existed long before the arrival of Europeans. Her casual reference to "the last few centuries" reveals a much larger time frame than any conventional western sense of American history encompasses, thereby undermining her white reader's comfortable and usually unexamined sense of primacy and national citizenship.

The end of the preface asserts more strongly that the legends Zitkala-Ša presents are not merely fairy tales, but express an entire belief system. Suggesting that the reality of the stories' figures should be taken seriously, as they are "not wholly fanciful creatures" (*OIL,* p. v), she hopes that through her tales her reader might be

> forcibly impressed with the possible earnestness of life as seen through the teepee door! If it be true that much lies "in the eye of the beholder," then in the American aborigine as in any other race, sincerity of belief, though it were based upon mere optical illusion, demands a little respect. (*OIL*, p. vi)

Although Zitkala-Ša's preface poses as nothing more than a courteous gesture of commonality and brotherhood, it subtly undermines the sense of superiority of "the little blue-eyed patriot" by challenging the comfortable assumptions on which this patriot builds culture and by asserting an alternative viewpoint, which operates from a different sense of history, with a different belief system, and in a different language.

Prepared for by Zitkala-Ša's trickster strategies in her carefully crafted preface, the tales in *Old Indian Legends* showcase the trickster Iktomi. While Iktomi is a major figure in Lakota tradition and his unbounded energy, greed, and foolishness make him especially appealing to young audiences, in most collections he shares the stage with myriad other beings, taking up a relatively small proportion of the stories.[6] However, in Zitkala-Ša's collection, Iktomi emerges as the central figure: The first five stories concern him exclusively, and he appears in ten of the collection's fourteen tales. Of course, Zitkala-Ša's focus on Iktomi derives partly from his obvious appeal to a young audience. Yet the serious undertones of her preface invite further speculation. John W. Roberts, in a study of tricksters in the African American tradition, suggests why the trickster might be so important in Zitkala-Ša's collection. Roberts associates the creation of mythic and folkloric figures like the trickster with culture-building, which he describes as "a recursive, rather than a linear, process of endlessly devising solutions to both old and new problems of how to live under ever-changing social, political, and economic conditions" (Roberts, p. 11). Writing in the face of enormous cultural threat, Zitkala-Ša seeks to preserve an oral tradition while modifying that tradition according to the culture's contemporary needs. The trickster, whose survival depends largely on techniques of masking, deceptive speech, and subversion, is a highly appropriate choice for an author faced with having to preserve her culture by publishing for an American audience in English, her "second tongue."

Although Zitkala-Ša's announced purpose is to retell traditional legends, her individual artistic choices also highlight her own political concerns. As a writer who must "transplant" Lakota tales into English while preserving their "native spirit," Zitkala-Ša is clearly aware that she, like any other individual teller, will alter the tale to fit her circumstances.[7] In recording her culture's oral tradition, she simultaneously creates her own work of art, and her choice of stories and of emphasis within those stories reflects her individual concerns and a contemporary response to historical change. While Zitkala-Ša values the trickster's rhetorical prowess and ability to survive, she also recognizes his potential for destruction, especially when infringement from an outside colonizing force threatens the Lakota culture in which Iktomi traditionally moves. Although Zitkala-Ša deals much more overtly with the danger of modern Iktomis in her contemporary short stories, she aligns Iktomi with cultural threat even in her legends. The stories in *Old Indian Legends* emphasize his undesirable and even dangerous characteristics; in fact, Zitkala-Ša omits Iktomi altogether from one of the few stories in which he traditionally plays a heroic role, "Iya the Camp-Eater."[8]

A particularly vivid example of Zitkala-Ša's revisionist storytelling is "Dance in a Buffalo Skull." The tale retells a traditional Iktomi story in which the trickster hears dancing and shouting coming from a buffalo skull at night. Peering into a lighted eye socket, he finds field mice dancing inside. As he thrusts his head into the skull to try to join them, they scatter, and he is left dancing ridiculously, trying to pry the skull from his head.[9] In Zitkala-Ša's version, the comic ending of the tale is entirely dropped as the story is told from the point of view of the field mice, who, dancing heedlessly in the skull, do not hear wolves howling or other omens of impending disaster. Iktomi, approaching, appears only as "two balls of fiery . . . fiery eyes." We are not told it is Iktomi: "It might have been a wild-cat prowling low on soft, stealthy feet. Slowly but surely the terrible eyes drew nearer and nearer to the level land" (*OIL,* p. 114). While the mice are oblivious to the looming threat, the narrator knows what's coming: "Ah, very near are those round yellow eyes! Very low to the ground they seem to creep—creep toward the buffalo skull. All of a sudden they slide into the eyesockets of the old skull" (*OIL,* p. 116). The story ends with the mice scattering in terror; in this version, to reveal the fiery eyes as those of the comic Iktomi would considerably reduce the story's ominous effect. Zitkala-Ša's revision of this familiar story turns Iktomi into a vast, impersonal, nearly invisible force sweeping over the plains, much like American expansion west: "They came farther and farther into the level land" (*OIL*, p. 114). In addition, she emphasizes the humanity of the "mice" dancers as "night people on the plain" (*OIL*, p. 113). Their dance in a buffalo skull further aligns the mice with the Lakota people, for whom the buffalo represented the means of subsistence. In this tale the unnamed Iktomi represents a genuine threat to the ongoing survival of the Lakota. Tricking the trickster, Zitkala-Ša presents this tale about the threat of devouring colonialism as a ghost story, charging the inherited narrative with more serious political implications that warn against the mice's easy, short-sighted sense of security.

Zitkala-Ša likewise connects traditional legend with contemporary issues in her revision of another well-known story in her trio of tales, "The Badger and the Bear," "The Tree Bound," and "Shooting the Red Eagle." In the first of these, a hungry bear enters a badger's lodge, accepts his hospitality, and returns every day until he grows strong and ousts the badger and his family from their home. The implications of this story for Native American history could not have escaped Zitkala-Ša, who notes ironically in "America's Indian Problem" that the hospitality of Native Americans to early English settlers was met not with gratitude but with claims of dominion (*AIL*, p. 185). Julian Rice points out in his discussion of the *Dakota Texts* version of the "Blood Clot Boy" tale that the bear traditionally comes from somewhere far away, "perhaps like the white man, and is therefore not related by blood or inclination" to the badger (Rice, p. 143). Displaced from his own home by the bear, the badger comes begging to the bear, now living in the badger's home, and is forced to leave with a clot of blood dropped from the bear's buffalo meat. From this clot grows the first human, who takes back the usurped hut for the badger and sends the bear away. In the traditional story Blood Clot Boy becomes a village hero by making the buffalo plentiful. Zitkala-Ša, however, changes the avenger's feat; she has him save the people from a more immediate threat: "every morning rose this terrible red bird out of a high chalk bluff and spreading out its gigantic wings soared slowly over the round camp ground. . . . The people, terror-stricken, ran screaming into their lodges" (*OIL*, p. 78). Whereas Blood Clot Boy helps the people secure the necessities of life, Zitkala-Ša's "avenger" saves the people from immediate external threat, a "man-hungry" red eagle.[10] As with "Dance in a Buffalo Skull," the people's sense of terror is quite vivid, and the threatening creature is "gigantic" and "indifferent" (*OIL*, pp. 78, 80). Clearly these tales have special resonance in the context of their 1901 publication, when the allotment act and the mission boarding schools were gigantically, indifferently swallowing up Lakota lands and culture.

In *American Indian Stories*, Zitkala-Ša connects trickster materials with politics to an even greater extent. The collection contains ten pieces, seven originally published separately between 1900 and 1902. While the book's title suggests they all should be considered stories, even representative "American Indian" stories, what we find inside is an eclectic mix of autobiography, personal essay, short story, and political tract. By grouping these diverse genres together under the label "stories," Zitkala-Ša oversteps the traditional boundaries of the short story form and suggests that all of these forms have equal validity. Indeed, like the many faces of the trickster, each piece presents a different facet of the same subject. For Zitkala-Ša the personal is inseparable from the political: Her individual story speaks to and comes out of other American Indian stories. In particular, one new piece included in the collection, "The Widespread Enigma Concerning Blue-Star Woman," to which I return later, suggests the relationship between the individual and her culture even in its title, which straddles the borders between fiction and political tract.

The short stories in *American Indian Stories* deal either overtly or covertly with contemporary issues. Reflecting the fact that an entire generation of Lakotas and other Native Americans became culturally displaced because of their experiences at mission boarding schools, the English-speaking Lakotas of Zitkala-Ša's generation, like the Lakota trickster Iktomi, possess the power to move between worlds. Like Iktomi, who is both a cultural savior and a greedy, treacherous thief, they also carry the potential for cultural survival or for chaos. In the stories, Zitkala-Ša explores the destructive element as well as the redeeming potential in the generation of tricksters, connecting their power, for good or ill, to the persuasive powers of language.

"The Soft-Hearted Sioux" presents in unequivocal terms the threat that the cultural displacement of a mission education poses to the individual and to the community. After a ten-year absence a young man returns to his tribe "with the white man's Bible in my hand, and the white man's tender heart in my breast" (*AIS*, p. 112). He finds his dying father attended by the medicine man, "the sorcerer of the plains," whom he bans from the home. Despite the convert's attitude, the story bears out his father's edict that "I cannot live without the medicine man" (*AIS*, p. 115). Unable to hunt, to help his people, or to save his father's life, the convert is unfitted for life; his homecoming causes a breach in the tribe, the death of his father, the murder of a white man, and finally his own execution. Zitkala-Ša strategically places this story just after the reprinted essay "The Great Spirit" (originally titled "Why I Am a Pagan"), an essay in which she explains her own spiritual views after a visit from a converted "native preacher," who mouthed "most strangely the jangling phrases of a bigoted creed" (*AIS*, p. 105). The narrator's barely contained self-contempt in "The Soft-

Hearted Sioux" shows the crippling psychological effect of mouthing the "bigoted creed" of an alien language and culture.

Displaced persons are not only self-destructive, Zitkala-Ša suggests, but can also destroy their communities. "The Widespread Enigma Concerning Blue-Star Woman" introduces a class of educated Lakota "tricksters" whose maneuverings serve them as individuals while undercutting the fabric of Lakota culture and society. Blue-Star Woman is a fifty-three-year-old Sioux woman faced with losing her home under the land allocation policies of the Dawes Act.[11] "In the eyes of the white man's law, it was required of her to give proof of her membership in the Sioux tribe," an almost impossible demand for a woman whose parents died in her youth and whose people kept no written records (*AIS*, p. 159). The story portrays intertribal conflict: Through the dealings of two young English-speaking Indians, Blue-Star Woman is allotted land on a distant Sioux Indian Reservation which can ill afford to spare it. "No doubt this Indian woman is entitled to allotment, but where?" wonders Chief High Flier; "We were not asked to give land, but our land is taken from us to give to another Indian" (*AIS*, p. 172).[12]

Zitkala-Ša uses this story, which is placed last in the collection before the political piece, "America's Indian Problem," to address the issue of the destructive potential of modern, educated tricksters. The two men arrive at Blue-Star Woman's cottage bearing all the marks of tricksters; like Iktomi they are disguised, wearing rusty, unpolished "white man's shoes" and "faded civilian clothes." And they know how to smooth-talk and adapt rapidly: Significantly, Blue-Star Woman trusts them because "these near white men speak my native tongue and shake hands according to our custom" (*AIS*, p. 165). They are also Iktomi-like in the foolishness of their stance: "'You see we are educated in the white man's ways,' they said with protruding chests. One unconsciously thrust his thumbs into the armholes of his ill-fitting coat and strutted about in his pride" (*AIS*, p. 166). Typically, they are ravenous: "Coyotes in midwinter could not have been more starved," and they quickly devour the impoverished woman's food (*AIS*, p. 167). Like typical greedy tricksters, they use their bilinguality to exploit an advantageous situation, convincing their host to split her land with them once they obtain it for her.[13] Blue-Star Woman realizes too late that "in her dire need she had become involved with tricksters" (*AIS*, p. 170). To be sure, because the story is a thinly veiled didactic fable, its language often slips into heavy-handed political discourse. Lest her reader miss the point, Zitkala-Ša reveals that the men's "solicitation for Blue-Star Woman was not at all altruistic. They thrived in their grafting business. They and their occupation were the by-product of an unwieldy bureaucracy over the nation's wards" (*AIS*, p. 168). Yet by drawing on Iktomi legends, Zitkala-Ša weds contemporary politics with an ongoing, vibrant cultural tradition.

With the shift to Chief High Flier's perspective in the second half of "Blue-Star Woman," Zitkala-Ša even more explicitly presents the danger of not knowing English. The chief must enlist the help of his granddaughter as the "interpreter and scribe" of his letter of protest. Written "in a child's sprawling hand," the letter is signed by the chief's "X" (*AIS*, p. 173). Convinced this letter will meet with the same defeat as all the others, the chief finally burns it on the way to the post office, preferring to entrust it to the "wings of fire" rather than to the postal service (*AIS*, p. 176). Adding insult to injury, the chief is imprisoned on the trumped-up charge of trying to set fire to the post office, and the two tricksters who had acquired the land for Blue-Star Woman conspire for his release from jail. As "words were vain," the chief signs away half his land to these same tricksters with his thumb print (*AIS*, p. 182). The story is an overwhelming indictment of both the reservation system and the "tricksters" who work within it to exploit their people for personal gain. U.S. Indian policy and its by-product, the grafters, have created a never-ending cycle of corruption and loss. In "Blue-Star Woman," Zitkala-Ša presents knowing English as a dubious but necessary power. Learning English is both a threat to culture and the only means of preserving her people from cultural disintegration. Blue-Star Woman and Chief High Flier, whom Zitkala-Ša calls the "voiceless man of America," are at the mercy of English-speaking translators and tricksters, and of the American government (*AIS*, p. 178). The tricksters themselves are "simply deluded mortals, deceiving others and themselves most of all" with their "flow of smooth words" (*AIS*, pp. 165, 169).

But Zitkala-Ša does not uniformly condemn strategies of disguise and deception. In "The Warrior's Daughter," she suggests the positive possibilities of trickster strategies. Seemingly unrelated to contemporary issues, this story tells of a young woman, Tusee, who rescues her captured lover from enemy territory by sneaking into their camp late at night in disguise. Watching from a distance as the warriors dance around their captive, she picks out her lover's captor as her target for revenge and smiles at him all evening from the edge of the campfire, captivating him with her dark eyes. Finally, she whispers to him "in his own tongue," luring him into the dark night, where she hisses in a husky voice, "I am a Dakota woman!" and kills him. Later that night as all go off to sleep, "a bent old woman's figure" with a bundle on her back enters the campsite and circles toward the captive. Appearing almost supernaturally before his eyes, "the old bent figure straightens into its youthful stature. Tusee herself is beside him" (*AIS*, p. 152). She cuts the cords that bind him, and carries her lover, too weak and numb to walk, triumphantly into the night.

Tusee is a powerful trickster/savior in this story. Her disguise as a bent woman with a bundle on her back echoes a Lakota trickster tale in which Iktomi throws grass into his blanket and carries it as if it is a great burden in order to trick and catch some ducks.[14] She enacts revenge, killing the enemy and rescuing her lover by masking herself in the harmless poses of a pretty maid and an old woman. Tellingly, it is Tusee's skill with language that brings her first success: She can lure the warrior only because she speaks softly "in his tongue," reserving her husky, truthful hiss for the moment before she kills him. Tusee's disguises skillfully manipulate gender roles. Because as a woman she is an observer at the victory dance rather than a participant, she can do what a man can't. No one would suspect that an appealing young woman at the edge of the campfire, or a wandering old woman humming to herself, is a murderous avenger. Zitkala-Ša closes the story with an image of womanly strength:

> A mighty power thrills her body. Stooping beneath his outstretched arms grasping at the air for support, Tusee lifts him upon her broad shoulders. With half-running, triumphant steps she carries him away into the open night. (*AIS*, p. 153)

Upsetting traditional role expectations, Tusee's trickster strategies save her lover's life, and by extension the honor of her people.[15] Unlike Zitkala-Ša's openly didactic attacks on trickster-grafters in "Blue-Star Woman," her message about positive trickster strategies here is more covert. Whereas she obviously feels she cannot afford to be ambiguous in her accusations against tricksters who would destroy her culture, perhaps she equally recognizes the dangers of revealing all of her own strategies to her enemies. As she suggests in her autobiographical writings, Zitkala-Ša carefully modulates her message for her audience: "However tempestuous this is within me, it comes out as the low voice of a curiously colored seashell, which is only for those ears that are bent with compassion to hear it" (*AIL*, p. 68).

Zitkala-Ša's most ambivalent use of trickster material involves her autobiographical sketches. The bilinguality that the tricksters in "Blue-Star Woman" use to swindle others, and that Tusee in "A Warrior's Daughter" uses to trick her enemy, also represents an ambivalent sign of power in the author's own life. For Zitkala-Ša, the conflict between cultures centered on learning the English language. An education in English was what originally split her from her heritage; yet even her mother saw this as inevitable if she was to survive: "She will need an education when she is grown, for then there will be fewer real Dakotas and many more palefaces. This tearing her away, so young, from her mother is necessary, if I would have her an educated woman" (*AIS*, p. 44). Before she speaks English, she must rely on the seductive language of a missionary translator, who plies her with trickster-like promises of "nice red apples . . . [and] a ride on the iron horse" to convince her to leave her home (*AIS*, p. 41). Once at the school, not knowing English leads to terror: She watches a playmate being beaten after giving the wrong memorized response in a language she does not understand. Only by acquiring a "second tongue" herself, so that she no longer has to rely on faulty or forked-tongued translators, can Zitkala-Ša gain a measure of power and control (*AIS*, p. 59).

If learning English is the crucial step in enabling Zitkala-Ša to negotiate the two worlds she lives in, Mikhail Bakhtin's conception of language as world view helps to explain the trickster's relationship to language. Because of their marginal cultural position, tricksters can parody languages, and therefore world views. Their location outside the confines of rigid social structures gives them a perspectival advantage. "Jokesters," as Bakhtin calls tricksters, are experts at double-voiced discourse; as masters of nuance and double entendre, they know that what matters is "the actual and always self-interested *use* to which . . . meaning is put and the way it is expressed" (Bakhtin, p. 401). Even the very young Zitkala-Ša senses this power involved in manipulating language, for once she understands English, she immediately uses it for revenge. In "School Days of an Indian Girl," she describes her first act of rebellion as involving the interpretation of verbal instructions, "mashing" turnips until she smashes the bottom of the jar (*AIS*, p. 60). Also Zitkala-Ša associates the power of the Christian devil with written and spoken English, and her actions on learning of this devil reveal both the power and the danger involved in that linguistic knowledge. After a missionary teacher shows her the "white man's devil" in a large book, she dreams of his coming to get her in her mother's cottage. "He did not speak to my mother, because he did not know the Indian language" (*AIS*, p. 64). Her mother can't be hurt by the devil because they do not speak the same language; they inhabit different worlds. But the girl, who inhabits both, is threatened by him and can't seek protection from her mother. Her literacy and fluency in English give her power, but also make her vulnerable to forces to which her mother is immune and from which her mother cannot save her. After the dream, Zitkala-Ša attacks the devil in his own world, a world of print, exacting her revenge by scratching him out of the children's picture Bible. In order to fight back against the white cultural powers which threaten her, she is learning that she must fight in their medium: spoken and written English.

Both empowered and marginalized by her education in English, Zitkala-Ša's return to the reservation was even more difficult than her immersion in the assimilationist missionary school. While learning English helped her to negotiate in a white world, it alienated her from her mother: "My mother had never gone inside of a schoolhouse and so she was not capable of comforting her daughter who could read and write" (*AIS*, p. 69). Her description of this period captures the painful personal isolation which comes from living within the gap between two cultures: "During this time I seemed to hang in the heart of chaos, beyond the touch or voice of human aid. . . . Even nature seemed to have no place for me. I was neither a wee girl nor a tall one; neither a wild Indian nor a tame one" (*AIS,* p. 69). Zitkala-Ša's liminal position, which derived not only from adolescence but also from cultural alienation, could not resolve itself with age. Cut off from her mother and her home by her education, Zitkala-Ša spent most of her life among non-Lakota Indians and whites, whose cultures and traditions were equally alien to her.[16]

Zitkala-Ša was certainly not alone in her reaction to mission schools, whose assimilationist policies were designed to guarantee that reentry into traditional cultures would be difficult, if not impossible (Welch, p. 16).[17] However, even among other educated, progressive Native Americans, Zitkala-Ša stood apart as a radical for her rejection of the pervasive assimilationist ideals of her era. Mary Stout notes, for example, that Zitkala-Ša's writing differs rather dramatically from autobiographies of other Sioux writers at the turn of the century, notably Charles Eastman's *Indian Boyhood* (1902) and Luther Standing Bear's *My Indian Boyhood* (1931), which are more concerned with representing Native peoples appealingly to a white audience than with expressing personal feelings (Stout, p. 73).[18] While Anglo perceptions surely affected Zitkala-Ša, her refusal to let them define her representation of herself speaks for her anti-assimilationist commitment. As Dexter Fisher observes, Zitkala-Ša and Eastman

> represented two divergent choices that educated Indians could make. . . . Zitkala-Ša was the reformer, the protestor, the one who refused to convert to Christianity or yield totally to assimilationist politics. . . . Her voice stands out all the more because she is writing early when other Indians, such as Eastman, were expressing themselves much more passively. (Fisher 1979, 27; quoted in Stout, p. 73)

Yet while Zitkala-Ša and Eastman may have represented two possible choices, the overwhelming majority of educated Native Americans in the first decades of the twentieth century chose Eastman's path. Zitkala-Ša's fierce commitment to her Lakota heritage led not only to her broken engagement to fellow progressive Carlos Montezuma, but to her eventual alienation from most of her Society of American Indians colleagues.[19] At the Carlisle Indian School where Zitkala-Ša taught, "she was an anathema because she insisted on remaining 'Indian,' writing embarrassing articles such as 'Why I Am a Pagan' that flew in the face of the assimilationist thrust of their education" (Dexter Fisher's foreword to *AIS,* p. viii). If, as she explains in her autobiographical essays "The School Days of an Indian Girl" and "An Indian Teacher Among Indians," her education, her writing career, her move to Washington, and her success in a white world represent a rejection of her mother, her writings themselves challenge assimilation and preserve the very traditions with which she herself can no longer live.

Zitkala-Ša's insistence on writing from the gap between tradition and assimilation ironically marginalized her in both Lakota and pan-Indian communities, as well as in non-Indian circles. Painfully aware of the tremendous personal cost of her refusal to live within the limits of any of her worlds, Zitkala-Ša must have recognized the affinity of her position to the trickster Iktomi's. Indeed, she could employ this likeness to her advantage. Gertrude Bonnin's careful manipulation of her own public image, renaming herself Zitkala-Ša and appearing at crucial congressional hearings in full Lakota dress, suggests her shrewd sense of the power of appearances.[20] Her self-naming, spurred by a family dispute, not only represents a violation of traditional naming practices but also an opportunity to craft the public persona of an educated Lakota woman.[21]

Her last autobiographical essay, "An Indian Teacher Among Indians" contains an elaborate metaphor that makes clear Zitkala-Ša's awareness of her own tricksterlike position, and suggests that, despite the danger posed by some contemporary "tricksters," she serves her people with her ability to move between worlds. She describes herself bleakly as a slender tree uprooted, shorn of its protective bark and branches, "planted in a strange soil." Yet she turns this image into a position of power, hoping "a day would come when my mute aching head, reared upward to the sky, would flash zigzag lightning across the heavens . . . dream of vent for a long pent consciousness" (*AIS*, p. 97). In Lakota myth, Iktomi the spider is closely associated with thunder and lightning and is often invoked for protection from lightning.[22] Like the spider, Zitkala-Ša moves between worlds, not belonging, because not limited, to any one realm. Capturing both the personal anguish and the potential power of her between-worlds condition, she envisions herself as a conductor, a tricksterlike mediator between worlds, a lightning rod to galvanize and direct the anger and frustrations of her people. Her voice, like the voice of Tusee, can whisper softly or hiss angrily, in her own language or in a second tongue, according to her purpose. While so many of her writings emphasize the chaotic consequences of the trickster's greedy scheming, Zitkala-Ša's works as a whole confirm that the trickster's voice, if well directed, carries electrifying power.

Notes

1. I consistently use the name "Lakota" in this essay, rather than the common appellation "Sioux," which is actually "a French corruption of the Ojibway word for 'snake'" (Rice, p. 1). Following biographer Deborah Welch, I refer to the author, known as Gertrude Simmons Bonnin, as Zitkala-Ša, the name under which she published her books and editorials.

2. James LaPointe, for example, claims that tales of Iktomi "illustrate what happens when one fails to heed the edicts and customs of social living," and his tales even include an explained moral at the end of each tale. The device seems motivated

to prove to LaPointe's predominantly white audience that "the Indian . . . lived a truly moral life" (p. 94). The Eastmans' collection also includes morals.

3. Zitkala-Ša expresses a sense of urgency in a 1901 letter to Carlos Montezuma: "As for my plans—I do not mean to give up my literary work—but while the old people last I want to get from them their treasured ideas of life" (quoted in foreword by Fisher; Zitkala-Ša, p. vi).

4. For Iktomi as namer, speaker, and culture-bearer, see Beckwith (pp. 429–430) and W. Powers (pp. 153–159). The great majority of Iktomi stories portray his lowly attributes; however, stories of Iktomi as benefactor appear in collections by Beckwith, McLaughlin, LaPointe, and Deloria.

5. For example, Mary McLaughlin more typically characterizes her 1916 *Myths and Legends of the Sioux* as the legacy of an "earnest, thoughtful, dignified, but simple and primitive people . . . now fast receding into the mists of the past," and Charles and Elaine Eastman's 1909 collection *Wigwam Evenings* emphasizes the stories' affinities to European folk tales (pp. ix–xii). Deborah Welch's 1985 biography abundantly shows that Zitkala-Ša's differences with her contemporaries on this point are typical of her life-long resistance to assimilation. Unlike most educated Native Americans of her time, Zitkala-Ša refused "to bend to the prevailing ethnocentrism of her time. In her view, Indian peoples possessed a cultural tradition not merely equal, but superior, to that of Anglo America" (Welch, *Zitkala-Ša: An American Indian Leader,* Ph.D. diss., University of Wyoming, Laramie, 1985, p. v).

6. Iktomi appears in five out of forty of McLaughlin's *Myths and Legends of the Sioux,* four out of twenty-seven of the Eastmans' *Wigwam Evenings,* three out of nineteen of LaPointe's *Legends of the Lakota,* and nine out of fifty-four of Deloria's *Dakota Texts.*

7. For a discussion of the role of the individual artist in shaping traditional materials, see Elaine Jahner, *Lakota Myth* (pp. 12–13).

8. See Eastman and Eastman, "Eya the Devourer," and Deloria, "Iktomi Conquers Iya, the Eater."

9. See "Iktomi in a Skull," *Dakota Texts,* p. 18 for a fuller account.

10. See Deloria (p. 50) and McLaughlin (p. 156) for other versions of this tale. Zitkala-Ša's version corresponds more closely to McLaughlin's 1916 version, "White Plume," in which White Plume saves the village from a white buffalo, a red eagle, and a white rabbit. Zitkala-Ša's version is unique, however, in its emphasis on the people's fear.

11. The Dawes Act, passed in 1887 and operational when Zitkala-Ša was writing in the early 1900s, "provided for parceling out land to individuals according to a formula and was billed as giving Indians the right to own land individually. . . . [The program] was in reality a strategy to open up Indian land for white settlement, since the allotment act specified that surplus lands—that is, lands remaining after individual allotments were made—could be sold to the United States. . . . During the time the Dawes Act was in effect, American Indians lost four fifths of their land" (M. Powers, p. 30).

12. The story of "Blue-Star Woman" in some respects closely resembles a case in which Zitkala-Ša was personally involved, that of Ellen Bluestone, who petitioned for a Yankton allotment in 1920. Zitkala-Ša was personally involved with land-allotment disputes on the Yankton reservation in 1920 and 1921 (see Welch, pp. 173–181).

13. Dell Hymes notes an association of tricksters with bilingualism in several tales of tribes in the Pacific Northwest (p. 115). While in the tales Hymes mentions

bilingualism does not benefit the trickster, in Zitkala-Ša's work and also in an Iktomi tale told by McLaughlin bilingualism always benefits the trickster, and sometimes also benefits the tribe (see McLaughlin, "The Bound Children," in which Iktomi, acting as translator between humans and crows, earns food for himself and reunites abandoned children with their relatives). In Lakota culture, at least, the trickster's ability to manipulate language is one of his greatest powers.

14. See Zitkala-Ša's "Iktomi and the Ducks," *OIL*; Deloria, "Iktomi Tricks the Pheasants"; and LaPointe, "Iktomi and His Bag of Songs."

15. Although, as Deborah Welch puts it, "Zitkala-Ša never felt any responsibility to work with or for her sex," her own life demonstrates her unwillingness to remain within the roles traditionally prescribed for women (p. 179). "Domesticity had never interested her," and from the early years of her involvement with the Society of American Indians, she broke through unspoken gender boundaries to become a recognized writer, editor, and secretary-treasurer (Welch, p. 58). Welch also suggests that the "Warrior's Daughter" may reveal Zitkala-Ša's own view of herself, and a wish for a warrior father. "There is nothing in the story to indicate that it is autobiographical. Yet, it is worth noticing that Zitkala-Ša wrote of a young girl exactly the age she had been when she first left her people. Moreover in choosing a heroine for her story, Zitkala-Ša depicted how a woman, just as a man, could act to save her people" (p. 63).

16. See Welch for a description of Zitkala-Ša's experiences among the Utes (pp. 47–60).

17. See Charles Eastman's "The School Days of an Indian," and especially James LaPointe's preface to *Legends of the Lakota* for similar accounts of the challenges the mission schools posed to a tribal identity.

18. For an interesting contrast to Zitkala-Ša's autobiography, see Sarah Winnemucca Hopkins's emotionally told *Life Among the Piutes* (1883).

19. While at times almost single-handedly sustaining the pan-Indian movement, Zitkala-Ša also maintained a lifelong loyalty to the Lakota, which at times endangered pan-Indian alliances. In 1919 she largely engineered a "Sioux coup" in the pan-Indian Society of American Indians (Welch, p. 165). Welch suggests that Zitkala-Ša's eventual alienation from almost all of her friends, family, and associates both contributed to and grew out of an ambitious, uncompromising personality (p. vii).

20. See Welch (pp. 133–138) for further discussion of Zitkala-Ša's public persona.

21. Dexter Fisher notes that Zitkala-Ša's creation of her own name asserts "at one and the same time her independence and her cultural ties" (*AIS*, p. x).

22. "One should never kill a spider lest he be struck by lightning," William Powers explains (p. 156). The spider protects against lightning because its own home is impervious both to lightning and rain (W. Powers, p. 159).

Works Cited

Babcock-Abrahams, Barbara. "'A Tolerated Margin of Mess': The Trickster and His Tales Reconsidered." In *Journal of Folklore Institute* 9 (1975): 147–186. Rpt. in *Critical Essays on Native American Literature,* ed. Andrew Wiget. Boston: G. K. Hall, 1985, pp. 153–185.

Bakhtin, Mikhail. *The Dialogic Imagination: Four Essays by M. M. Bakhtin,* ed. Michael Holquist. Austin: University of Texas Press, 1981.

Beckwith, Martha Warren. "Mythology of the Oglala Dakota." *Journal of American Folklore* 43 (1930): 339–42.

Deloria, Ella. *Dakota Texts,* eds. Agnes Picotte and Paul Pavich. Vermillion: Dakota Press, 1978.

Eastman, Charles. "The School Days of an Indian." *Outlook* (April 1907): 851–855, 894–899.

———. *Indian Boyhood.* 1902. Rpt. Williamstown, Mass.: Cornerhouse, 1975.

Eastman, Charles, and Elaine Goodale Eastman. *Wigwam Evenings.* 1909. Rpt. Eau Claire, Wis.: E. M. Hale, 1937.

Fisher, Dexter. "The Transformation of Tradition: The Study of Zitkala Ša and Mourning Dove, Two Transitional American Indian Writers." Ph.D. diss., City University of New York, 1979.

———. "Zitkala-Ša: The Evolution of a Writer." In *American Indian Quarterly* 5, no. 3 (1979): 229–238. Rpt. as Foreword, *American Indian Stories,* Zitkala-Ša. Lincoln: University of Nebraska Press, 1985, pp. v–xx.

Hopkins, Sarah Winnemucca. *Life Among the Piutes.* 1883. Rpt. Bishop, Calif.: Chalfant Press, 1969.

Hymes, Dell. "Use All There Is to Use." In *On the Translation of Native American Literatures,* ed. Brian Swann. Washington, D.C.: Smithsonian Institution Press, 1992, pp. 83–124.

Jahner, Elaine, ed. *Lakota Myth,* by James Walker. Lincoln: University of Nebraska Press, 1983.

LaPointe, James. *Legends of the Lakota.* San Francisco: Indian Historian Press, 1976.

McLaughlin, Marie. *Myths and Legends of the Sioux.* Bismarck: Bismarck Tribune Co., 1916.

Powers, Marla N. *Oglala Women.* Chicago: University of Chicago Press, 1986.

Powers, William K. *Sacred Language.* Norman: University of Oklahoma Press, 1986.

Rice, Julian. *Deer Women and Elk Men: The Lakota Narratives of Ella Deloria.* Albuquerque: University of New Mexico Press, 1992.

Roberts, John W. *From Trickster to Badman.* Philadelphia: University of Pennsylvania Press, 1989.

Standing Bear, Luther. *My Indian Boyhood.* 1931. Rpt. Lincoln: University of Nebraska Press, 1988.

Stout, Mary. "Zitkala-Ša: The Literature of Politics." In *Coyote Was Here: Essays on Contemporary Native American Literary and Political Mobilization,* ed. Bo Scholer. Aarhus, Denmark: Seklos, Department of English, University of Aarhus, 1984, pp. 70–78.

Welch, Deborah Sue. *Zitkala-Ša: An American Indian Leader, 1876–1938.* Ph.D. diss., University of Wyoming, 1985.

Zitkala-Ša. *American Indian Stories.* Washington, D.C.: Hayworth, 1921. Rpt. Lincoln: University of Nebraska Press, 1985.

———. *Old Indian Legends.* Boston: Ginn, 1901. Rpt. Lincoln: University of Nebraska Press, 1985.

ERIC ANDERSON

Manifest Dentistry, or Teaching Oral Narrative in *McTeague* and Old Man Coyote

Jack London begins *The Call of the Wild* (1903) by announcing that "Buck did not read the newspapers." No one, to my knowledge, has ever suspected that he *did*. Though more sentient and competent than some of London's human characters, Buck is literally a naturalist brute, and naturalist brutes, whatever their species, don't spend much time reading. For some, verbal expression in general is puzzling, frustrating, fragmentary, impossible. McTeague, for example, struggles to articulate himself—and as I'll suggest, his difficulties with speaking and self-representation manifest his inability to position himself historically. As David Wyatt remarks in a chapter titled "Norris and the Vertical," *McTeague* (1899) deals "with steady devolution in time, but it registers that process as failed transcendence in space. Attention to the self in landscape diverts us from the fate of the self in history" (p. 107). It diverts McTeague as well: the fate of this particular self in history is to be destroyed not only by the punishing landscape of Death Valley but also by the genealogical or thermodynamic imperatives that lead him there. These imperatives direct the dentist to be unaligned historically, unable to recognize, let alone to behave as though he inhabits, linear western narrative history. The most intensified moments in the novel register his inability to stay between (or inside) the lines: he is dislocated from the careful, particular documentary realism of late nineteenth-century Polk Street, San Francisco.

The novel's cultural-historical frames cannot contain and control its main character. Too bulky and awkward to fit comfortably inside realistic interiors even when he tries, McTeague has an uncontrollable habit of reverting to wild, animalistic urges and forces that violently contravene time, and these animal transformations take place at odd critical intervals. Ordinarily the "poor crude dentist of Polk Street, stupid, ignorant, vulgar, with his sham education and plebeian tastes" (p. 28) suggests "the draught horse, immensely strong, stupid, docile, obedient" (p. 3). But at times of genetic and emotional crisis, nature and heredity mix frighteningly to produce a very different sort of brute: "It was the old battle, old as the world, wide as the world—the sudden panther leap of the animal, lips drawn, fangs aflash, hideous, monstrous, not to be resisted" (p. 30). Lurking latent and ready beneath the placid equine surface, these mixed animal and human identities generally portend uncontrolled and uncontrollable violence.

Clearly, the dentist's animal nature diminishes his humanity while also, at its very worst, disrupting and violating the culture that surrounds him. That is, Norris's evolutionary paradigm sets forth an unquestioned hierarchy, and that hierarchy figures the animal as qualitatively less than human and at times positively malevolent and dangerous. The man must contest the animal that prowls somewhere inside him, must try to ward off the wolf that cannot be warded off: "That night he walked the streets until the morning, wondering what now he was to do to fight the wolf away" (p. 366). But this very antagonism between the human and the wolf, grounded in the assumption that animal characteristics do violence to human identity and that animalized humans do violence in turn to the culture that categorically fears and loathes such shape-shifting, needs to be rethought and indeed reimagined. The white Euroamerican recoiling from the werewolf needs to be recontextualized alongside Native American celebrations of tricksters like Old Man Coyote, and the trickster energy that informs and negates indigenous cultures is well worth remembering in the face of the dentist's violent and violating savagery.

The trickster-transformer is of course different from the dentist transformed. McTeague's animal howls sound nothing like native oral traditions, and the trickster's explicitly scandalous behavior facilitates and energizes his culture's most vital stories, while the dentist's brutality, more often implied than manifest, threatens to demolish his already tenuous sense of language, narrative, and community. McTeague's demolitions, like his animalizations, are humorless and largely unschemed and finally deadly; for these reasons, they do not tap into trickster energy, and do not work as subversions. But trickster's would, and trickster's still do, and Coyote, insatiable as ever, occasionally wanders through naturalist landscapes, overturning and subverting and reinventing what otherwise often pass for determined fictions. As is typical of the many trickster figures of North American Indian cultures, Coyote is an originator, an interpreter, an improviser, a mediator, in sum an "inexhaustible creator of situations and episodes" (Ramsey, p. 27), as brilliantly unpredictable as the dentist is, with the possible exception of his destructive rages, numbingly predictable. Yet they share the tendency, often associated with oral narratives, of disrupting what I call (for want of a better term) linear history. By not constructing or inhabiting such a notion of history, the trickster and the dentist make potentially useful critical and pedagogical bedfellows. In this essay Old Man Coyote, he of many shapes and guises and appetites and stories, meets the brute/dentist McTeague, who has the greatest difficulty articulating, let alone developing, any one of his fumbling selves—especially his animal selves. As I bring this humanlike animal figure and this animalistic human character together, imagine if you will a classroom where manifest destiny and the grand, monumental, imperial manner of history give way to something genuinely stranger and more surprising: a classroom more like a true frontier, where cultural contacts are unpredictable and often unresolved, where the terms and lines and figures change shapes and positions constantly.

Begin with a taxonomy of the trickster. Taxonomies, rather, for his classifications characteristically change from tale to tale, telling to telling, tribe to tribe, region to region, race to race, and while the trickster Coyote (for example) is often in a sort of mythic-narrative shorthand referred to as male, his cheerful promiscuities and all-around insatiable appetites lead him to disguises and transvestism just as his twentieth-century cousin Wile E. Coyote is led to the Acme Company and batman suits. Trying again and again to impress, Coyote hatches scheme after scheme, only to have his plans shattered by his would-be victims, who invariably expose him and thereby outtrick the trickster. Old Man Coyote, whom the linguist and anthropologist William Bright deems the "most important trickster figure of native North America" (p. 342), seems to have a wife and children, but because he is relentlessly, imperturbably horny, he pursues (for example) his daughters and, in one remarkable act of autofellation that I discuss later, himself. He cross-dresses and crosses species unabashedly, seducing and impregnating (among others) mice, frogs, and humans of all ages. He is truly, in ethnologist Barre Toelken's words, "the exponent of all possibilities" (Bright, p. 349), including the perpetual possibility of being found out, tricked back, humiliated, outfoxed. Residing preeminently in this realm of the ever-possible, he takes on a much more pivotal, central cultural role than do the wily, tricksterish animals we call coyotes; among the Salish of the northwest coast and the Flathead of the plateau, for example, he truly is both trickster and creator.

Bright argues persuasively that for many such native communities, Old Man Coyote was one of the "prehuman" First People, shape-changers involved in, among other things, the creation of humankind itself; Coyote, the "marplot" as well as the most popular First Person in the mythic stories, "lays down cultural roles for men and women, and even ordains death" (p. 348). In his most recent book on the subject, *A Coyote Reader* (1993), Bright adds a modest but important clarification: Coyote "does not create the world of the First People, but rather 'fixes it up' so that it becomes the world of humanity" (p. 35). Jarold Ramsey's sense of trickster as bricoleur—as handyman or "fixer" who cobbles reality out of the available materials[1]—concurs with Bright, just as Ramsey's general definition of the trickster bears close family resemblance to Bright's characterization of Coyote:

> A Trickster is an imaginary hyperbolic figure of the human, irrepressibly energetic and apparently unkillable, whose episodic career is based upon hostility to domesticity, maturity, good citizenship, modesty, and fidelity of any kind; who in Freudian terms is mostly id, a little ego, and no superego; who is given to playful disguises and shape-changing; and who in his clever self-seeking may accomplish important mythic transformations of reality, both in terms of creating possibility and in terms of setting human limits. From a structural standpoint, Tricksters are important *mediative* figures. (p. 27)

Like Bright, Ramsey finds Coyote the most transgressive trickster figure as well as the most popular among native audiences, and like Bright, who calls Old Man Coyote "an especially apt 'mediator' between culture and nature" (p. 379), Ramsey calls particular attention to the trickster's crucial cultural position, his "mediating between the realm of human society and the realm of nature, effecting imaginative accommodations of the former to the latter and vice versa without blurring or weakening the distinctions whereby 'the People' maintain their identity *as* people, one distinctive form or life in a variously changing world" (p. 30). Thus, as a mythic figure, he remains an enabler rather than a moral examiner; he is neither dictatorial nor particularly demanding, and he consistently subverts any authority he affects to have—or *is* subverted when spotted putting on such airs.

Ramsey follows Lévi-Strauss's *Structural Anthropology* by understanding this mediation as a "continuing process" of developing, among other things, "historical self-consciousness" (p. 39). Tricksters "seem to function as sources of a kind of tribal historical perspective" (p. 38), inventing strategies for negotiating history as perpetually present, origins as always continual. Seen in this light, tricksters, especially Coyote, transgress not so much morally as temporally in order to help the community and the culture recharge itself. However unwittingly, they dramatize the culture's spatial and temporal understanding of itself, defining what it is by acting out its boundaries. Their troublemaking figures as performance, their disruptions as spiritual continuities. As Andrew Wiget writes, trickster's

> behavior is always scandalous. His actions were openly acknowledged as madness by the elders who performed the stories with obvious relish on many winter evenings. Yet these same respected voices would solemnly assert the sacredness of these very tales, which always involved the most cavalier treatment of conventionally unassailable material like sexuality or religion. To many Westerners reading these stories for the first time, it seemed at best a puzzling inconsistency and at worst a barbaric mystery that in many tribal mythologies this idiot and miscreant was in some unaccountable way also the culture hero. (p. 16)

McTeague, of course, is no "culture hero." Though he is, like Old Man Coyote, a shape-changer "overcharged with biological energy," these two extraordinary, anthropomorphic supercanines are astonishingly different in their roles as figures in and out of cultural history—as figures, that is, formed and nourished by their familiar, particular cultural habitats, and also as figures who cross over into different habitats with markedly different success.

As many critics have noted, animal imagery suffuses naturalist texts; the "brute" as a sort of category conjures up what June Howard describes as "the dumb beast, the animal who does not use language and is named but never names" (p. 81). American literary naturalism often preoccupies itself with showing the process by which a character gradually or explosively *becomes* brutal; though inherent, the condition of brutality happens *to* the character, and is measured dramatically against, for example, his or her more placid, tame ("domesticated") behavior. Most importantly and paradoxically, I think, the brute "who does not use language" *is* language; the fictive brute, unlike the real-life abusive husband and murderer Pat Collins, is an image, a metaphor. We tend not to think of McTeague, let alone naturalist brutes in general, metaphorically, believing that they resist and destroy such schemes and tropes and the vast possibilities figurative language implies, as they so easily destroy so much else in and around them. But when McTeague leaves off "just looking" out the window of his "Dental Parlors" and, splintering the temporal as well as the spectatorial frame, batters Trina to death, he paradoxically exchanges his latent brutality for manifest, public, journalistic narratives *about* his brutality, narratives that organize, historicize, diminish, and in effect dispose of the brute by transposing him—or, better yet, exposing him—as just language.

In sharp contrast, Coyote is not by nature figurative, or "just" figurative; he invents and reinvents himself into being as he is invented and reinvented into being, and that being *is* Coyote: neither *Homo sapiens* nor *Canis latrans,* but rather some complex and compelling mixture. In brief, Coyote's invaluable cultural role as an originator and dramatizer of both the people and their cultural memory is very different from the naturalist character whose latent brute nature periodically and often inevitably leaps to the surface, violating the character's human and evolutionary development. The dentist McTeague never develops the fundamentally human ability to remember, to know and perpetuate his own as well as his community's history; he simply cannot historicize by (for example) developing personal emotions such as remorse. Neither can he construct and sustain larger historical memories. Instead, the lurking brute inhabits him and extracts the potential materials of his history as roughly and violently as he extracts teeth from his patrons in the "Dental Parlors" with bare hands.

Wrenching out teeth, expelling a billiard ball from his distended mouth, breaking and emptying his wife Trina's battered treasure chest, beating her to death, mining, prospecting for gold, and finally entering Death Valley with nothing of his eradicated past except the canary "chittering feebly" in a gilded cage, McTeague's is a life of extractions but a life unaware of history. Coyote, much more the prankster, is also much more paradoxical, embodying and creating both chaos and order, both disruption and continuity. To put it another way, Coyote mediates (according to Ramsey) between fiction and morality:

> Tricksters . . . effect complex mediations whereby human polarities are imaginatively held together and indeed in a fashion integrated—Nature as against Society, social collectivity as against individuality, "Id" as against "Superego," Childhood as against Adulthood and the individual's experience as against that of the race, prehistory against "history," and finally, on the level of mythic transformations, what could have been in the world as against what is. (p. 43)

To this catalogue of contesting yet mixing and integrating polarities, I propose adding another, cross-cultural and cross-racial: Coyote in relation to dentist, or, Indian in relation to white.[2] Such a positioning looks at first blush extremely tricky; for one thing, McTeague comes to us sharply polarized and unmediated, inarticulate and sometimes borderline unconscious. Despite Frank Norris's precise documentary-style handling of the dentist's Polk Street neighborhood and of other parts of San Francisco and California, "Doctor" McTeague is, in a profound sense, *out* of history. As such, he seems to inhabit worlds irreconcilably different from Coyote's. But in asking how the process of being, performing, and hearing Coyote differs from the experience of reading the tenuously linear narrative history of an individual brute in a discrete printed text, I implicitly raise the possibility of complex mediation, of commerce or confluence, between them. In other words, I invoke Ramsey's link between two very powerful things—cultural stability and a "variously changing world"—and I take both figures (and their texts) seriously as shape-shifters, as examples and reflections of cultural power and possibility.

Because they are so deeply grounded in oral traditions (and also because there are so many of these traditions, and so many breeds of trickster inside them), it is difficult to assign dates, to historicize Native Americans and their literatures according to the conventions and manners of western linear history. It is also largely unnecessary. For while we know pretty much exactly when *McTeague* was written, right down to the dates on Frank Norris's Harvard theme papers,[3] Indian tales work differently. One of the nearest English-language approximations of Coyote in the "perpetual present" is Barre Toelken's description of Ma'i, as quoted by William Bright:

> There is no possible distinction [for the Navajo] between Ma'i, the *animal* we recognize as a coyote in the fields, and Ma'i, the *personification* of Coyote power in all coyotes, and Ma'i, the *character* (trickster, creator, and buffoon) in legends and tales, and Ma'i, the symbolic character of *disorder* in the myths. Ma'i is not a composite but a complex; a Navajo would see no reason to distinguish separate aspects. (p. 348)

Coyote's various schemes and exploits are told and retold in an extraordinarily rich and still actively growing array of stories whose very nature—as oral narrative—underscores not their fragility but their incredible vitality and sustenance. As Leslie Marmon Silko makes abundantly clear in the following line but also in the larger form and construction of *Ceremony* (1977), "You don't have anything / if you don't have the stories" (p. 2). Further, "in the belly of this story / the rituals and the ceremony / are still growing," gestating history created and named by Thought-Woman, nurtured by people, and tended, always constant yet always in process, by particular storytellers and listeners. As ethnologist Dell Hymes points out, "Myths are performed and thereby shaped, both in performance and in reflection between performances, by individuals" (p. 79); like the dynamic integration of masculine and feminine to effect the creation, safekeeping, and necessary revising of stories, the performance of a particular story is shaped by the dynamic relations between mythic traditions, the style and skill of the teller, and the nature of the audience. As Bright puts it in *A Coyote Reader,* these oral traditions develop and are "transmitted . . . sometimes with relatively accurate memorization, sometimes not. Thus most stories have no single complete and 'correct' form" (p. xiii).

Coyote's shape-changing thus becomes a sort of collaboration between himself and the person telling the story about him; the trickster manipulates as he is manipulated—as Hymes emphasizes by printing two very different transcriptions of the same tale—and the unwritten history of a trickster tale involves the changes and flexibilities of the narrative over time. The tales also develop by repetition, repetition that works not as linear, causal narrative but as something closer to a homing-in or a savoring of the narrative in process: the "now then . . . again" sequence rather than the "Once upon a time" story. Repetition is inextricably linked to variation and improvisation, not only in the various responses to the tale but in the tale itself on a fundamental level. Here, then, is Coyote, recontextualized yet again but still (as always) recognizable, this time in the Santiam Kalapuya form of John B. Hudson's irresistibly autoerotic "The News Precedes Coyote" (collected by Melville Jacobs from the late 1920s to the 1930s).

> Coyote was going along [down the Willamette],
> he wanted to go to the [Oregon City] falls here.
>
> Now then he made camp,

now then it became morning,
now then he went on again.

Now then it became dark,
now then he camped again,
now then at morning he went on again.

Now then it was dark,
now then he camped again,
now then at morning he went on again.

Now then at dark he camped again,
now then he slept in a sweathouse.
Now then in the sweathouse he made it rock.

Now then he was licking his penis,
now then he came out:
"This sweathouse will be a rock."

Now then he went along.
Now then he was going along,
now then he saw a lot of people in a canoe.

Now then Coyote called out,
"What's the news?"
Again he called out,
"What's the news?"
"What's the news?"

Now then one of those people said,
"What can be calling you?
Oh it is that Coyote!"
Now then that person called back to him,
"Hello!"

Coyote said,
"What news is there?"

Now then that person said,
"There is no news at all,
"The only news [is] Coyote was sucking his penis."

"Ah! Wonder where the one who saw me was standing?
"Ohhh, I will go back.
"I will see where he could have been standing, I wonder."

Now then he went back,
Now then he got to the sweathouse here,
Now then he examined his sweathouse;
Now then he saw
where the rock had been cracked apart.

"Ohhhhh! I suppose this is where the news came out from it.
"That is how it is going to be,
"That is the way it will always be,
"Nothing will ever be hidden,
"That is the way it will always be."[4]

Unlike the familiar opening line of western myths and fairy tales, "Once upon a time," Coyote tales usually begin in process, with "Coyote was going there" or "coming along" or "going along." In this tale, Coyote travels on and on, performing tricks along the way, toward conclusions that paradoxically both predict and explain continuing things; uncommon behaviors lead to explanations of the common, why bull frogs live near the water, why news travels fast: "That is the way it will always be." But what more specifically is "it" here? "It" seems to involve the relations between the important repetitions of "Now then . . . again" and the conclusion's "That is how it is going to be, / That is the way it will always be." The tale's paradoxical sense of news as both specific act (of autofellation) and perpetual circumstance ("Nothing will ever be hidden") is pointed up by the arresting contrast between the preparatory, repetitive stanzas and the sudden breaking of the narrative pattern with "Now then he was licking his penis." And about this autofellation—it is clearly more than an isolated masturbatory act. It is not introspective. It is in the public domain, and, most importantly, it "will always be" in the community: "Nothing will ever be hidden." Coyote is, on the one hand, the victim here, the exposed and humiliated traveler. But, more importantly, he is resolutely unembarrassed as he takes in the news about himself and, with winning curiosity and a remarkably understated self-consciousness, transforms personal exposure into social meaning—or rather, into prophecy that assumes the deep natural relation between individual act and larger community, between now and always as reflected in the relation between storyteller and audience as the story, the "news," is transmitted, perpetuated yet improvised and varied across time. My presentation of "The News Precedes Coyote" essentially does this too, the story enabling me to "go back" to "the news," to see the ways Coyote and his stories generate and regenerate historical consciousness.

As exemplified by this particular tale, Coyote stories themselves are well aware of how they are situated in time and space, in part because Coyote himself, whether he fully understands his circumstances or not, crosses time and keeps going along, presently. Not so *McTeague,* though, wherein the news fixes, tames, and finally disposes of the unruly brute. While the Coyote tale exclaims that "Nothing will ever be hidden," the action of *McTeague* suggests that what's hidden is nothing; the dentist spends a whole lifetime extracting—he is by turns a miner, a toothpuller, a robber and murderer, a prospector for gold—without ever understanding his own extraction. His limited family memories—of his father, the usually responsible but periodically alcohol-crazed shift-boss, of his mother, the "overworked drudge, fiery and energetic for all that," and of the aptly named Big Dipper mine—are mediated for McTeague by the helpful and much more articulate narrator. As June Howard points out, naturalist brutes cannot tell their own stories, precisely because their brutishness crushes their speech and language; yet because these brutes are so arresting, "critics of American literary naturalism have spent more time dissecting the characters victimized by determinism than they have discussing the perspective that complements them" (p. 104). Granted, Coyote does not directly tell his own story, either; but he takes a much more active part than the dentist in collaborating with the storyteller, inventing what happens, and subverting his own susceptibility to victimization. For Norris, though, the point of view of the naturalist spectator or narrator makes possible the more or less coherent construction of the brute's story, and places the brute in perspective. The narrator frames in words that McTeague "framed no words; in the rush of high-pitched sound that issued from his wide-open mouth there was nothing articulate" (p. 234).

But to what end? Certainly not the end of the Coyote tale, where the mythic figure himself takes part in the ever-changing shaping of his stories, and where this figure himself mediates between individual and community, always toward community. In *McTeague,* the work of mediation serves primarily to make the individual main character comprehensible to the individual reader, by finding metaphors for this character's difference, his separation from any sense of larger community. What is being mediated is, essentially, the gap between dentist and reader rather than the link; the naturalist narrator, in other words, maintains the gap, while the Coyote tale reduces and even (in the very nature of its oral performance in front of a group) eliminates it. To figure the gap I'm describing in *McTeague,* consider the novel as oral narrative; it is oral not only because one of its sources is Thomas Fillebrown's 1889 *A Text-Book of Operative Dentistry,* but also because each significant character in the book—including the miserly Trina, the dreamily tawdry old folks Grannis and Miss Baker, the rag man Zerkow, and Maria Macapa—clings to one obsessive idea or image and obsessively repeats that image, even if, as in Maria's enigmatic "Had a flying squirrel an' let him go," the repeated line makes absolutely no sense to anyone else.

And the book is obsessively, graphically oral, too, serving up very specific descriptions of chewing, gnawing, biting, gnashing, swallowing, grinding, gorging. *McTeague* begins with a gray meal and a pitcher of steam beer, then moves through dental examinations and operations to the doggedly orgiastic centerpiece wedding feast ("McTeague's cheeks were distended, his eyes wide, his huge, salient jaw moved with a machine-like regularity; at intervals he drew a series of short breaths through his nose.") Early in the book, McTeague on Marcus's dare shoves a billiard ball in his mouth; later, in the dark sadomasochism of their deteriorating marriage, he tortures Trina by biting her fingers. And any time a character gets angry or frustrated, he or she invariably grinds and gnashes teeth, loses all power of speech, and in McTeague's case, is transformed into a howling, maniacal werewolf. Of course, many of the characters' calmer rhetorical performances are markedly abysmal; Norris perversely gives McTeague not only the wedding dinner but two marriage proposals and a speech at the celebration of Trina's winning the lottery:

> I don' know what to say—I—I—I ain't never made a speech before; I—I ain't never made a speech before. But I'm glad Trina's won the prize—. . . I—I—I'm glad Trina's won, and I—I want to—I want to—I want to—want to say that—you're—all—welcome, an' drink hearty, an' I'm much obliged to the agent. Trina and I are goin' to be married, an' I'm glad everybody's here to-night, an' you're—all—welcome, an' drink hearty, an' I hope you'll come again, an' you're always welcome—an'—I—an'—an'—That's—about—all—I—gotta—say. (p. 120)

McTeague accomplishes just what he sets out to accomplish here; what he means, he says, and what he says, he means. Even so, the sweating dentist's halting repetitions mark the impossible contest between his embarrassed self-consciousness and his genuine attempt to develop a linear speech; more than a matter of rhetorical inexperience, the speechlessness of this speech exposes an intellect that simply adds one thing to one other thing to accumulate an undifferentiated, unshaped pile of stuff. His "an'" conjunctions make for a repetition significantly more painful than the "now then . . . again" repetitions in the Coyote tale, and they mark the difference between a comfortable sense of storytelling as stylistically in process and a distressed, faltering participation in one's own narrative history.

While extraction for Coyote is a present and skillfully articulated community concern, extraction for McTeague is not so much meaningless as unspeakable. The naturalist narrative never really gets underway as a linear story of a character's development, and therefore, to my reading, the critical argument that *McTeague* charts the deterioration of the dentist and his wife needs to be qualified and complicated: "deterioration" is too linear, and presumes too much about the characters'—and the novel's—beginnings. William B. Dillingham, for example, undertakes to defend Norris's Death Valley ending by tracking down various ways Norris "foreshadows" the ending and carefully works out a "progression . . . always away from the more civilized to the more primitive" (p. 138), so that McTeague's desert surroundings act as "a counterpart to McTeague's personal movement toward bestiality" (Dillingham, p. 138). But how can he move toward something so clearly lodged inside him from the very beginning of the novel, his unfortunate genetic map or, as Norris more graphically puts it, "the foul stream of heredity evil" that runs, below his surface, "like a sewer" (p. 32)? And as such, how linear and orderly is this deterioration? Are the dentist's periodic brutal rages themselves "orderly"? The beast always latent in the dentist leaps to the surface early in the novel (p. 30) and becomes most thoroughly tamed around the middle of the book, during what Dillingham himself calls the "somewhat dull courtship" (p. 135) of McTeague and Trina, through the bland domestic scenes between the newlyweds, before greed and miserliness insinuate themselves thoroughly.

McTeague does not, as *Sister Carrie* does, plot a more or less symmetrical chiasmus, where one character's resigned fall contrasts and complements another's ambivalent rise and where the economic affairs of both Carrie and Hurstwood change much more dramatically across class borders than Trina and McTeague's ever do. A distinction must also be made between the urban deterioration—the gradually widening gap between the amount of money Trina has saved and the poverty level of their lodgings and neighborhoods, until the couple, mostly under her miserly direction, move toward and finally into slum housing—and the later, more "rural" scenes, set in "untamed" landscapes that the dentist enters as a fugitive *from,* among other things, that deterioration. (Though he doesn't remember it once he leaves San Francisco, he rails noisily against what he sees as needless poverty when in it and avenges Trina in part because of it.) And when he plunges into the desert, he is in some ways at his sharpest and most alert. Though still bewildered, he hardly seems "crop-full, stupid, and warm," as Norris describes him in paragraph two of the book. Instead, we find a McTeague capable of some alertness and vigilance: at one point, for example, the dentist "slowly turned his head and looked over one shoulder, then over the other. Suddenly he wheeled sharply about, cocking the Winchester and tossing it to his shoulder" (p. 409). Though not really in control of these vague yet insistent forces that urge him to keep moving, he responds to them actively and energetically. As he moves over land through brutal terrain, his "bestial" instincts point toward self-preservation, not toward the more brutal acts of sexual assault, battery, robbery, and murder he commits earlier in the book. Focusing on McTeague running for his life, Norris in fact modestly expands the dentist's range of mental activity, showing him planning, reflecting, dreaming, and suffering. All in all, though, he remains if anything fundamentally unchanged throughout the novel, particularly in his stunted historical relations—and as such, the so-called "plot of decline" and its punitive implications do not strongly apply.

The empirically derived continuities urged by Dillingham and others[5] assume that *McTeague*'s characters inhabit a literary narrative very different from their world and experiences; there's a vast and unbridged gulf between what Norris tells and what his characters know. Artistic and critical standards, in other words, unify the book, while Norris's naturalist characters, much more turbulently and uncontrollably obsessive, do not domesticate as readily. In a way, the critics are more determinist than the determinist. Still, as Walter Benn Michaels's "double logic" or Mark Seltzer's "double discourse" posits,[6] the disjunctive, dislocated experiences of these characters can also be understood as deep, latent continuities, continuities made up of what the characters typically don't see or do or know. As such, take McTeague's tendency to behave as though outside of anything resembling a historical consciousness. That is, he rarely remembers things on the strength of his own volition, and his links to the past are instead passive, the result of genealogical imperatives and uncontrollable brute instincts. This continuity is, paradoxically, the sum total of numerous absences and emptinesses, compounded by McTeague's various occupations in the novel, all of which—dentist, prospector, miner, thief, murderer, fugitive—involve extraction. He is both consistently removing and consistently removed. Placed in a documentary-style setting throughout much of the novel, surrounded by particular details painstakingly researched and realistically observed, the dentist alternately shatters and forgets this time frame, and in so doing reminds us, quite by accident, of its fragility but also of its consequences. Thus the closing chapters of the novel, though they seem disjunctive to some readers, actually exemplify, by magnifying, McTeague's fundamental, continuous emptiness. He is of course not a vacuum, but he is, especially in the perverse sublimity of Death Valley, "the empty spirit in vacant space," the empty container unaware of the possibility of being filled, for better or worse, by the demands and problems and recognitions of history.

Old Man Coyote, though certainly different from McTeague in ways I have suggested, is also similar in his "ahistorical" role as a sort of signpost or maker of how and where things are in the text and in the world. Granted, Coyote inhabits many more worlds than the dentist, and manipulates them as actively and consciously as he is manipulated by them. Granted, Coyote tales as oral performances speak to groups of listeners who talk back, and participate in the ever-moving community created and reaffirmed by the tales and their tellings. Moreover, McTeague is supposed, according to powerful western conventions of linear narrative, to be headed somewhere quite specific, in structural terms: the explosive climax and somewhat more relaxed resolution of the story he inhabits. Coyote, in contrast, both goads and welcomes us to imagine him occupying, shaping, passing through, and scrambling in a habitat that's much more broadly understood; both oral and written trickster narratives judge themselves and their audiences beyond and outside them, over and over again. Dell Hymes in *A Coyote Reader* (Bright, 1993) underscores this characteristic circumstance wonderfully in Part IV of his celebratory poem "Fivefold Fanfare for Coyote":

never will he go from this land,
   here always, as long as the land is,
      that is how Coyote is in this land
         (Coyote, surviving all names);
            now I know only that far. . . . .

The people coming are near now. . . . .
Story! Story! (p. 51)

In this, the next-to-last section of the poem, Hymes brings together a "composite of lines from endings" (Bright, p. 54) of various Coyote tales. And these endings typically point toward unending things: first and foremost the sheer presence and staying power of Coyote, who lives as far and as long as the land itself, beyond even language, "surviving all names."

Compare the Hopi/Miwok poet Wendy Rose's "Trickster":

Trickster's time
is not clicked off neatly
on round dials nor shadowed
in shifty digits;
he counts his changes slowly
and is not accurate.
He lives in his own mess of words,
his own burnt stew; he sees
when the singers are spread
and trapped by their songs,
numbed by the sounds of space
and reach their limit
so they can't hear the frozen music
circle above us like ravens or
like grubs flow into fleshy thrums
as their feet.

Trickster turns to wind,
Trickster turns to sand,
Trickster leaves you groping,
Trickster swings walking off
            with your singer's tongue
            left inaudible,
Trickster dashes under cars
            on the highway and leaves
            the crushed coyote,
Trickster bounces off whistling
            with his borrowed coat of patches
            and upside-down kachina mask,
Trickster licks stolen soup from his face
            and counts the slaps
            that hover in the silence
            near the place where
            they missed his face.

> We only see his grey tail
> bird-disguised
> like a moving target
> as he steals all the words
> we ever thought
> we knew. (Bright, *A Coyote Reader,* pp. 87–88)

Again (and this is of course far from an isolated example), trickster/ Coyote's pranks and disguises and transformations help him break free of the constraining boundaries of history, language, even death. By shape-changing, he steals his own and by extension his people's survival. At the same time and in the same way, the mixed-blood Native American woman poet, doubly (perhaps trebly) a cultural "other," reinvents language by stealing it; with Coyote as a characteristically eager accomplice, *she* "steals all the words," including the oppressors' languages, and subverts them. Rose's poem, and the poet herself, are "trickster." These stories about Coyote typically contain traces of and invitations to realities larger than their particular narrative or textual worlds, often through reported "sightings" of Coyote; Rose spots him as roadkill, the Acoma Pueblo writer Simon Ortiz sees him on Route 66, "just trucking along,"[7] and so he keeps going and going along, tricking time, inhabiting the silences, and helping to change the noise of language and culture.

McTeague, on the other hand, enjoys no such unpredictable, requickening life on roads not yet mapped or written. Indeed, at novel's end he is as if frozen to the desert ground, even as his head moves helplessly around:

> As McTeague rose to his feet, he felt a pull at his right wrist; something held it fast. Looking down, he saw that Marcus in that last struggle had found strength to handcuff their wrists together. Marcus was dead now; McTeague was locked to the body. All about him, vast, interminable, stretched the measureless leagues of Death Valley.
>
> McTeague remained stupidly looking around him, now at the distant horizon, now at the ground, now at the half-dead canary chittering feebly in its little gilt prison. (p. 442)

As the novel ends its linear movement, the main character loses his ability to move; literally as well as figuratively stuck, the dentist can no longer make his way horizontally through time and space. Death Valley thus remains "measureless" (in and as space) and "interminable" (untimed as well as timeless). *McTeague* does shape-change into the movie *Greed* (1924) and the Chicago opera production of 1992, but such changes in media and consequently in form do not double as changes toward a genuinely Coyotean lifeway. And we should not expect them to: rather than faulting either one for not being the other, I suggest that, their differences notwithstanding, both the dentist and the trickster remain, in problematic and complicated ways, out of history, the one because of his inability to create and comprehend it, the other because of his inability to stop creating and fix it. Both the novel and the Coyote tales, in other words, verge on the hazy borderlands of several major cultural processes. And as such, McTeague and Coyote can be pedagogically useful together.

Consider, for example, the one moment in *McTeague* when a Native American enters the narrative and encounters the dentist. This moment points to the problems of language and history in cross-cultural conversation. The Indian remains speechless and subsumed, though acknowledged:

> once in the northern part of Inyo County, while they [train/crew/passengers] were halted at a water tank, an immense Indian buck, blanketed to the ground, approached McTeague as he stood on the roadbed stretching his legs, and without a word presented to him a filthy, crumpled letter. The letter was to the effect that the buck Big Jim was a good Indian and deserving of charity; the signature was illegible. The dentist stared at the letter, returned it to the buck, and regained the train just as it started. Neither had spoken; the buck did not move from his position, and fully five minutes afterward, when the slow-moving freight was miles away, the dentist looked back and saw him still standing motionless between the rails, a forlorn and solitary point of red, lost in the immensity of the surrounding white blur of the desert. (p. 393)

The silence here is mutual, as is the odd, almost surreal passivity of both the animalized "buck" and the lurking animal McTeague. Striking, too, is the narrator's insistence on so animalizing Jim; captivated by the highly charged reflections of Indian in dentist and dentist in Indian, Norris is himself unreflectively racist in his hypersexualized "buck." Big Jim stands both literally and figuratively between the lines, standing stock still as the lines—marks of "history," of "progress," of western industrial technology—both contain him and leave him behind. McTeague and the train look back at the vanishing red point as it recedes into the "white blur of the desert," made accessible by the "white blur" of manifest destiny but attributed mostly to the sheer nature of perception in a blinding desert rather than to any humanly constructed determinist paradigm. Still, the ideological links between ways of seeing and ways of not seeing overwhelm both Jim and McTeague. The process of making Big Jim invisible and of watching him literally vanish from sight in the book as he vanishes from the book enacts with remarkable efficiency the actual political plans of most turn-of-the-century Indian fighters, be they military or governmental. This process is perhaps best encapsulated in the illegible signature on the letter Big Jim carries; the signature has been marked on him, presumably by a white authority, as a way of recommending him as a "good" Indian to other whites who, one assumes, imagine a world full of "bad" Indians but remain unable to differentiate between "good" and "bad" without the help of written documents. Here, though, the signature itself is illegible—white in at least two senses—and its absence efficiently and quickly renders Big Jim invisible as well, a process probably begun when he was first "marked," written on, interpreted, caricatured. Yet a very similar fate awaits McTeague as well; all that he sees around him in Death Valley is predicated on all that he has not seen throughout the novel, and his repeatedly emphasized activity in the final scene of the novel—his *looking* up, down, and all around him—looks very much like a prelude to his own fading away out of sight. The process of becoming invisible is of course not simply self-induced, but in *McTeague,* such a washing out and paring down of visual perception makes, finally, for an emptying out that both literally and figuratively freezes the life history of this brutal male object in its tracks.

But "Trickster turns to wind, / Trickster turns to sand, / Trickster leaves you groping." Groping for what? I suspect, and invite, something like a sense of, and a confidence in, the "variously changing world" trickster so joyfully inhabits. Bringing the trickster Coyote and the dentist McTeague into contact helps illuminate various quiet and suggestive transactions within and across texts while doing productive violence to cultural boundaries. This changefulness in turn dramatizes that cultural processes, including critiques, take many shapes and forms, and that cultural stability, whatever its motives or benefits or dangers, traffics undeniably in the power of imagination. As a vital and important result, McTeague and Old Man Coyote together present to our students and to ourselves a very great mystery, a mystery both naturalist and Indian, both contemporary and untemporary: what *is* history? What does it mean to naturalists and Indians, considered both separately and together? *Does* it mean anything to them? How might the very different mediatory roles of McTeague and Coyote be mediated in turn? And what is manifest to us, mediated as we are? The answers to such questions, I suggest in closing, point us toward a *process* of teaching and a *process* of imagining. For however unlikely the conjunction of Coyote and dentist, and in fact precisely *because* it still seems unlikely, it is all the more important as a beginning toward a classroom where shape-changing both happens and matters. Otherwise, we have nothing but the same old lines and the same old loaded silence.

Notes

1. In addition to Ramsey's own discussion in *Reading the Fire* (p. 41), see Bright's *A Coyote Reader,* Chapter 5, titled "Coyote the Bricoleur" (pp. 35–55).

2. Other crossings, these interdisciplinary, are suggested by William Bright: because *Canis latrans* is "an especially appropriate actor—biologically, ecologically, and ethnologically—to play the trickster role," it is useful to consider "how some

of the attributes of Coyote as trickster and survivor are reflected in correlations between zoological observations, Native American myth, and contemporary poetry" (*A Coyote Reader,* p. 23).

3. For detailed information about Norris's Harvard English 22 themes and their compositional relationship to *McTeague,* see James D. Hart, *A Novelist in the Making: A Collection of Student Themes and the Novels* Blix *and* Vandover and the Brute (Cambridge: Harvard University Press, 1970).

4. My source for "The News Precedes Coyote" is Ramsey's *Reading the Fire* (pp. 44–45). Bright in *A Coyote Reader* prints a remarkably similar Clackamas Chinook tale, "Coyote Sucks Himself" (pp. 70–72); the autoerotic Coyote of the Santiam Kalapuya tale I read is, in yet another sense, not isolated or alone.

5. See, for example, Donald Pizer's *The Novels of Frank Norris* (pp. 81–82).

6. Walter Benn Michaels discusses the "double logic" of naturalism in the eponymous fifth chapter of *The Gold Standard and the Logic of Naturalism* (p. 174); Mark Seltzer introduces his concept of a naturalist "double discourse of the natural and the technological" (p. 4) early in *Bodies and Machines.*

7. Ortiz is quoted in Bright, *A Coyote Reader* (p. 30).

Works Cited

Bright, William. *A Coyote Reader.* Berkeley: University of California Press, 1993.

———. "The Natural History of Old Man Coyote." In *Recovering the Word: Essays on Native American Literature,* eds. Brian Swann and Arnold Krupat. Berkeley: University of California Press, 1987.

Dillingham, William B. *Frank Norris, Instinct and Art.* Lincoln: University of Nebraska Press, 1969.

Howard, June. *Form and History in American Literary Naturalism.* Chapel Hill: University of North Carolina Press, 1985.

Hymes, Dell. "Anthologies and Narrators." In *Recovering the Word: Essays on Native American Literature,* eds. Brian Swann and Arnold Krupat. Berkeley: University of California Press, 1987.

Lévi-Strauss, Claude. *Structural Anthropology,* trans. Claire Jacobsen, Brooke Grundefest Schoepf, and Monique Layton. New York: Basic Books, 1963.

London, Jack. *The Call of the Wild.* 1903. Rpt. *Jack London: Novels and Stories.* New York: Library of America, 1982.

Michaels, Walter Benn. *The Gold Standard and the Logic of Naturalism: American Literature at the Turn of the Century.* Berkeley: University of California Press, 1987.

Norris, Frank. *McTeague: A Story of San Francisco.* 1899. Rpt. New York: Penguin, 1982.

Pizer, Donald. *The Novels of Frank Norris.* Bloomington: Indiana University Press, 1966.

Ramsey, Jarold. *Reading the Fire: Essays in the Traditional Indian Literatures of the Far West.* Lincoln: University of Nebraska Press, 1983.

Seltzer, Mark. *Bodies and Machines.* New York: Routledge, 1992.

Silko, Leslie Marmon. *Ceremony.* New York: Penguin, 1977.

Swann, Brian and Arnold Krupat, eds. *Recovering the Word: Essays on Native American Literature.* Berkeley: University of California Press, 1987.

Wiget, Andrew. *Native American Literature.* Boston: Twayne, 1985.

Wyatt, David. *The Fall into Eden: Landscape and Imagination in California.* Cambridge: Cambridge University Press, 1986.

JULIA B. FARWELL

Goophering Around: Authority and the Trick of Storytelling in Charles W. Chesnutt's *The Conjure Woman*

He [the African priest or Medicine Man] appeared early on the plantation and found his function as the healer of the sick, the interpreter of the Unknown, the comforter of the sorrowing, the supernatural avenger of wrong, and the one who rudely but picturesquely expressed the longing and disappointment of a stolen and oppressed people.[1]
W. E. B. DU BOIS

It has become common practice to describe Charles W. Chesnutt's *The Conjure Woman* (1899) as a politically strategic text, designed by an African American author to inspire a certain amount of humanistic sympathy in a largely white readership. This is a book that operates in dual rhetorics, speaking across the boundary between oral and written voices, African and European literary traditions, realistic and mythic universes.[2] Such oppositions meet at the divisive line of race, a line that polices racial distinctions in favor of white hegemony, thereby reinforcing the authority of "race" itself. From these distinctions, thematic and narrative confrontations develop in *The Conjure Woman* to question such constructed oppositions, demonstrating that Chesnutt ultimately finds the distinctions arbitrary. He asserts racial pride and trickster energy in the twin powers of conjure and "signifying," self-authorizing rituals that challenge the surviving black-white relationships inherited from slavery. What I hope to demonstrate is that while *The Conjure Woman* performs the critically acknowledged cultural mission of affirming a group identity bound by speech, experience, and tradition, its most important task may be to use a trickster strategy to confront white hegemonic misrepresentations of that group as distinctly "other."

Traditionally, tricksters live on their wits; lacking the strength of their opponents, they are always in jeopardy, always hungry, always needing something to survive. Early African American traditional animal tricksters, such as Br'er Rabbit, were models of opportunism within a moral code compromised by the perils of slavery,[3] and certainly Chesnutt's Julius is legible as such a trickster figure because of his opportunism. But Chesnutt's conjure tales also expand the traditional African American trickster from the appetites of Br'er Rabbit's (and Julius's) food-getting to the communal interests of both Uncle Julius and Chesnutt himself. Whenever Julius profits from his cunning, it is usually for someone other than himself. He seeks a job for his nephew, a meeting place for his church group, or renewed health for Annie. Through his tales, Julius is forming a community within which the conjure work of story is both a creative agent and an invitation to the listener to join. Specifically, in Chesnutt's narrative, trickster energy takes the form of conjure, or "goopher." A religion of diasporic Africa, conjure transplanted into the American context became a system for cultural survival within slavery, a means either to escape harsh treatment or to administer justice within an integral community. It could provide geographically scattered Africans with cultural continuity, solidarity where identity was fragmented, influence with nature, and power within a social system which would deny them humanity. According to John W. Roberts, conjure doctors functioned multiply as priests, disaster specialists, spiritual intercessors, consultants, removers of obstacles, and practitioners of all important magic. They were integral lifelines of history, culture and survival.[4]

To transmit a concept of conjurers as folk heroes, Africans recounted the actions of conjurers in oral narratives, a tradition—like the Br'er Rabbit tales—that Chesnutt draws upon with Julius's stories in *The Conjure Woman.* Roberts, for example, notes "the frequency with which enslaved Africans reported the intervention of conjurers in their interactions with the masters, especially to secure supernatural protection."[5] Of the seven stories in *The Conjure Woman,* there are several in which conjure circumvents the master's orders: in "Sis' Becky's Pickaninny," a child is turned into a bird in order to visit her distant mother; in "Po' Sandy," a man is turned into a tree to avoid being loaned away yet again from his wife. In addition, conjure's signs operate as metaphors for the injustices and prejudices that the "reality" of slavery enforces. The conjure doll in "Hot-Foot Hannibal" represents the title character as a racist stereotype, "light-headed en hot-footed." Primus's term as a mule in "The Conjurer's Revenge" signifies the allegiance between slave and reluctant beast of burden. Henry's personification of the scuppernong vines, or Sandy's transformation into a tree, and ultimately lumber, suggests that a slave is nothing more than a "raw material" to be consumed by the master with no more feeling than he would have for harvested crops. The skill of the conjure doctor offers escape from and commentary upon the inhumanity of the situation.

These signals may be lost on John, but their design should not be missed by the reader. The metaphoric play of conjure belongs to the African American rhetorical mode of "signifying" that Henry Louis Gates, Jr., speaking of the traditional figure of the signifying monkey, describes.

> The Signifying Monkey, he who dwells at the margins of discourse, ever punning, ever troping, ever embodying the ambiguities of language, is our trope for repetition and revision, indeed our trope of chiasmus, repeating and reversing simultaneously as he does in one deft discursive act.[6]

As a cultural strategy employed to represent against misrepresentation, to perform dominant expressive models while reinventing them, signifying is a verbal skill, an art form that couples an apparent meaning with an equal and contrary one. As John Edgar Wideman explains, "in the street a skillful signifier can talk behind a victim's back while looking him in the face."[7] Thus a writer who signifies can speak on several levels at once, appealing to different audiences who belong to distinct communities of understanding. *The Conjure Woman* speaks double on several levels at once, creating a dense fabric that signifies ceaselessly. Just as Julius's stories mean differently to John and Annie within the narrative, so does the text appeal to diverse cultural sympathies among readers; yet these meanings are not ultimately separate, for the text works to desegregate cultural understanding by enlightening the reader to its own design. Chesnutt *mediates* between the conflicting power systems of slavery and conjure, between the European and African expressive idioms, between the black and white racial communities in which he operates simultaneously. Signifying becomes an inclusive, interracial strategy, so that whether Chesnutt speaks to our face or behind our back, we as readers see that there are other layers, other meanings that we might come to understand. To illustrate, I will examine several of Chesnutt's dynamics (keeping in mind that no layer operates independently of the others). My point will be to demonstrate the complexity of *The Conjure Woman* and the power of the conjure doctor, be it Aun' Peggy, Uncle Julius, or Chesnutt himself, to signify upon empirical reality and thus transform it for the empowerment of author and reader alike.

John employs Julius as an "appurtenance" of the plantation, conditioned, as John would have us think, "to look upon himself as the property of another" (p. 65). But any possibility that we should regard Julius similarly is undercut by his manipulation of the Uncle Tom role. Julius's status with his employer depends upon his ability to fulfill John's degrading expectations. As William L. Andrews observes, "to *sound* authentic to whites requires [African Americans] to adopt a mask, to play a role, to feign authenticity in and through a carefully cultivated voice."[8] The authenticity of Julius's speech pattern is something that many contemporary notices mentioned: For example, the *St. Louis Globe Democrat* said Chesnutt had "perfectly captured black dialect"; the Boston *Saturday Evening Gazette* said Chesnutt was "very successful in his dealing with negro dialect"; the *Boston Courier* crowed that the dialect was "used without a flaw"; and the *Minneapolis Journal* allowed that the Negro dialect was "pretty generally the real thing."[9] However, we should be careful of such evaluations.

Julius's dialect differs from the textual experience of standardized modern English; it is more like the words of Chaucer, or another language altogether. Thus Julius's speech represents almost a barrier to reading, difficult going for readers accustomed to the standardized voice of John. Some words may have no standardized meaning at all; if we can't understand that "afternoon is 'evening' in Southern parlance" as John interprets for us, how are we to know what Julius means by a buckrah, a shote, or a junesey? Terms are purposefully difficult. Because the language is written as it is spoken, to make sense of the stories, readers have to convert the transcription into the sound of Julius's voice, maybe reading aloud to *hear* what words Julius might be "approximating," thus returning the language to its proper oral context. That is, Chesnutt's deployment of black speech itself signifies, demanding that the reader confront both the comfort of reading what should be heard, and the expectations of how an "ol' darky" would sound and what his stories would say. And once we decode, the apparent serenity and quaintness of dialect refuse to hide the atrocities of families separated and men flogged for clumsiness.

By playing with genre conventions of the slave narrative and of southern plantation fiction, Chesnutt skillfully manipulates reader—and publisher—expectations; in this way he opens a space for the African American vernacular of conjure, not as a marginalized dialect, but as a language with its own historical necessity. Language here stands for experience. Chesnutt makes a distinction between normative white language and vernacular black language in order to distinguish white from black experience.[10] For Chesnutt, what it means to be black is best represented by being able to speak "black." The phonetics and abbreviations on the page contrast with, and disrupt, the inconspicuous voice of John's narration, signifying the difference of slave experience from the nostalgic portraits of white plantation fiction, even signifying upon what John mistakes as material consistent with that genre.[11] Chesnutt's language also expands what has previously been read as authentic slave experience, what has been recorded by Frederick Douglass or Harriet Jacobs, for example, in a language mastered yet inadequate to record the details of life as a slave. Here we witness an attempt to represent slavery in its own vernacular. Julius's stories may not be autobiographical in the strictest sense like Douglass's or Jacobs's, but it is possible to read the characters in Julius's stories as stand-ins for him, friends with whom he shared the experience of slavery. Further, even though Julius never shows up as a character in the stories, he is their protagonist. As the story *teller,* Julius is never absent from his tales. The transcribed voice—visual, foregrounded, difficult—reminds us of his presence and appeals to us on behalf of his past. His is a legitimate slave narrative.

If the African American oral tradition—indeed any oral tradition—is limited by the capacities of voice and audience, Chesnutt's fictionalization intends to bring a larger audience to, and expand the didactic potential of, his story. In his own words:

> The subtle almost indefinable feeling of repulsion toward the Negro, which is common to most Americans . . . cannot be stormed and taken by assault; the garrison will not capitulate: so their position must be mined, and we will find ourselves in their midst before they think it.
>
> This work is a twofold character. The negro's part is to prepare himself for social recognition and equality; and it is the province of literature to open the way for him to get it—to accustom the public mind to the idea; and while amusing them to lead them on, imperceptibly, unconsciously step by step to the desired state of feeling.[12]

As Andrews observes, slave narratives were accompanied by letters of introduction by white editors or abolitionists, verifying that the content of the black author's chronicle was true. That is, the "truth" of the tale relied upon white voices testifying to the character and dignity of the author, which was otherwise suspect. This petition to a white readership from "one of their own" opened a space for black voice and experience, and such framing seemed to be the only position from which a black author might gain access to a white reading audience.[13] This hierarchical relationship established white skin as a hypostasis of transcendent truth, as the measure of all other possibilities—a position that John, as the only white man in *The Conjure Woman,* occupies. Indeed, he inhabits both of the roles reserved for white men in slave narratives: editor and master—which identifies John as the power that must be subverted according to the trickster paradigm. Before I discuss how Chesnutt manipulates John's editorial function, however, it's important to survey how the legacy of slavery positions the white man for his commentary role.

Without a white landlord, the plantation in *The Conjure Woman* is a neglected landscape filled with signs of decay: the rotting rail fence, the spacious mansion reduced to ruined chimneys, the soil exhausted by "shiftless cultivation." For John, this is a space emptied of purpose. Since the departure of McAdoo, the grapevines have grown in "unpruned luxuriance" and have been the "undisputed prey of the first [no doubt black] comer" (pp. 5–6). The chaos of the vineyard requires a disciplining (read "white") hand to restore its productivity. All the plantation needs is John to rescue it and to enforce meaning. Hence, like the master, he systematically stakes out his territory, clearing the woods to expand his cultivation and adding corn and melon crops to his grape vines. Yet John also fills much of his narrative with what he and Annie do in their spare time: read, take drives, play the piano; and it is clear that, for Annie, having nothing to do aggravates her frail condition. Since we never see her doing anything but passing time, we can only assume that domestic chores are performed by hired help. Predicated on the labor of others, John and Annie's excessive leisure is itself part of the white stereotype; like the plantation, it is a legacy of the departed slave owners.

Even if slavery is no longer legal, John fits easily into the southern plantation stereotype he's mapped out for himself as a gentleman farmer; he's deeply protective of his delicate (read feminine) invalid wife, paternalistic and condescending toward Julius, and indulgent of his storytelling. However, all other entertainments must first be exhausted: Novels fail to entertain (p. 104), reading aloud has no cheering effect (p. 133), and philosophy, even in the "simplest and most lucid form," seems nonsense (p. 163). Boredom is the only excuse for humoring Julius:

> The man had not yet finished cleaning the spring, and we *might as well* put in time listening to Julius as in any other way. We had found some of his plantation tales quite interesting. (p. 70, my emphasis)
>
> The prospect of a long, dull afternoon was not alluring, and I was glad to have the monotony of Sabbath quiet relieved by a plantation legend. (p. 108)
>
> I was *willing to humor* the old man's fancy. He had not told us a story for some time; and the dark and solemn swamp around us . . . made the place an ideal one for a ghost story. (pp. 203–204, my emphasis)

According to Chesnutt, boredom is a prominent feature of the proprietary white lifestyle in the South: "It was often necessary to wait awhile in North Carolina; and our Northern energy had not been entirely proof against the influences of climate and local custom" (p. 68). Finding elaborate justifications for requesting Julius's stories, John deflects all responsibility for the situations he finds himself in, so that even the "wild extravagance" of Julius's tales is better than nothing; listening is more often than not a matter of surrender.

Although John is willing to indulge the old man his "ingenious fairy tales," he's convinced that Julius's opportunism is always a debit, always an attempt to trick John out of something that is "rightfully" his. John characteristically seeks the materialistic motivation behind Julius's tales, which invite commodified solutions from the Yankee entrepreneur obsessed with the efficiency of his crops and confident that all things have a profit function. He discovers Julius's material gains and satisfies himself that desire for a new suit or for a new building for church temperance meetings is reason enough for the black man to tailor lies. Meanwhile, Julius's experience is one shaped by the material reality of chattel slavery, a system that allows one man to own another, where sweethearts, wives, and mothers can be sold or traded for a race horse. If such things occur, then can anything *not* be possible? Slavery's transformation of an entire race into property makes conjure's transformations of children into birds and men into trees comparatively simple. Perhaps what John enforces by doubting Julius is nothing more than his authority on the plantation, his assertion of final word on what is truth and what is impossible. Put another way, what John refuses to believe is the extent of slavery's atrocity. For him Julius's tales are outrageous lies, not simply for the transformations within them of people into animals, but for what the stories signify about white authority.

It is Chesnutt's most powerful performance as trickster-author to question the position of whites to judge black experience. With John's editorial nay-saying, Chesnutt signifies upon the structural and political designs of the genre of the slave narrative, which traditionally petitioned for white recognition of horrors of chattel slavery, the presence of a shared humanity, and the inclusion of black people in the white capitalistic system of authority and self-authorization. In *The Conjure Woman,* the white editor's voice is no longer supplemental to the story; rather, John's testimonial attempts to overtake Julius's narrative, trying to discredit the conjure tales. John's incredulity directly contrasts with, for example, William Lloyd Garrison's acclaim of Frederick Douglass's "union of head and heart, which is indispensable to an enlightenment of the heads and the winning of the hearts of others," or Lydia Maria Child's testimony about the seventeen years of high esteem of "a distinguished family of New York" for Harriet Jacobs.[14] Chesnutt's white narrator is "skeptical of his [Julius's] motives"; he accuses Julius of disguising material ambitions with elaborate lies. Yet this anti-testimonial eventually undermines John's authority, as Julius's wit outshines John's (merely) racial advantage with the white reader, who comes to acknowledge the legitimacy of black conjure power in context. As John continues to be duped and Julius continues to triumph, John's skepticism and stubborn adherence to the archaic lifestyle of plantation master become laughable, his epistemological powers deflated. John's notion of reality is itself lampooned by a passage in his philosophy book:

> The difficulty of dealing with transformations so many-sided as those which all existences have undergone, or are undergoing, is such as to make a complete and deductive interpretation almost hopeless. So to grasp the total process of redistribution of matter and motion as to see simultaneously its several necessary results

in their actual interdependence is scarcely possible. There is, however, a mode of rendering the process as a whole tolerably comprehensible. Though the genesis of the rearrangement of every evolving aggregate is in itself one, it presents to our intelligence. . . . (pp.163–164)

Through this satire on European rhetoric and John's pretentious enjoyment of such language, we understand the passage as a description of the very improbabilities to which John objects in Julius's stories. Deaf to the lessons of the conjure tales because they come from black experience, John fails to notice what should by now be a familiar subject even when confronted with his favored idiom. He cannot apprehend the lesson of the fluidity of reality, regardless of which rhetorical tradition would have him learn it. Chesnutt suggests that the nature of reality is not divided along racial boundaries but that, as Annie and Julius show us, the apprehension of reality is a matter of sensitivity, of an open-mindedness that accepts uncertainty.

The truthfulness of Julius's tales would be completely lost on John were it not for his wife's insight and sympathy. Affected by the tragic stories of lovers and families torn apart by slave masters' requisitions, Annie is deeply moved and acts accordingly, giving Julius's nephew a second chance to work or choosing a route to "conveniently" meet up with Murchison on the way to a neighbor's. She begins, early in the book, with "is that story true?" (p. 33) but then eventually comes to discover meaning on her own when she recites the moral of "Sis' Becky's Pickaninny" herself. For Annie, Julius's stories are an education. She understands that they are "true to nature, and might have happened half a hundred times, and no doubt did happen, in those horrid days before the war" (p. 159). She hears the tragedies of slavery (thinly veiled, but veiled nonetheless); as even John must admit, these stories, "poured freely into the sympathetic ear of a Northern-bred woman, disclose many a tragic incident of the darker side of slavery" (p. 41). However, Annie is not a perfect reader for the stories. She rejects "The Conjurer's Revenge" as falling short of Julius's "usual mark": "It is n't pathetic, it has no moral that I can discover, and I can't see why you should tell it. In fact, it seems to me like nonsense" (p. 127). Puzzled by Annie's dismissive pique and her sentimental taste, Julius learns immediately and follows up in "Sis' Becky" with a tale of an infant torn from its mother's breast. Annie's evaluation of a story for its sentiment reduces her—like John—to a white stereotype, unreliable unless her expectations are pandered to.[15]

While part of the reality that Julius favors may be supernatural, he nevertheless endorses a morality that should be easily comprehended by all listeners. His black characters act out of the most universal and understandable desires to protect, avenge, or be near the people they love. It's the white folks Chesnutt seems to be concerned about. In his journal, Chesnutt anticipated the legacy of slavery's corruption that he would have to overcome.

> The object of my writings would be not so much the elevation of the colored people as the elevation of the whites—for I consider the unjust spirit of caste which is so insidious as to pervade a whole nation, and so powerful as to subject a whole race and all connected with it to scorn and social ostracism—I consider this a barrier to the moral progress of the American people; and I would be one of the first to head a determined, organized crusade against it.[16]

We can use this to understand how affecting the moral progress of whites is one cultural mission of *The Conjure Woman*. Enslaved Africans generally considered conjure ineffectual toward whites, attributing their immunity to disbelief.[17] Not surprisingly, in Julius's stores, conjure is usually intraracial, practiced only for fellow Africans. Only in "Mars Jeems' Nightmare" is conjure directed at a white man, since, as Aun' Peggy warns, "I has ter be kinder keerful 'bout cunj'in' w'ite folks" (p. 77). Whites may hire Aun' Peggy to fence off grapevines from pilfering field hands or to discover a "voodoo" doll underneath the kitchen steps. But whites have no business meddling with conjure. They misunderstand it in the stories with destructive results, leading, as we see in both "The Goophered Grapevine" and "Hot-Foot Hannibal," for example, to the death of a slave. In the antebellum context, whites exploit all aspects of black culture, so when masters are given access to conjure, they can see only economic potential. For them, conjure is either a shortcut to bigger profits or a superstition whose indulgence must be prohibited because it interferes with the efficient management of the plantation.

While conjure and white folks may not mix often in the stories, the combination operates differently in the frame tale. Annie is sensitive to the suffering around her, as we see in the relapses and complications of the illness she came South to cure. Her initial recovery is replaced by a somnolent spirit; her mood falls prey to the anxieties of postwar southern culture and Yankee opportunisms. The suffering around her affects her health. Only through the administration of Julius's conjure stories does she achieve her ultimate recovery, without which John would miss their instructive benefit. He acknowledges the stimulating effect of the entertainment upon Annie's languor:

> My wife had listened to this story with greater interest than she had manifested in any subject for several days. (p. 158)
>
> My wife's condition took a turn for the better from this very day, and she was soon on her way to ultimate recovery. (p. 160)

Conjure is medicine. The rabbit's foot Julius gives to Annie may or may not have contributed to her elevation of spirits, yet it seems that John does perceive the conjure quality of Julius's stories. It is no coincidence that Aun' Peggy's warning about white folks comes in the story that John recognizes as being "powerful goopher" directed at him (p. 101). The "goopher" John refers to is both Aun' Peggy's transformation of Mars Jeems into one of his own slaves and the power of the story itself, which has not only transformed John and Annie's boredom into satisfaction, but also persuaded them to give Julius's awkward nephew a second chance as a plantation farm hand. In other words, John finally recognizes what we've known for a while. Julius is leading John out story by story, like the educable white reader in Chesnutt's journal, "imperceptibly, unconsciously step by step to the desired state of feeling," that is, to the recognition of Julius as a man of authority.

Julius's stories use conjure to promote cultural understanding. The trope of conjure functions metonymically, representing a legitimate black culture with an Afrocentric system of authority and expression and an ability to understand, shape and control the natural and social environment. It is a system of faith. If white folks, readers of and characters in *The Conjure Woman* alike, could be persuaded to believe in goopher, they would be just as susceptible to it as black folk. Julius is a conjure evangelist who, through the "powerful goopher" of story, indoctrinates John and Annie into sympathy with, if not faith in, the possibility of transformation. The book is an invitation to the white audience from Julius (and behind him, Chesnutt) into conjurability, into a trickster-suffused reality that need not be divided along racial boundaries. Rather than blacks applying for position in white racist society, whites can become part of a black system. It's not a perfect system that Julius offers here, but it does offer alternatives to hegemonic notions of signifiers, authenticity, and authority. While slave narratives appealed for the inclusion of blacks by whites, Chesnutt's inverted structure beckons whites into a conjure belief-system. The rationalizations of western metaphysics, of which John is so fond, are parodied as pretentious "nonsense," while Julius makes more sense with each passing chapter. Freed from their limited perceptions of material reality, sympathetic white readers like Annie can be persuaded of the "truth" of the tales and come to regard "goopher" as a matter of faith. With the stories providing Annie with relief from boredom and from her debilitating languor, the charmed rabbit's foot—"de lef' hin-foot er a grabe-ya'd rabbit, killt by a cross-eyed nigger on a da'k night in de full er de moon" (p. 135)—finally cures her condition. Health is the reward for her proper understanding of conjure's lesson, and for her interventions with John on Julius's behalf.

As *The Conjure Woman* progresses, John and Annie find themselves increasingly susceptible to conjuration, less as dupes than as beneficiaries. John's conclusion to "Hot-Foot Hannibal," the last story in the book, suggests that perhaps he has learned something after all. Resolving the lovers' quarrel between Mabel and Malcolm, Julius's tale, perhaps more opportune than the others, takes immediate effect. Listening to the story, Mabel cannot help but see in Chloe's fatal treatment of her sweetheart Jeff a fictional reflection of her own situation; she realizes she may be throwing away her last chance with her estranged fiancé, Malcolm, by allowing him to leave for New York. Mabel is dispatched, and Annie and Julius pick flowers to delay the horse-drawn cart. The lovers reunited, John speculates about Julius's motive and, quite significantly, fails to find his usual economic interpretation:

> I do not know whether or not Julius had a previous understanding with Malcolm Murchison by which he was to drive us round by the long road that day, nor do I know exactly what motive influenced the old man's exertions in the matter. He was fond of Mabel, but I was old enough, and knew Julius well enough, to be skeptical of his motives. It is certain that a most excellent understanding existed between him and Murchison after the reconciliation, and that when the young people set up housekeeping over at the Murchison place, Julius had an opportunity to enter their service. For some reason or other, however, he preferred to remain with us. The mare, I might add, was never known to balk again. (pp. 228–229)

So ends *The Conjure Woman*. If John does indeed know Julius well by now, why is he unable to understand Julius's reason for staying with him and Annie? He doesn't offer money as a possibility. John has prided himself throughout the narrative on his solutions to the puzzles of the stories. While he has managed to get them only half right, satisfied with locating the material profits, he's missed what Annie has gotten all along. He's missed the pleasure of the story, the enchanting rhetoric of conjure, while fixating on the rational, the what-can't-possibly-be-right, and the commercial. When Julius turns down a job offer from Malcolm, preferring, as John cannot fathom at first, to stay in his current employ, Julius's motivation finally becomes so clear that maybe John hasn't missed it: Julius chooses the community he has with John and Annie over however attractive an offer Murchison may have made. Like Mars Jeems, who wakes from his nightmare suspecting that something strange has happened to him, John is careful before he defames Julius this time.

In the last line, John states that the mare was never known to balk again. Because this is the final image of the book, an image of a harnessed yet reluctant animal now accepting directions willingly, there is room here for the suggestion that John, reined in by Julius for some time now, never hesitates to follow Julius's lead again. According to this reading, the book is—after all—the story of John's coming to accept the value and authority of Julius's conjure tales, as if not true to fact, then certainly true to spirit. It doesn't matter that John may not understand the nuances of conjure; what seems clear is that conjure, whether through actual metamorphosis or mere words, can work magic. John is a most resistant listener, and his "conversion" is consistent with Chesnutt's project of "leading out" the white reader "to the desired state of feeling."

For nineteenth-century white readers, white documentation was required for black narrative to be considered historical evidence. Without that testimony from the margins, the narrative would be incomplete, invalid, at best a curiosity. In Chesnutt's text, the margin of white testimony attempts to overtake the story of black experience, but finally the narrative traces not so much the story of Julius's coming into voice, as John's gradual acceptance of Julius's already authoritative telling. The tales do not rely upon the frame for their meaning; it is Julius's triumph that he manages to tell in spite of John's double guess. Julius the trickster stays ahead of his officious editor, always signifying, always offering opportune stories that improve communal conditions and that represent an African American culture in spite of, or because of, John's misinterpretations. Perhaps finally, we are allowed to infer and hope (if not to know with absolute certainty) that John recognizes that the community that benefits from such representation does include himself. With this qualified reading, I myself hope to avoid John's error of mastery, his reduction of Julius's motivation to simple terms. I do not wish to mistake the conversion of a white readership or the invitation to communal identity as the only two meanings of the text. Unlike John, I am aware that stories have multiple appeals and effects that do not depend upon a white audience or the interpretive work of critics for their value. However, I think it is possible to read the ending as an indication of a change in John; if he can be persuaded to believe in the possibility of conjure and, by implication, the contributions of African American culture to an enriched understanding of the world, then so might the most stubborn reader be able to follow his example.

The title *The Conjure Woman* is a textual commentary, naming the book itself as a conjure doctor, a trickster whose supernatural influence can circumvent the obstacles of slavery's legacy and set the world of the fiction's readers back on course. Chesnutt challenges the jurisdiction of white discourse over black expressive modes, and offers alternative African American models of authority in conjure and signifying. This writing opens questions of who's in control, especially since Chesnutt, as a black man, is the author of a white voice who tells a black man's stories of a black conjure woman. Ultimately, the who's in control of the text becomes unassignable because Chesnutt, John, Julius, and Aun' Peggy are inseparable. Power flows between and among fluid levels of narrative: Aun' Peggy affects Julius's reality, and Julius narrates Aun' Peggy's story; Julius manipulates John's authority in ways not dissimilar to Aun' Peggy's conjure. John controls Julius editorially; Chesnutt is inseparable from both Julius and John; and *The Conjure Woman* is Chesnutt's book. The text itself is a trick that Chesnutt uses to suggest that the elements of race, language, and experience—all continuous and dependent upon one another—may contribute to a sense of reality, but that reality is by no means limiting. Chesnutt legitimates the speech community of black dialect by locating the most influential wisdoms in the book in Julius, and champions the black rhetoric of signifying and the power of conjure as cultural symbols for anyone who would recognize them.

Notes

1. W. E. B. Du Bois, *The Souls of Black Folk* (1903; New York: NAL Penguin, 1982), p. 216.

2. For example, John Edgar Wideman lucidly analyzes Chesnutt's parity construction in "Chesnutt and the WPA Narratives," *The Slave's Narrative*, ed. Henry Louis Gates, Jr. (New York: Oxford University Press, 1985). Wideman's analysis and language were influential for this paragraph.

3. For more on the animal trickster figure, see John W. Roberts's essay "The African American Animal Trickster as Hero" in *Redefining American Literary History* (New York: Modern Language Association, 1990), eds. A. LaVonne Brown Ruoff and Jerry W. Ward, Jr., or Roberts's own book, *From Trickster to Badman* (Philadelphia: University of Pennsylvania Press, 1989).

4. Roberts, *From Trickster to Badman*, p. 73.

5. Ibid., p. 92.

6. Henry Louis Gates, Jr., *The Signifying Monkey* (New York: Oxford University Press, 1988), p. 52.

7. Wideman, p. 66.

8. William L. Andrews, "The Novelization of Voice in Early African American Narrative," *PMLA* 105 (1990): 24.

9. Curtis W. Ellison and E. W. Metcalf, Jr., eds., *Charles W. Chesnutt: A Reference Guide* (Boston: G. K. Hall, 1977), pp. 5–11. As Houston Baker notes, Chesnutt was defensive of the term "dialect," writing to his editor at Houghton Mifflin, Walter Hines Page, that "what we call by that name is an attempt to express, with such a degree of phonetic correctness as to suggest the sound, English as an ignorant old southern Negro would be supposed to speak it" (Baker, *Modernism and the Harlem Renaissance* [Chicago: University of Chicago Press, 1987], p. 42).

10. James Baldwin writes (*The Price of the Ticket: Collected Nonfiction, 1948–1985* [New York: St. Martin's/Marek, 1985], p. 651):

> Blacks came to the United States chained to each other, but from different tribes: Neither could speak the other's language. If two black people, at that bitter hour of the world's history, had been able to speak to each other, the institution of chattel slavery could never have lasted as long as it did. Subsequently, the slave was given, under the eye, and the gun, of his master, Congo Square, and the Bible—or, in other words, and under these conditions, the slave began the formation of the black church, and it is within this unprecedented tabernacle that black English began to be formed. This was not, merely, as in the European example, the adoption of a foreign tongue, but an alchemy that transformed

ancient elements into a new language: *A language comes into existence by means of brutal necessity, and the rules of the language are dictated by what the language must convey.*

11. For a history of southern plantation writing, including Chesnutt's place in its development, see Lucinda H. Mackethian, "Plantation Fiction, 1865–1900," in Louis D. Rubin, Jr., ed., *The History of Southern Literature* (Baton Rouge: Louisiana State University Press, 1985), pp. 209–218.

12. *The Journals of Charles W. Chesnutt,* ed. Richard Brodhead (Durham, N.C.: Duke University Press, 1993), p. 140.

13. Andrews, pp. 23–34.

14. Frederick Douglass, *Narrative of the Life of Frederick Douglass. An American Slave* (New York: Penguin Books, 1982), p. 36. Harriet A. Jacobs, *Incidents in the Life of a Slave Girl* (Cambridge, Mass.: Harvard University Press, 1987), p. 3.

15. I am indebted to Kathleen Gillespie both for her help in the fine tuning of this essay, and for her interest in Chesnutt's characterization of Annie's sentimentality.

16. Chesnutt, *Journals,* pp. 139–140.

17. See Roberts, pp. 91–92.

Works Cited

Andrews, William L. "The Novelization of Voice in Early African American Narrative." *PMLA* 105 (1990): 23–34.

Baker, Houston A., Jr. *Modernism and the Harlem Renaissance.* Chicago: University of Chicago Press, 1987.

Baldwin, James. *The Price of the Ticket: Collected Nonfiction, 1948–1985.* New York: St. Martin's/Marek, 1985.

Chesnutt, Charles Waddell. *The Conjure Woman.* Ann Arbor: University of Michigan Press, 1969.

———, *The Journals of Charles W. Chesnutt,* ed. Richard Brodhead. Durham, N.C.: Duke University Press, 1993.

Douglass, Frederick. *Narrative of the Life of Frederick Douglass. An American Slave.* New York: Penguin Books, 1982.

Du Bois, W. E. B. *The Souls of Black Folk.* 1903. Rpt. New York: Signet, NAL Penguin, 1982.

Ellison, Curtis W., and E. W. Metcalf, Jr. *Charles W. Chesnutt: A Reference Guide.* Boston: G. K. Hall, 1977.

Gates, Henry Louis, Jr. *The Signifying Monkey.* New York: Oxford University Press, 1988.

———, ed. *The Slave's Narrative.* New York: Oxford University Press, 1985.

Jacobs, Harriet E. *Incidents in the Life of a Slave Girl.* Cambridge, Mass.: Harvard University Press, 1987.

Roberts, John W. *From Trickster to Badman: The Black Folk Hero in Slavery and Freedom.* Philadelphia: University of Pennsylvania Press, 1989.

Rubin, Louis D., Jr. *The History of Southern Literature.* Baton Rouge: Louisiana State University Press, 1985.

Ruoff, A. LaVonne Brown, and Jerry W. Ward, Jr., eds. *Redefining American Literary History.* New York: Modern Language Association, 1990.

ALEXIA KOSMIDER

Reinventing Trickster: Creek Indian Alex Posey's Nom de Plume, Chinnubbie Harjo

Woetcoh Micco, Waboxie Harjo and Chinnubbie attended Sunday school at Frozen Rock last Sabbath afternoon. For some reason or other they did not return when they were expected, and, as a result, were given one or two demerits. "But," said Waboxie, "what of that? We recieved [*sic*] an introduction to the chief's daughter!" CHINNUBBIE[1]

Alexander (Alex) Posey, a Creek poet, short story writer, and journalist, dons the mask of Chinnubbie Harjo, his trickster persona who frequently finds himself in embarrassing circumstances or as the hapless observer of numerous local events in Indian Territory. While Posey was attending Bacone Indian University (1889–1894), located near what is now Muskogee, Oklahoma, he also was a reporter for the monthly *B.I.U. Instructor,* the school newspaper.[2] Here, as he wrote gossipy news about school meetings and other activities, Posey gave birth to his persona Chinnubbie. It was a delivery into an exciting, always ironic, humorous life in which Chinnubbie continuously becomes entangled in awkward predicaments such as the church meeting referred to above, with his friends Woetcoh Micco and Waboxie Harjo, who scoff at the school authorities. For Chinnubbie is a "humorist of unquestioned excellence, as well as being renowned for other traits of character" ("Chinnubbie and the Owl"). Moreover, he is a versatile storyteller, and when he speaks his listeners are charmed by his eloquence, for Chinnubbie could spin a yarn that "captivated the gravest of his audience." A truly renowned storyteller, even "his actions when delivering a tale were as comical and laughable, almost, as the story he told" ("Chinnubbie and the Owl").

Posey's persona Chinnubbie is derived from his Creek heritage.[3] A complex person—he kept one foot in the Euroamerican literary world as a reporter and a student and the other grounded in Creek culture—Posey attributed his love of Creek tribal stories to the influence of his full-blood Creek mother, Nancy Posey, who, although a devout Baptist, lived in a world steeped in Creek tradition (Littlefield, *Alex Posey,* p. 24). Nancy was an excellent storyteller and kept her twelve children, including young Alex, amused with Creek tales; it is highly probable that she had a good repertoire of stories about the Creek trickster Rabbit,[4] whose pernicious and resisting nature probably appealed to Posey's sensibilities as a writer. In any case, like the trickster, Posey had a talent for observing the comic side of situations; and through his detached third-person voice as Chinnubbie Harjo, he entertained his readers with his whimsical and often humorous renditions of local happenings (Littlefield, "Evolution of Alex Posey's Fus Fixico Persona," p. 138).

Through the persona Chinnubbie, Posey wrote humorous comments that appealed to his readers. For example, after mentioning the various students and faculty members who were on the university's sick list, he wrote, "Chinnubbie is not feeling so very well himself" (Littlefield, *Alex Posey,* p. 55). In another instance, as he describes the local school newspaper picnic, he states that "Chinnubbie sat quietly in the shade, meditating about the weather and the prospects of the farmer" (Littlefield, "Evolution of Alex Posey's Fus Fixico Persona," p. 138). Like a clever trickster, Chinnubbie shows an uncanny talent for tricking his audience into his chicaneries. In one issue of the Bacone school newspaper, Chinnubbie mentions that the editor recently had received many positive comments about his paper and adds that "Chinnubbie received a compliment also, but he wisely protests against having it published for he knows he does not deserve it, and even if he did, the step to have it printed would be egotistical."[5] Like Rabbit, who boasts about how much property he owns, Chinnubbie brags about his own editorial skills; tricksterlike, he pokes fun at conventions yet successfully outwits his readers by getting his name mentioned in the newspaper nevertheless. At an early age, Posey discovered how effective and useful it was to write behind the mask of a trickster figure.

The Creeks are fond of Rabbit, a wily character who has a tendency to get himself tangled up in ridiculous situations, but who, more often than not, still manages to come out relatively unscathed. It is very probable that Nancy Posey told Alex one of the numerous stories about Rabbit outwitting and outmaneuvering Wolf, such as "The Rabbit and the Wolf." In this well-known tale, Rabbit brags to some girls that he is a big "man" and owns property and a horse. Of course, the girls question Rabbit's truthfulness; he therefore sets out to make a favorable impression on them. Rabbit whines to his friend, Wolf, that he can't walk to the council meeting and wants to ride there on his back. Wolf, being a good friend, lets Rabbit climb on. But then Rabbit tricks Wolf further by persuading him to let Rabbit put a saddle and then a bridle on Wolf. Finally, Rabbit convinces Wolf that he will feel better wearing his spurs, even though he promises not to gouge Wolf's side with them. Before Wolf knows what's going on, Rabbit plunges his steel spurs into his sides, then madly gallops by the girls' houses, showing them that he indeed has some "horse" (Swanton, p. 64).

While some of Rabbit's actions may be conceived as inane or foolish, other behaviors represent dangerous individualistic expressions that could threaten or undermine existing customs and traditions. For instance, maybe Posey's mother told him the tale of "How Rabbit Won His Wife's Sister for His Second Wife," which not only shows Rabbit besting his wife but also pokes fun at existing marriage conventions. The story begins with Rabbit posed romantically: He reclines his head in his wife's lap, while she gently massages his head. Rabbit then sees his wife's younger and more beautiful sister stroll by. Making some feeble excuse, he runs out of his house and hides in the bushes until wife's sister passes by. Then, in a disguised voice, he whispers to her that the people have agreed to undertake a big bear hunt, where all the men will go to a designated camping spot with their wives' sisters, instead of with their own wives. The young woman runs back to Rabbit's house and tells him and her sister the camp news. She, of course, leaves out the most important part, however. But with Rabbit's prodding, she reluctantly reveals the information, specifying that each man should leave his wife at home and instead take his wife's sister to the hunt. Rabbit and his wife make the proper preparations for his departure. When Rabbit and his wife's sister arrive at the arranged camping spot, Rabbit feigns surprise that none of the other hunters has arrived yet. As the sun slowly begins to set, Rabbit tells his sister's wife to make her bed on the other side of the fire, apart from him. Wily Rabbit knows that a big anthill is situated there; wife's sister tosses and turns all night, scratching at her ant bites. At this crucial moment, Rabbit "began his wooing, and succeeded in winning his second bride" (Swanton, p. 57).

These trickster tales demonstrate that there is no limit to Rabbit's mischievous nature or his vivid imagination. He is clever and creative, as he ropes Wolf into acting like a horse or deceives his wife's sister into thinking that he is a kind and caring being. Rabbit demonstrates that he is determined to get what he wants and ends up, in each of these cases, impressing women. In the first tale, he is clearly the underdog (or should we say underrabbit) as he triumphs over the larger and stronger Wolf. In the second, Rabbit snubs his nose at conventions and gets the "girls," not through his strength, but because he uses his "brains." Trickster is a small creature, but he walks tall among his fellow animals: He is able to outwit them and get what he wants, whether from larger animals, or even from humans.

Rabbit demonstrates a range of cultural possibilities. As he comes up against what every culture envisions as distinct limits, he shows how far these limits can be extended, and by extension, how far human actions or emotions can go. Trickster treads the line between what is viewed as the "sacred" and the "secular," as his texts both reaffirm and deconstruct societal norms. As Yellowman, a Navaho storyteller, says in trying to pinpoint how this somewhat contradictory figure functions in the Navaho world: "If [Coyote, the Navaho trickster] didn't do all those things, then those things would not be possible in the world" (Wiget, p. 94). The trickster is a cultural metaphor that allows Native Americans to envision themselves and their existence. He is a "gut" response to the paradoxical nature of culture: the need to remain within the confines of society and the need to ridicule or reduce societal constraints. It is not surprising that trickster's mask is the mask that Posey adopts when he writes about his cultural experience in Indian Territory.

If we look for the site of Posey's tricksterlike tendencies, we see that he enjoyed foolish pranks, whether destructive or playful. He and his father, Lewis Henderson (Hence) Posey, both loved a good joke. In June 1897, Posey went to visit his father at his farm near Bald Hill, where he recorded in his journal this moment:

> My father and I scared the renters on the farm into fits with false faces. We run [them] out of the cotton patches and out of their home and out of their wits. I played the part of the hag and my father that of the devil before day. (Dale, p. 428)

While playing tricks appealed to Posey's humorous side, he also was an avid reader, enjoying such subjects as ancient history and the biographies of the Roman politicians, Marcus Antonius, Marcus Brutus, and Artaxerxes, a Persian king. Posey also was interested in Creek history, as he spent long afternoons chatting about Creek politics and history with Captain Belcher, an old and gregarious gentleman who was a local history enthusiast.

Along with his interest in history, Posey was a voracious reader of literature. He read current magazines including work by writers and poets such as Walt Whitman, Washington Irving, and Emily Dickinson. But more than anyone, Robert Burns appealed to his sensibilities as a writer and poet. Posey describes Burns's impact on him:

> I find some new pleasure, some new thought, some new beauty heretofore unseen everytime I read poems of the "Ayrshire Plowman." His warm heart, his broad and independent mind "glint" like the daisy in the "histie stubble field" in every song he coraled [sic]. (Dale, pp. 415–416)

Posey's attraction to the "Ayrshire Plowman" parallels his own paradoxical stance. Burns creates a dichotomous self-representation—on the one hand, he becomes a larger-than-life super-Scot, a national hero, while on the other, he assumes the figure of a man struggling, barely surmounting the harsh economic conditions characteristic of his class and dying relatively young (McGuirk, p. 219). Further, Burns looked at himself calculatingly and understood what the Edinburgh gentry desired. From the numerous letters he wrote to fellow poets, and to some of the established gentry, it becomes apparent that his position was painful. David Sampson points out that Burns was frustrated by a society that denied him entrance because of his lack of aristocratic birth.

It is probable that Posey, who admired Burns's poetry, identified unconsciously with the "Ayrshire Plowman." Like Burns, Posey sought to be accepted in a world that tried to deny him a literary voice. Both Posey and his hero, Burns, understood their positions between two worlds. In several of Burns's verse-epistles, he vacillates between condemning and confirming the gentry's position (Sampson, p. 35); yet, in spite of his apparent vacillation, Burns's poetry remains political. Burns, estranged from the English gentry, appealed to Posey's sensibilities as a fellow poet, and most likely Posey was sustained emotionally by the poetry of Burns, a person also alienated socially. Perhaps this is why Posey continually reread and reappreciated Burns's poetry. For, like Burns, Posey in his own manner makes his writings the site of political argument and exploration. As he reproduces a strange and powerful commentary about "real" Native peoples living in Indian Territory, he uses language and plotting that do not follow mainstream American conventions.[6]

Posey continued his newspaper reporting, along with his studies at Bacone Indian University, until he graduated in 1895 (Littlefield and Parins, p. 28; Dale, p. 395). Also, along with his propensity for newspaper reporting and for a Euroamerican education, he was actively involved with the Creek nation, holding a position in the legislature of the House of Warriors, the lower house of the Creek National Council, shortly after his graduation from college. He also served as Superintendent of the Creek National Asylum at Okmulgee (Littlefield and Parins, p. 28; Dale, p. 395). After serving as the Superintendent of Public Instruction of the Creek Nation (Challacombe, p. 1014), he concentrated on writing poetry and most likely wrote the two short stories that were later published in *Twin Territories*: "Uncle Dick's Sow," published in January 1900, and "Mose and Richard," in November 1900. Using his nom de plume, Chinnubbie Harjo, "a notorious wit and drone" who possesses "every trait common to man, with a strong unnatural leaning to traits characteristic of neither man nor beast," Posey wrote frequently for *Twin Territories,* effectively situating his stories in his Creek world (Littlefield, p. 50).

In "Uncle Dick's Sow" and "Mose and Richard," Posey writes tricksterlike stories in which the deep structure of the narrative radically interrogates the rules and structures of the dominant culture. Further, given the fact that Posey's stories are situated within the historical context of Indian Territory, it does not seem unusual that the central characters in both "Uncle Dick's Sow" and "Mose and Richard" are black men. Posey's use of black characters reflects the racial composition of his own Creek heritage and the dramatic population changes in Indian Territory just prior to Oklahoma's statehood.

Before the Civil War, the Seminole, Cherokee, Creek, Choctaw, and Chickasaw owned black slaves; the Creek, especially, were known for their benign form of slavery. After the war, freedmen lived in villages, often near their former owners. In the 1870s, the majority of the blacks within the territory were ex-slaves, but by the 1890s, many of the blacks came from neighboring states. Even though Euroamericans by the 1890s became the dominant population (in 1870, Euroamericans were 3 percent of the total population of Indian Territory; by 1890 they were 61 percent; Grinde and Taylor, p. 217), the Native groups were more distressed by an influx of "outside blacks," frequently calling them "state negroes" to identify them as a racial group that threatened the status quo. Native peoples as well as freedmen disliked these new immigrants, fearing that they would usurp political power and tribal lands, which had already diminished considerably after the Civil War (Grinde and Taylor, p. 218). The attempt by the Oklahoma Immigration Association to encourage blacks to immigrate into the Oklahoma district fueled the fire for racial hostility. In the 1890s, many Native people were antagonistic toward blacks.

Posey's discourse with his black characters Uncle Dick and Uncle Will in "Uncle Dick's Sow" and with Mose, Richard, and Aunt Cook in "Mose and Richard" represents Native people's fears, whether real or exaggerated, about the shrinkage of tribal lands and the loss of political power. The Native people's problem as they attempted to hold on to their position and at the same time not be the "other," reflects their complicated struggle with conflicting ideologies and the issue of how as Native Americans to position themselves.

It seems clear that Natives were afraid of losing their "place," which had become precarious with Euroamerican expansion into their lands. They were "allowed" to stay in the territories (where they had already experienced a diminishment in their position), by the sufferance of Anglos. Indians must have felt that the influx of "outside" blacks threatened what limited "place" they had. It is therefore little wonder that Native people were anxious and eager to displace their anxieties onto blacks, who up to this point had been "other" to them. Posey senses these paradoxes and creates a means for his predominantly Native American audience to react to their own fears by projecting Native people's phobias, fears, and desires onto blacks.

Posey's strategy relies on the conventions of the Creek world. He wears the mask of the trickster, Chinnubbie Harjo, and tricks the reader into accepting his paradoxical world, where tricksterlike characters fool and warn their readers. Like Rabbit, who reveals a vast range of actions and emotions, Posey demonstrates in his stories the spectrum of possibilities of Native Americans. At some points, he shows his people behaving like Euroamericans, at other times being aligned with blacks, and at still other times despising them. His position fluctuates and reflects the complicated nature of the changing world of Indian Territory. Posey's amusing "simple" stories appear on the surface to render merely the flavor of his rural locale, but in fact they reveal a complex Creek culture that few people even today seem aware of: He speaks about his people as oppressors, as people who have their own prejudices about blacks and freedmen.

"Uncle Dick's Sow" deals with an uppity pig, which belongs to Uncle Dick, who desperately tries to control her. His pig, though, breaks out of her pen and wanders off, eating the potatoes of Uncle Dick's friend, Uncle Will. Aggravated with this unruly pig, Uncle Will has his dog, "majah," chase the pig until she is captured. When Uncle Dick gets wind of what has happened to his prize pig, he seizes Uncle Will's musket, which is hanging over the door, and fires it over his friend's head. The story ends with Uncle Dick and Uncle Will's reconciliation, and the pig is restored to its pen. The narrator sums up the pig's life:

> The sow's career thereafter was smooth and uneventful. Realizing that she was leading a bad life and being a wise sow, she resolved to cut loose from her wickedness, and she did. She became a devoted mother and replenished Uncle Dick's larder with numerous fat shoats—some of them weighing not less than fifty pounds. (p. 33)

If we look closely at the pig's words and actions in context within this story, Posey works out the contradictions inherent in his people's position as the "other." The narrator alludes to the pig's exceptional characteristics, suggesting that she is radical, by equating her with a contemporary revolutionary figure, Emilio Aguinaldo, a Filipino freedom-fighter who was active during the Spanish-American War. The pig demonstrates her tendency to be transgressive, since she "wernt bo'n in no pen, kaze she lub liberty better'n de white folks" (p. 32). Furthermore, like trickster, the pig reveals that she also has her own bag of tricks. The narrator continues, "Cunnin? She's cunnin's cousin Dick hiself an' dat's sho gibin' huh lots o' cunnin!" (p. 32).

It is significant that Posey identifies the pig with a non-Euroamerican hero, for the pig comes to represent Native people in the story. The narrator points to the rascally nature of Uncle Dick's pig and notes the difficulties of keeping this kind of "cunnin'" pig confined. Posey transforms the pig to signify the actions of Native people by further identifying the pig's actions and behaviors with her owner, Uncle Dick; she possesses a discriminating palate, preferring such foods as yams and "rostin' ears." In other words, the pig desires the food of blacks. Yet Posey reveals the transitory position of Native people as he also says that his pig "was no common sow. She was rapidly approaching 'refinement'" (p. 32). Just as the pig is identified with blacks, she also desires to displace blacks.

The pig identifies with the manners and the practices of the dominant group, the Euroamericans, including their attitudes and beliefs about the "other." Before, however, we can understand how Posey tricks his reader into a dangerous discourse that exposes his own people's fears about blacks, it is important to clarify how the word "sofky" is used in the context of this story. "Sofky," a Creek word, denotes a traditional dish of hominy that Creeks are fond of eating. Posey relished this corn dish, but it symbolizes much more than a native delicacy, at least in Posey's mind, where "sofky" becomes synonymous with Creek identity. As he notes in his journal when his wife, Lowena, a non-Native American, learns how to make sofky:

> I must compliment my wife on the sofky she made today—this being her first effort. She, by some hook or crook, contrived to give it just the proper flavor. No one but an Indian can make sofky; Lowena can make sofky: therefore Lowena is an Indian! (Dale, p. 409)

In "Uncle Dick's Sow," however, Posey states that this sacred word, "sofky," became dramatically transposed; he says that "sofky is a Creek word . . . but it has been corrupted by the white man and is made to denote a contemptible dog. Therefore, the sofkies . . . are pupy [*sic*], whelp and hounds and curs of low degree" (p. 33). The pig, like "the white man," uses "sofky" in a negative manner to refer to blacks.

Behind his trickster mask, Posey has his pig speak derogatorily about blacks, aligning herself with Euroamericans. The narrator says that the pig's "attitude toward 'sofkies' in general was not calculated to breed familiarity. She despised them individually, collectively and as a race" (p. 32). The pig thus does not identify with the common people; she thinks of herself as being above the common "cur." In other words, the pig thinks of herself as above blacks. Furthermore, she shows aggressive behavior toward them. The narrator continues, "nothing gave her [the pig] greater pleasure than to make a vain young cur run over himself" (p. 32). In effect, Native Americans' fear and anxiety are projected onto blacks. The narrator adds that the pig's obsession with such foods as yams and "rostin' ears" inevitably leads to her downfall. The narrator also warns his audience about transgressive behavior by discouraging Native people from trying to erase their "otherness" by donning the "skin" and "tastes" of the dominant society.

Uncle's Dick's pig, in desiring forbidden food and putting down "curs," is punished for her unconventional behavior. Because the pig "lub liberty" and refuses to sleep in her pen, or metaphorically oversteps preexisting racial lines, she "gave her neighbors something to talk about" (p. 32). Uncle Will's dog, "majah," chases her until she is captured, but not without having a violent confrontation with Uncle Will. With a bloody nose, the pig "grunting and in deep dejection, struck a bee line for home" (p. 32). For her rebellion, the pig is beaten to submission.

Posey (re)produces a means for his predominantly Native American audience to react to their own fears and anxieties about encroachment. He aligns the pig with a Filipino freedom-fighter, with blacks, and with Euroamericans. In the first instance Posey shows Native Americans rebelling. But his ending suggests that this is not the action to take, for Uncle Will beats the pig into obedience. Posey also shows the pig closely identifying with the actions and behaviors of blacks. Yet this position suggests that Native Americans will become even more "invisible" if they are not distinct from African Americans. Finally, Posey aligns his pig with Euroamericans, including their attitudes and beliefs about blacks. This position, of course, reveals dangerous assumptions about Native Americans' fears and desires about blacks. Posey, in "Uncle Dick's Sow," makes tracks across convoluted and ambiguous racial boundaries. Though he seems to vacillate, he persists in interrogating and subverting existing racial stereotypes, reflecting the conflicting and paradoxical nature of Indian Territory.

Posey continues his tricksterlike tactic of exposing people's fears of the "other" in the short story "Mose and Richard," which further interrogates the notion of hegemonic power. "Mose and Richard," although a humorous story about two boys' mischievous escapades, reaffirms some Native Americans' desires and fears about blacks and reveals how certain Native Americans felt about educating blacks. Many Native Americans greatly valued education, and writers such as Posey recognize the importance of establishing a literary space where Native American voices could be heard. This was evidently the desire of Cherokee and part owner of *Twin Territories* Orna Eddleman, as she published and brought to the foreground other lesser known Native American writers and poets in her magazine. Native American attitudes about educating blacks and former slaves were various. Posey's story "Mose and Richard" deals with the controversy surrounding blacks and education as he unmasks his people's beliefs and anxieties about blacks.

In the story, Uncle Dick tells his two sons, Mose and Richard, that they must go to school, because as a former slave, he never had the opportunity. On the first day of class, Uncle Dick takes Mose and Richard aside and tells them:

"I want you to learn somet'ing kaze de time done get heah w'en if you grows up ignonat, de white man an Mistah Injin gwine to get the best ob you; an' dey may git de best ob you anyhow, but hit aint gwine hu't you to go to school." (p. 226)

Here Uncle Dick exposes his position as being doubly oppressed by "de white man" and "Mistah Injin." His words indicate that he is skeptical about getting out from under oppression; he does know, though, that education is a weapon that might be able to change his boys' position. Mose and Richard listen to their father's speech, but like most boys, they can't stay out of trouble. Richard, the more mischievous, comes home with a swollen lip and with his shirt sleeve ripped off. He barely survives the close scrutiny of Aunt Cook, who tells him "youse sinful" as he concocts a woeful tale about "de bresh whut try to hol' me we'n de ho'nets git at me" (p. 226) to conceal the fact that he had been fighting with his classmates. But the boys are most worried about what their father will say if he finds out about their behavior. In order to placate Uncle Dick, Mose and Richard contrive stories about their school work. Before church every Sunday, Uncle Dick asks his boys to recite what they have learned:

Richard opened his blue-black speller, wound one leg around the other and made out to spell "g-o go" and "h-o-g" allowing each letter plenty of territory. Mose, likewise, spelled "c-l-i-n-g."

"Boys, dat's sho good," said Uncle Dick greatly pleased. (p. 227)

At first impressed with his boys' learning, Uncle Dick soon realizes that they are playing tricks on him. On the third Sunday when he again asks Mose and Richard to recite to him their school learning, he knows that they have duped him. He asks Mose what he has learned. "'Doan know nut'n' replied Mose, 'cep dat word c-l-i'" (p. 228). When Uncle Dick finds out that instead of learning, his boys have been daydreaming and fighting with their classmates, he sends both to work in the cotton fields, and the story ends with his humorous but deadly harangue about their incompetency:

"Mose" interrupted Uncle Dick, "I has er notion to break yo head an' be done wid you . . . I talk to you an' talk to you . . . but hit ain't do no good . . . I wants yo to take dem books to de teachah . . . an' cling to er plow Monday mawnin' . . . er I'll cling to yo' back wid er stick!" (p. 228)

In this story, Richard, in what Uncle Dick refers to as "tricks and devilment," exhibits one-upmanship in his ability, like trickster, to deceive

Aunt Cook and Uncle Dick. But again like trickster, who spends his time duping others and being duped himself, Richard and Mose are also being "duped" by mainstream society; they are being tricked out of a formal education. Both boys, like their father, Uncle Dick, are the products of double colonization; they are downtrodden both by the "white man" and by "Mistah Injin." Perhaps even more revealing is the implication that Native people have political authority over blacks, since Uncle Dick refers to the Indian as "Mistah Injin" (Littlefield and Parins, p. 29). Uncle Dick tells his boys: "De fus t'ing you gwine grow up, an' if you caint hol' up yo' end wid de white man an' Mistah Injin, hit gwine be yo' own fault, kaze I sen' you to school an' gin you good advice" (p. 226). Posey thus reaffirms blacks' position within the racial hierarchy.

Posey's short story exposes the problem facing blacks as they vie for an equal position within the rapidly changing territory, but he also replicates some Native American readers' desires to keep blacks in their place. For Posey wrote at a time when interracial tension had greatly accelerated, ending in what the local newspapers called a "race war" (Grinde and Taylor, p. 220). In "Mose and Richard," Posey, whether inadvertently or intentionally, places blacks into what many Native people viewed as their rightful position, as slaves working the cotton fields. Furthermore, he depicts his black characters, Mose and Richard, as unworthy of a proper education. Richard, like trickster, is too preoccupied with getting into trouble, and Mose is "lazy" and "easy-going." Posey, behind his own trickster mask, reinforces many Native people's desires to separate themselves from African Americans.

In both stories, we see that blacks definitely hold a position lower than Native Americans and are perhaps even despised by Native people. In "Uncle Dick's Sow," through tricksterlike strategies, Posey shows Native Americans trying to take on the actions and the behaviors of Euroamericans as they attempt to create distance between themselves and blacks and freedmen. In "Mose and Richard," Posey further exposes his own aversion, whether conscious or not, to empowering African Americans through education, and suggests that if blacks are educated they may pose a threat to Native people. Here, Posey seems to say that blacks, like his fictitious characters Mose and Richard, are not worthy of elevation. In doing so, he expresses some negative and uncomplimentary beliefs about blacks.

Posey's short stories reveal that he has undertaken a very "tricky discourse," a strategy that attempts to make his people visible and distinct and, at the same time, confront and arrest the negative imagery of Native peoples at the expense of his black brethren. It is a discourse that, relying on trickster strategies, shows contradictions and vacillations in his own thinking. Posey, in these narratives, reproduces the turn-of-the-century reality of the Creek world—where black men and Creek pigs trick and warn and discard the conventions of society, with ambiguous results.

Notes

1. This excerpt is taken from a clipping from the Bacone newspaper, dated approximately between 1889 and 1895. This is part of the Alexander L. Posey Collection, no. 4126, Thomas Gilcrease Institute of American History and Art, Tulsa, Oklahoma.

2. For a thorough description of Alex Posey's life, see Daniel Littlefield's *Alex Posey: Creek Poet, Journalist, and Humorist* (1992).

3. Interestingly enough, William E. Connelley, who wrote the introduction of *The Poems of Alexander Lawrence Posey* (published by Crane and Topeka, 1910), stated that "Chinnubbie" originally was derived from Creek mythology, which Posey changed considerably. Connelley states that Chinnubbie had been a supernatural hero endowed with some human traits; Posey, according to Connelley, transformed Chinnubbie into the "evil genius of the Creeks." However, after investigating various ethnographic sources and other collections of Southeastern Native American folktales such as John R. Swanton's *Myths and Tales of the Southeastern Indians,* James Mooney's *The Myths of the Cherokee,* and Jack E. Kilpatrick and Anna Kilpatrick's *Friends of Thunder* (Dallas: Southern Methodist University Press, 1964), it is evident that Connelley is mistaken; Chinnubbie is not a traditional Creek trickster figure that Posey reshaped to fit his own literary taste, but is indeed Posey's own literary invention. According to Daniel Littlefield, it is likely that Posey probably heard trickster tales from his mother Nancy and reinvented Chinnubbie as his persona. It is possible, as Littlefield believes, that the name Chinnubbie also could have been one of his mother's story characters.

4. Rabbit as a trickster figure is very pervasive and is found throughout the Southeast. Similar stories about Rabbit's adventures can be found in Cherokee, Chickasaw, Choctaw, and Seminole tribal lore. See *Friends of Thunder* (eds. Jack F. Kilpatrick and Anna G. Kilpatrick) for examples of Cherokee rabbit tales and the ethnographic material already mentioned. Furthermore, it should be noted that Rabbit appears as Br'er Rabbit, a familiar figure of African American stories; there is much debate, dating back to the publication of Joel Chandler Harris's *Uncle Remus: His Songs and Sayings* (1880), as to whether African-American tales were of European, African, or Native American origin. For an overview concerning this debate see Florence Baer's introduction to *Sources and Analogues of the Uncle Remus Tales* (Helsinki: Sumalainen Tiedeakatemus, 1980). Also, *American Folklore Scholarship* (ed. Rosemary Levy Zumwalt, Bloomington and Indianapolis: Indiana University Press, 1988, pp. 130–135), provides a similar synopsis concerning the debate over the origins of the trickster Rabbit.

5. This particular newspaper clipping is from the Bacone newspaper dated approximately between 1889–1894. It is from the Alexander L. Posey Collection, no. 74, located in the Thomas Gilcrease Institute of American History and Art, Tulsa, Oklahoma.

6. Not only does Burns seem to have inspired Posey, but the Scottish poet's use of dialect appears also to have influenced him. Daniel Littlefield in *Alex Posey: Creek Poet, Journalist and Humorist* mentions that Posey, in order to persuade his friend George Riley Hall, who detested Burns's use of dialect, that Burns was a

great poet, recast "To A Mountain Daisy" in "good English." Posey later writes that "In doing so, I fear I have spoiled the poem; for it is in his dialect that Burns is sweetest" (Littlefield, *Alex Posey*, p. 87). Posey's use of black and Creek dialect, not only in his short stories but in his Fus Fixico letters, is indeed one of his greatest achievements.

Works Cited

Baer, Florence. *Sources and Analogues of the Uncle Remus Tales*. Helsinki: Sumalainen Tiedeakatemus, 1980.

Challacombe, Doris. "Alexander Lawrence Posey." *Chronicles of Oklahoma* 11 (1933): 1011–1018.

Dale, Edward Everett. "The Journal of Alexander Lawrence Posey." *Chronicles of Oklahoma* 45 (1967–68): 398–432

Grinde, Donald, and Quintard Taylor. "Red vs. Black: Conflict and Accommodation in the Post Civil War Indian Territory, 1867–1907." *American Indian Quarterly* 8 (1984): 211–229.

Kilpatrick, Jack E. and Anna. *Friends of Thunder*. Dallas: Southern Methodist University Press, 1964.

Littlefield, Daniel. *Alex Posey: Creek Poet, Journalist and Humorist*. Lincoln: University of Nebraska Press, 1992.

———. "Evolution of Alex Posey's Fux Fixico Persona." *Studies in American Indian Literature* 4 (1992): 136–144.

Littlefield, Daniel, and James Parins. "Short Fiction Writers of the Indian Territory." *American Studies* 21–23 (1980–1982): 23–37.

McGuirk, Carol. "Scottish Hero, Scottish Victim: Myths of Robert Burns." In *The History of Scottish Literature*, ed. Andrew Hook. Vol. 11. Aberdeen: Aberdeen University Press, 1987.

Mooney, James. *The Myths of the Cherokee*. Washington, D.C., 1900. Rpt. Asheville, N.C.: Historical Images, 1992.

Posey, Alexander. "Uncle Dick's Sow." *Twin Territories* (January 1900). Sam Publishing Co., Muskogee Creek Nation.

———. "Mose and Richard." *Twin Territories* (November 1900). Sam Publishing Co., Muskogee Creek Nation.

———. "Chinnubbie and the Owl." Ms. 4627.32, scrapbook. Alexander L. Posey Collection. Thomas Gilcrease Institute of American History and Art, Tulsa.

———. Clippings from Bacone newspaper. 4126.217 ts. Alexander L. Posey Collection. Thomas Gilcrease Institute of American History and Art, Tulsa.

———. *The Poems of Alexander Lawrence Posey*. Intro. William E. Connelley. Crane and Topeka, 1910.

Sampson, David. "Robert Burns's Use of Scots Verse-Epistle Form." *Modern Language Review* 80 (1985): 17–37.

Swanton, John R. "Myths and Tales of the Southeastern Indians." *Bureau of American Ethnology Bulletin* 88 (1929): 1–86.

Wiget, Andrew. "His Life in His Tail: The Native American Trickster and the Literature of Possibility." In *Redefining American History*, eds. A. LaVonne Brown Ruoff and Jerry W. Ward. New York: Modern Language Association Press, 1990.

Zumwalt, Rosemary Levy. *American Folklore Scholarship*. Bloomington and Indianapolis: Indiana University Press, 1988.

YUKO MATSUKAWA

Cross-Dressing and Cross-Naming: Decoding Onoto Watanna

Ever since their discovery as two of the first Asian American writers,[1] Edith and Winnifred Eaton (sisters of Anglo-Chinese descent) have intrigued scholars because of the pseudonyms they adopted: writing at the turn of the century, the elder, Edith (1865–1914), assumed the pen name Sui Sin Far, identified herself with her mother's Chinese ancestry, and wrote short stories about the Chinese American communities of the west coast; the younger, Winnifred (1875–1954), took the pseudonym Onoto Watanna and a Japanese identity to write a number of popular romances set in Japan with Japanese and American characters.

Given the current interest in women's studies and feminist theory, it comes as no surprise that Edith Eaton is the one who is of academic interest, because we can read her assumption of Chinese identity as her attempt at recovering her mother's heritage and her mother's tongue, as speaking out for a voiceless minority. It also helps that her short stories are of convenient length for teaching: she now is fast turning into *the* turn-of-the-century Asian American writer of choice in major literature anthologies.[2] Winnifred Eaton and her work, on the other hand, do not lend themselves to easy theoretical categorization. It is tempting to dismiss her for appropriating an identity that she had no "authentic" reason for taking, and for exploiting that identity to sell her books; in this light, Winnifred, the writer of fanciful formulaic romances (which are all out of print), becomes the foil to the serious and righteous Edith. That Winnifred's works are too long to anthologize—she did not seem to write anything under two hundred pages—may also be a reason for her relative unfamiliarity.

However, there is more to Winnifred Eaton than meets the cursory dismissive eye, prompting my invocation of the "cross-" in the title of this essay. In choosing to write as Onoto Watanna, Winnifred Eaton crosses cultural lines to challenge what we perceive as the conventional boundaries of ethnicity and authenticity. "Crossing" or "passing" are loaded terms in understanding Winnifred Eaton's writing persona, Onoto Watanna: it is through examining these activities that I will attempt to decode the culturally and literarily constructed facade of this orientalist popular romance novelist in order to reveal a writer far more subversive than she is usually credited to be. For the purposes of this essay I will concentrate on exploring a few important instances in Eaton's non-fiction and autobiographical writing where she is tricksterlike in her self-representation.

Amy Ling suggests that the peculiar pen name "Onoto Watanna" is only a Japanese *sounding* name, not an "authentic" Japanese name as it was long assumed to be, and that her autograph is an illegible scrawl.[3] Indeed, the symmetry of the repetition of letters and the phonetic quality of the name suggest that this may be a cipher-code, or may possibly be taken from one of the artificial languages that were so popular during the late nineteenth and early twentieth centuries. But no words remotely resembling this name appear in any of the Esperanto dictionaries or Volupuk lexicons, and if it is a code, I certainly have not been able to break it. The key to decoding the name, surprisingly enough, lies in that illegible scrawl, which, as it turns out, is at least half legible after all.

The facsimile of the author's autograph, found in the frontispiece of one of her earlier novels, *The Wooing of Wistaria* (1902), is written not only in Japanese but also in the order in which Japanese names are written: surname first and then the first name. Out of the five characters that comprise the signature, the first two represent the last name "Watanna" written in *kanji* or Chinese ideograms and the remaining three spell "Onoto" in *hiragana*, one of the Japanese phonetic alphabets, though this part of the signature is more illegible than the first. The legible half, the top two characters, represents the last name "Watanna," composed of the Chinese ideograms (Japanese pronunciation) for "to cross": *wata[ru]*, and "name": *na*. The first character not only means simply "to cross" but also "to cross a body of water and reach the other side," "to convey," "to pass," "to go abroad." "Watanna" is a contrived name in that the ideograms were probably chosen for their meaning and then someone determined how to pronounce them. In any event, the characters that represent her last name suggest that she is indeed deliberately crossing boundaries and that her name allows her to cross over or pass.

Cross-naming as a pun on her adopted last name foreshadows Winnifred Eaton's career as a tricksterlike figure who assumes multiple identities in order to straddle different spheres and disrupt the sense of reality and complacency of those worlds. There is always an element of deceit involved in how tricksters operate, for they are at once playful and duplicitous in raising havoc. Winnifred Eaton fits this description, since the factors that could possibly serve to define her—ancestry, name, profession, and places of residence—emphasize the adroitness with which she adapted to the constantly changing circumstances of her life. As Onoto Watanna, she

Onoto Watanna, frontispiece from *Me* (1915), including facsimile of author's autograph in Japanese. Reprinted from the original publication (New York: The Century Co., 1915).

claimed Japanese ancestry,[4] though she presents to her audience variations of this and of her actual heritage (her mother was Chinese, her father British) throughout her life. Her sundry names collectively comprise a book cataloguer's nightmare; not only did she have a cryptic pseudonym, she married twice, each time taking her husband's name. So though she was born Lillie Winnifred Eaton, she soon dropped the Lillie to become Winnifred Eaton, who in turn engendered Onoto Watanna. Then with her first marriage she became Winnifred Eaton Babcock, and after her second marriage, Winnifred Eaton Babcock Reeve. Moreover, her many careers mirror the difficulty in trying to pinpoint her name: She was a wife (of first an alcoholic reporter and later a Canadian cattle rancher) and mother of several children as well as an office worker, a newspaper reporter, a fiction writer, and finally a scenarist for Hollywood movie studios. Her nomadic life, which took her from Canada to the Caribbean to the Midwest to the East Coast and then Canada and the West Coast, also reflects the trickster trait of traversing many physical worlds and societies with dexterity.

The bottom half of the signature that purports to be that of Onoto Watanna is not as clearly legible as the first part; however, the name Onoto takes on great significance when one realizes that this was the name of a celebrated fountain pen manufactured by Britain's De La Rue company from about 1905 to the late 1950s. "Crossing" and "passing," strangely enough, also figure in the birth of the Onoto pen, since it was a transvestite roller-skating vaudevillian inventor named George Sweetser who sold his patent for a self-filling fountain pen piston to De La Rue. According to fountain pen collectors as well as books on the history of fountain pens,[5] the company chose the name Onoto because it would be pronounced the same in languages around the world and would easily be assimilated into those cultures. By the time the first Onoto pens were introduced in 1905,[6] Onoto Watanna was a best-selling writer of several romances, all published by major American and British publishing houses. Amy Ling, in a footnote to an essay published recently, informs us of the discoveries made by Yoshio Ando, a Japanese scholar, that the name "Onoto" is used in a story by Lafcadio Hearn and that "Winnifred Eaton was asked by the manufacturer of the [Onoto] pen, Thomas de la Rue Company, for permission to use her name; she gave them permission and disclaimed any credit or royalties" (Lim and Ling, p. 317). In any case, given Eaton's predilection for playfulness and crossing, it is curiously appropriate that Winnifred Eaton's *pen name* turned out to be, for most of her life, also *the name of a pen*.

Winnifred Eaton's efforts in her self-representation as a "Japanese" writer do not end with the Japanese-sounding pseudonym. There are other examples of Eaton authenticating this persona: One strategy was in her "cross-dressing" as a Japanese woman writer. The photograph that accompanies her autograph facsimile in the frontispiece of the novel *The Wooing of Wistaria* (New York: Harper & Brothers, 1902) shows her with her hair arranged in a turn-of-the-century Japanese style; she is "properly" and "authentically" dressed in a kimono and *hakama* (a Japanese split skirt sometimes worn over a kimono), an outfit associated with scholarly women of the time. She is facing sideways and is looking at a book that she holds in her hands. Although with more careful examination we realize that her facial features look more Caucasian than Asian, in this instance (with the assistance of the half-legible signature), Onoto Watanna at a casual glance passes effectively. In short, she cross-dresses for success. The orientalized bindings of the book, the illustrations, and of course the contents of the novel contribute to the overall packaging of Onoto Watanna as an "authentic Japanese" writer.

By looking closely at what constituted her "Japanese-ness," however, we see that deliberately or not, Eaton leaves traces of discrepancies that are begging to be read, and when read, provide the key to deconstructing her seemingly innocuous authorial persona as "Onoto Watanna." In another photograph[7] the remarkably Caucasian-looking "Onoto Watanna" wears her kimono "unauthentically": not only is it too loosely worn as if it were a dressing gown, but the front panels of the gown overlap right over left in the photo, instead of left over right. Furthermore, she seems to be sitting Japanese-style with her legs tucked under her, but she is directly on the grass, usually an unlikely place to sit if only because of the bothersome stains one acquires.

Other examples of Winnifred Eaton's perpetuating her "Japanese" identity while at the same time leaving clues for us to unravel her impersonation have to do with her writing. For instance, in the obituary she wrote for her sister, she sustains this "Japanese" identity by referring to their mother as a Japanese noblewoman from Nagasaki, though her sister adopted a Chinese pseudonym, Sui Sin Far, and their mother was actually Chinese.[8] And while her knowledge of Japanese seems extensive, her novels often belie the fact that she is relying on information garnered from other sources—travel books, friends' stories perhaps?—than from a native speaker's understanding of the language. And as Amy Ling has noted, her Japanese characters, when speaking English, speak a peculiar pidgin that sounds as if they have stuffy noses (Ling, p. 54).

But the discrepancies that I have described in Winnifred Eaton's construction of the "oriental(ist)" writer Onoto Watanna can not have been pure carelessness. As C. W. Spinks, Jr., in his study on semiosis and the trickster figure, notes, "Wherever the culture has drawn a line of demarcation, Trickster is there to probe the line and test the limits. . . . he reminds us that the cultural boundaries are arbitrary, and he releases the desire, at

Winnifred Eaton, circa 1914. From the collection of Paul Rooney and reprinted with his permission.

least vicariously, to challenge those boundaries. He both exercises and exorcises the negation of the Cultural Other" (Spinks, p. 178). Like the archetypal trickster, in exposing the slippage between what she is supposed to be (a Japanese woman writer) and what she appears to be (a biracial woman mimicking a Japanese woman writer), Winnifred Eaton playfully questions our assumptions of how we construct anyone's identity—especially that of an "Oriental" subject—and challenges us to acknowledge that she is critically aware that this is a role she is playing.

Very early on in her career, Winnifred Eaton tested her persona as Onoto Watanna in a small pamphlet of poetry published in 1898 called *Love Lyrics,* written by a Chicago journalist named Frank Putnam.[9] In her fictionalized autobiography, *Me, A Book of Remembrance,* Eaton catalogues the admirers of the protagonist, Nora Ascough, and mentions in passing that a poet had written verses to her that were published in the Chicago newspapers.[10] Frank Putnam may have been the poet to whom she referred or he may have been one of the men to whom Nora was engaged—one of them was, according to *Me,* a journalist who went to work in Cuba, a description which also fits Putnam; in any case, it is evident that Putnam and Eaton knew each other well because *Love Lyrics* is dedicated to Winnifred Eaton and has a laudatory introduction by Onoto Watanna.

What is intriguing about this arrangement—we must imagine their glee in indulging in such an inside joke—is that Winnifred Eaton/Onoto Watanna actively represents herself as one who is knowledgeable about Japan by intoning judgments such as, "Every poem is a song that lingers in the ear like Japanese music" (Putnam, p. 7). Therefore, because of this persona, she serves to authenticate Putnam's intentions and aspirations in poetry not because she is a famous author—her first book was published a year after Putnam's poems—but because she seemed authentically Japanese or exotic enough to pass for an "Other."

Hence, her introductory appreciation of Putnam's poems strikes us now as tongue in cheek. It opens with the detached assertion, "Only a lover could have written 'Love Lyrics,'" but it is a hilariously disingenuous sentence, since he was clearly an admirer of hers. The following comment about Putnam's poetry, "In these days of poseurs and affected poets it is refreshing to pick up a little volume that vibrates with its genuineness" (Putnam, p. 7), written in a tone of admiring sincerity, acquires a comical double edge because Eaton as Onoto Watanna could not help but be cognizant of herself as a poseur and Putnam as an affected poet. Putnam's poetry drips with maudlin affectations and schmaltzy sentimentality ("Love is the spirit's dream of beauty, / Love is the flower of dear desire; / Love's call is man's supremest duty, / Hope glows in Love's immortal fire" starts the poem entitled "Onoto-san"; Putnam, p. 27).

Onoto Watanna's favorable introduction assists in the packaging of Putnam's poems as expressive, sincere, refreshing, genuine, and melodious, "like Japanese music." Furthermore, it presents us with a titillating counternarrative of authorial complicity, and paves the way for her sustained writing career as Onoto Watanna, the romance novelist. Her involvement in *Love Lyrics* was also a preview of other things to come: Winnifred Eaton further explores the trickster potential of how her pseudonym simultaneously signifies and de-signifies, discloses and conceals, and how it connects with the problem of self-representation and authenticity in two texts: a cookbook she compiled with her sister Sara Bosse, and a memoir she published anonymously entitled *Me, A Book of Remembrance.*

Sixteen years after *Love Lyrics,* Winnifred Eaton and her sister Sara Bosse co-authored the *Chinese-Japanese Cook Book* (1914). The title of this cookbook is misleading to our late-twentieth-century eyes; the *Chinese-Japanese Cook Book* does not present a crossing of national cuisines that in turn produces a new category called "Chinese-Japanese cooking." Instead, the 120-page *Chinese-Japanese Cook Book* is a compilation of recipes that begins with a preface and then is divided into two parts: Chinese Recipes (with the following subheadings: Rules for Cooking, Soups, Gravy, Fish, Poultry and Game, Meats, Chop Sueys, Chow Mains [*sic*], Fried Rice, Omelettes, Vegetables, Cakes) and Japanese Recipes (Soups, Fish, Poultry and Game, Omelettes and Custards, Vegetables and Relishes). In the table of contents, the following seem to be under "Japanese Recipes"—Cakes, Candies, Sweetmeats; Bean Sprouts and Beverages; List of Chinese and Japanese Groceries; Index—but they actually include both Chinese and Japanese recipes and information.

Susan J. Leonardi, in her essay on the discourse of cookbooks, notes that "the root of *recipe*—the Latin *recipere*—implies an exchange, a giver and a receiver. Like a story, a recipe needs a recommendation, a context, a point, a reason to be" (Leonardi, p. 340). The *raison d'etre* for this cookbook is explained in the preface, which starts by noting the popularity of Chinese and Japanese restaurants and goes on to declare:

> There is no reason why these [Chinese and Japanese] dishes should not be cooked and served in any American home. When it is known how simple and clean are the ingredients used to make up these Oriental dishes, the Westerner will cease to feel that natural repugnance which assails one when about to taste a strange dish of a new and strange land. (*Cook Book,* p. 1)

The authors' goal is to make the exotic and unfamiliar familiar, so after a brief description of the food and eating habits of the Chinese and Japanese, they note that the "dishes have been selected as would appeal to the Western palate, and which can be prepared with the kitchen utensils of Western civilization" (*Cook Book,* p. 4). However, the *Chinese-Japanese Cook Book* is a peculiar and unsatisfying cookbook because of what it lacks: Though it systematically presents recipes under the subheadings in a cut-and-dried manner, it is devoid of both the imprint of an authorial voice—or in this case, an authorial sororial dialogue—and a narrative that engages the reader in a cultural and culinary exchange. What is missing, it seems, is a context that would make this text come to life.

The *Chinese-Japanese Cook Book* is a very early example of the publication of Asian cuisine recipes in the United States.[11] Unlike most of the subsequently published Chinese or Japanese cookbooks, which made it a point to self-orientalize through visual representations of the food, the author, and the names of the dishes in calligraphy, and which reinforced the self-representation of the author as an engaging culinary authority, the *Chinese-Japanese Cook Book* resists this kind of reading because it has none of the visual representations that mark ethnic cookbooks, and the short preface lacks the cookbook author's personality. In fact, Onoto Watanna's romance novels, with their fanciful calligraphy, beautiful layouts, and in the case of the novel *The Wooing of Wistaria* mentioned earlier, a frontispiece photograph of the author, are more cookbook-like than this cookbook she co-wrote. Published by Rand McNally, a publisher then engaged in the publishing of trade books but now specializing in maps and guidebooks, the *Chinese-Japanese Cook Book* is of a size (8.8 × 17 cm) and color (dark brown with gilt lettering: simply *Chinese-Japanese Cook Book* on the cover and the title plus "Bosse-Watanna" on the spine) that is reminiscent of utilitarian travel guides or glossaries of foreign words and phrases for travelers. Indeed, though we may view the *Chinese-Japanese Cook Book* as a guide through the unfamiliar terrain of cooking Chinese and Japanese food, as a handbook for a very specific kind of cultural reproduction, it leaves much to be desired because in its insistent reticence, it refuses to be the site for introducing and reproducing the cultures it claims to represent.

Cooking, as Anne Goldman suggests, is a metonym for culture (p. 169), but as with all metonyms it needs explication, a narrative to connect the part to the whole. It is this contextualizing narrative that is conspicuously absent in the *Chinese-Japanese Cook Book*. Except for the rare "delicious" appended to the end of a recipe or "a favorite of Japanese children" that opens a candy recipe, we do not hear the voice of the authors: There are no personal anecdotes; no annotations; no information as to when, where, and why a dish may be consumed; no "special helps" as Betty Crocker would call them, to aid the cook in the serving, the presentation, and the menu-making for a meal. That Onoto Watanna, who reveled in the art of storytelling, would refrain from constructing a narrative in this book is unnerving. The text, except for the matter-of-fact preface, is eerily impersonal and silent.

Perhaps the question to ask is: if cooking is a form of cultural reproduction, whose culture is being reproduced and by whom in the *Chinese-Japanese Cook Book*? The title combines the two "other" ethnicities that figured largely in Winnifred Eaton's life: Chinese, through a maternal genealogical biological connection, and Japanese, through her self-constructed writing persona. By 1914, when this cookbook was published, Onoto Watanna had produced the bulk of her popular fiction and was a best-selling writer who had perpetrated her pseudo-Japanese identity through her novels and an obituary she wrote for her sister, Sui Sin Far. Given her writing persona and fame, that Onoto Watanna's name would serve to authenticate the Japanese recipes was to be expected. However, the unevenness and carelessness of the compilation do not necessarily suggest that Onoto Watanna was invested in reproducing Japanese cuisine. In the text of the cookbook, there are 55 pages devoted to Chinese recipes and 33 pages to Japanese ones (excluding candy recipes), and though there are "Rules for Cooking" for Chinese recipes, there are none for the Japanese recipes. There are also strange translations for the Japanese recipes (under "Kinoko Tamago Yaki," which means Mushroom Omelette, it says "Shrimp Omelette," and there are other slightly corrupt names that are perhaps the product of typographical errors ("yohan" for "yokan" and "kanton" for "kanten").

Given the sisters' background, then, was it Chinese cuisine that was being reproduced here? Granted, there were more Chinese recipes than Japanese ones and more instructions to go with them. Unlike the Japanese recipes, for which we are given no source, the preface to the cookbook informs us whence the Chinese recipes came:

> No cookbooks, so far as the authors know, have ever been published in China. Recipes descend like heirlooms from one generation of cooks to another. The recipes included in this book (the Chinese ones, that is) have been handed down from Vo Ling, a worthy descendant of a long line of noted Chinese cooks, and himself head cook to Gow Gai, one time highest mandarin of Shanghai. They are all genuine, and were given as an especial expression of respect by a near relative of the famous family of Chinese cooks. (*Cook Book*, p. 5)

Anne Goldman, in her essay discussing the relationship between cooking, culture, and colonialism, states, "If it provides an apt metaphor for the reproduction of culture from generation to generation, the act of passing down recipes from mother to daughter works as well to figure a familial space within which self-articulation can begin to take place" (Goldman, p. 172). Goldman also stresses the importance of how the culinary metaphor recuperates "a female legacy [that] enables self-assertion at the same time it celebrates the lives of women family members as role models" (Goldman, p. 191). Clearly one of the silences, then, is related to the absence of Sara and Winnifred's own genealogy, their Chinese heritage, though much attention is paid by them to the Chinese recipes. Amy Ling writes that "Their mother . . . was Chinese, abducted from home at age three or four, presumably by circus performers, and later adopted by an English missionary couple who gave her an English education" (Ling, p. 26). Whether or not their mother cooked Chinese dishes for her many children when they were growing up is questionable, given her unorthodox upbringing and harried and impoverished life married to Edward Eaton, with whom she had sixteen children. Sara and Winnifred do not invoke their mother's culinary practices in order to authenticate their cookbook, and in failing to do so, they forfeit an occasion to celebrate this female legacy that enables self-assertion. Maybe there were no culinary secrets passed on from mother to daughters and maybe this is why the sisters are unable to contextualize the cookbook: They are not as familiar as they might have been with Chinese cuisine and culture.

Is the silence of the *Chinese-Japanese Cook Book* the silence of uneasiness then, of the difficulty of culinary representation and self-representation when one is unfamiliar with a specific food culture, or did the authors' reticence mask their unwillingness to appear to be culinary tour guides, or what Goldman would call cultural plunderers and colonizers (Goldman, p. 172)? This silence may also be related to the double bind in which Winnifred Eaton may have found herself: To explicate more about Japanese food might reveal that she was unversed in it; conversely, to write about Chinese food personally and familiarly would have destroyed the carefully constructed writing persona that she had cultivated for over a decade. What the sisters invoke is someone else's familial culinary tradition, which, though slightly exotic, is detached and alienating.

But is it another family's heritage, after all? The passage that attributes the Chinese recipes—"all genuine"—to Vo Ling, head cook to a Shanghai mandarin, is a quaint touch to authenticate them. However, most of the Chinese recipes are far from approximations of eclectic, sophisticated Shanghai cuisine; they are instead what we would now call genuine Chinese-American cooking, developed in the major metropolitan areas of the United States around the turn of the century. The "all genuine" American faux-Chinese chop sueys and chow meins, with their deep-fried noodles, celery, bean sprouts, and the ubiquitous gravy reminiscent of the brown sauce one encounters over roast turkey belie the assertion that these are recipes handed down generation to generation somewhere on the other side of the world. If the sisters' mother did not transmit Chinese food recipes to them, what they may have done to compile their cookbook is to collect recipes from Chinese and Japanese restaurants they frequented at the time. This is a strong possibility, given that Sara Bosse and Winnifred Eaton lived in Boston and Chicago for a while, and that both places have distinct styles of Americanized chow mein named after them.[12] Given this hypothesis, the practical advice they dispense in the preface takes on a decidedly comical tone:

> The authors advise any one who intends to cook "Chinese" to go to some Chinese restaurant and taste the various dishes he desires to cook. A good cook always should know what a dish tastes like before he tries to cook it. (*Cook Book,* p. 4)

If the recipes they introduce in their cookbook were indeed authentic Shanghai recipes, readers who followed the above advice would have been hard pressed to find restaurants that served those dishes, since most immigrants from China were from Canton and cooked the food of their region and culture. However, if, as I suspect, the recipes were culled from Chinese restaurants already catering to American tastes, readers would be pleased and satisfied by the correspondence between the recipes in the cookbook and what they were served at their local Chinese restaurant.

So the joke is on the reader: The *Chinese-Japanese Cook Book,* an ambitious but flawed endeavor, actually passes off Americanized Chinese food as authentic Shanghai cuisine and ends up crossing into new territory to give the unwitting reader a glimpse of food culture in turn-of-the-century Asian America. True to her pen name, Onoto Watanna playfully crosses and blurs the boundaries of food culture and ethnicity and in doing so complicates the issue of authenticating culinary authority. Hence, even though circumstances compelled her to be silent, Onoto Watanna takes the impossibility of creating a narrative to contextualize Chinese and Japanese food discourses and transforms it, through consuming identities and then producing her own, into an opportunity to covertly satisfy her passion for creating fictions.

If co-authoring this cookbook temporarily stunted the development of Winnifred Eaton's trickster narratives of self-representation, the writing of her fictionalized memoir the following year furnished her with the opportunity to return to them with a vengeance. *Me, A Book of Remembrance* is a fictionalized memoir published anonymously by Winnifred Eaton in *The Century* in five installments (April–August 1915) and later in the year published in book form by Century. It chronicles a year in the life of Nora Ascough, a seventeen-year-old Canadian girl who leaves home to seek her fortune as a journalist in Jamaica and then journeys to the United States to work briefly as a secretary in Richmond and then as a stenographer in Chicago. In this narrative, we follow her education in the ways of the world: She has many admirers and at one point manages to be engaged to three men at the same time while pining away for a wealthy man who is kind to her on the train to Richmond. By the end of the story, Nora learns that her beloved is a philanderer. Though disillusioned, she is determined to succeed as a writer. On the last page, we see her on the train to New York City to start her life anew.

The reviews for *Me* were mixed: The *Literary Digest* welcomed the book enthusiastically,[13] *The New York Times Review of Books* was lukewarm,[14] and the *Boston Transcript* panned it.[15] Though the reviewer for the *New York Times* guessed that Nora's mother was from Japan, only the reviewer for *The Dial* seemed to be aware that this was written by Winnifred Eaton: "Although published anonymously, the author of 'Me' is believed to be Onoto Watanna (Mrs. Winnifred Eaton Babcock)."[16] Both the reviewers for the *Times* and *The Nation* expressed misgivings about what the former called "that curious hybrid, the autobiographical or semi-autobiographical novel." The reviewer for *The Nation* declared,

> Personal narratives of this type are embarrassing to the reviewer. . . . Shall he accept them at their face value as bits of autobiography or construe them as pieces of realism in a familiar disguise? . . . We doubt if the novelist ever existed who could make a piece of pure reporting out of the events of his own life. However closely he may stick to his material, there will come moments when, willy-nilly, the figure of his former self becomes "our hero," an object of art.[17]

This discomfort about the duplicitous nature of the "semi-autobiographical novel" relates to how trickstering operates on two levels in *Me*: first in the way Winnifred Eaton's self-representation is further complicated by the production of the text, and second in the way the figure of Nora Ascough functions as trickster in the narrative.

Me, A Book of Remembrance, which is dedicated "To / 'LOLLY' my friend who was / and to JEAN my friend who is," opens with a short five paragraph preface by Jean Webster, the author of the popular children's book *Daddy Long Legs*. Webster begins by expressing amazement at the length of the story ("one hundred thousand words long") and the celerity with which it was written ("The actual writing occupied two weeks, the revision another two"), and she applauds the writer's stamina: "The writing of this book seems to me one of the most astounding literary feats I have ever known."[18] However, rather than considering it a piece of fiction, Webster calls it "pure reporting" (p. [i]) and regards the work as "not only . . . an intensely interesting human document, but as a suggestive sociological study," and she focuses on the veracity of the author's account of past events, saying "I have known the author for a number of years, and I know that the main outline of everything she says is true, though the names of people and places have necessarily been changed in order to hide their identity" (p. [ii]).

Webster and the preface she writes serve to substantiate and frame the text of *Me* much in the same way that Onoto Watanna's preface to Putnam's poems and her introduction to the cookbook do. Nevertheless, Webster authenticates and mystifies at the same time: Though she will quote the author verbatim, Webster does not tell us who the author is; likewise, all other clues—names of people and places—have been altered in order to confound us: Webster conspires to maintain the aura of mystery surrounding Onoto Watanna/Winnifred Eaton even as she purports to reveal more about her. As Amy Ling notes, "because Onoto Watanna's novels are well-known, Winnifred Eaton cannot tell the truth about herself" (Ling, p. 36) or, in this case, cannot have Webster tell it for her.

Webster relays to us the author's words, "As I lay on my back and looked at the ceiling, the events of my girlhood came before me, rushed back with such overwhelming vividness that I picked up a pencil and began to write" (p. [i]). By presenting us with the figure of the writer recuperating from an operation, scribbling furiously in her hospital bed, Webster inadvertently reminds us of the complicated relationship between turn-of-the-century women writers and illness, between writing and subjectivity, and between writing and oppression. This romanticized tableau leads us into an equally romanticized *bildungsroman* in which naive Nora Ascough gradually acquires the survival skills necessary for a young single woman to make career choices. Despite the romantic narrative of infatuation with the philandering Roger Hamilton and the descriptions of other men pursuing the protagonist, *Me* is a story of shifting identities and of writing and rewriting. It is this self-inscription and self-fashioning that inform the trickstering in *Me*.

Not surprisingly, Nora Ascough's genealogy is a site of romanticization and concealment. Though we do not learn Nora's full name until she arrives in Jamaica, we are told about her genealogy in the second paragraph of the text:

> My father was an artist, and we were very poor. My mother had been a tight-rope dancer in her early youth. She was an excitable, temperamental creature from whose life all romance had been squeezed by the torturing experience of bearing sixteen children. Moreover, she was a native of a far-distant land, and I do not think she ever got over the feeling of being a stranger in Canada. (p. 3)

Though the sentences seem to be descriptive, much information is concealed from us: What kind of artist was the father and where exactly did the mother hail from? In the next paragraph, the author mentions that her father was "an English-Irishman" who had "sojourned in China and Japan and India in the days when few white men ventured into the Orient" (p. 30). Later she exclaims:

> Was I not the daughter of a man who had been back and forth to China no fewer than eighteen times, and that during the perilous period of the Tai-ping Rebellion? Had not my father made his journeys from the Orient in the old-fashioned sailing-vessels, being at sea a hundred-odd days at a time? What could not his daughter do? (p. 5)

The protagonist identifies with her father and a picaresque tradition, but the mother is again vaguely dismissed and suppressed. She is simply a "creature" from a "far-distant land" and in the description here as with the cookbook, the mother is rendered invisible and does not seem to be helpful in constructing the protagonist's identity.

By not identifying her mother as Chinese (or as in her sister's obituary, Japanese), Winnifred Eaton avoids the complications of writing about race and ethnicity; rather, she simply alludes to her personal appearance by describing herself as "a little thing, and, like my mother, foreign-looking" with black hair and black eyes (p. 6). This visual difference made all the difference in the world to Nora, who "[i]n all [her] most fanciful imaginings and dreams . . . had always been golden-haired and blue-eyed" (p. 41). She later compares herself to her blue-eyed blond friend Lolly, and exclaims, "I would have given anything to look less foreign. My darkness marked and crushed me, I who loved blondness like the sun" (p. 166). This insistent self-othering as "dark foreigner" provides Nora with the space to define herself through the different professions she pursues and not solely by visual difference.

Interestingly, Nora shifts shape as a trickster by the clothes that she wears: Visually, it is these sartorial changes that indicate the different roles that she assumes in the narrative. We first see her as a naïf in heavy woolen Canadian clothes unsuitable for the tropics (p. 15) who, upon arrival, exchanges clothes with the girl whose place she is to take at the Jamaican newspaper (p. 30). This change marks the professional journalistic debut of Nora, who then proceeds to put her hair up to play the part of the young, earnest reporter. When she starts secretarial work in Chicago, she receives compliments on her looks, which she self-deprecatingly attributes to her simple sailor-suit clothes (p. 184). Her foray into finery is contrived by her admirer Roger Hamilton, who takes her to a shop where they charge her ridiculously low sums for clothing because he makes up the difference behind her back. Hence, he has the satisfaction of convincing himself that he is keeping her while maintaining for her the illusion that she is an independent woman. However, being kept does not sit well with Nora, and when she discovers that her beloved Roger is front-page news as an adulterer in Virginia, she packs not "those clothes he had paid for, but [her] manuscripts" (p. 350) and, with the encouragement of her friend Lolly, goes off to New York City to pursue a writing career.

From the very first pages Nora speaks of the importance of writing in her life. It was because one of her stories was published in a Quebec newspaper when she was sixteen that she was recommended for the job of a journalist for a Jamaican newspaper called "The Lantern" where she writes and edits articles on all aspects of political and social life. After settling in Chicago as a stenographer and typist, Nora continues writing in her spare time and tells Roger Hamilton of the stories she was writing about her mother's land: "I feel as if I knew everything about that land, and when I sit down to write—why, things just come pouring to me, and I can write *anything* then" (p. 176). Following a period of continuous rejection, gradually Nora's stories are accepted at magazines around the country and she is inspired to write her first novel: "I lived now with only one avid thought in my mind—the story I was writing. It infatuated me as nothing I had ever done before had infatuated me" (p. 321).

Roger lets slip his feelings for Nora when he pretends to toss the manuscript into the fireplace. Though Nora screams "like an outraged mother" (p. 335), she tells him, "Burn it if you wish to, then. It represents only the product of my fancy; but *you* are my life" (p. 335). Earlier in the narrative, Nora decides that it is up to her and her talent in writing to make up the class difference between Roger, the successful businessman, and herself:

> I realized that he belonged to a different social sphere. He was a rich, powerful man, of one of the greatest families in America, and I—I was a working-girl, a stenographer of the stock-yards. . . .
>
> My only hope lay in pulling myself up by my talent. If I achieved fame, that perhaps, I felt, would put me on a level with this man. (pp. 183–184)

However, at the end of the story, Nora is disillusioned by Roger's sordid private life. Her position is radically transformed in that writing for her is no longer a means to an end—that is, marrying Roger—but an activity from which she derives pleasure. There is a shift in signification: Whereas prior to Roger's scandal her manuscript was a product of her fancy and Roger, she declares, was her life, at the end of the story, disappointed though she is, it is clear that she has been deluding herself about her beau, and that her manuscripts and writing are indeed her life.

The moment of catharsis occurs when Nora, with her bag of manuscripts, trudges through the snow to the lake shore where a policeman thinks she is about to commit suicide. Nora contemplates her fate:

He had destroyed something precious and fine; he had crushed my beautiful faith, my ideals, my dreams, my spirit, the charming visions that had danced like fairies in my brain. Worse, he had ruthlessly destroyed Me! I was dead. This was another person who stood there in the snow staring at the waters of Lake Michigan. (p. 351)

The policeman urges her to go home, but she replies "I have no home" (p. 352). In this homeless state, she visits her friend Lolly, who tells her, "*You* have something to *live* for. . . . You can *write*. . . . You have a letter in your pocket addressed to posterity. Deliver it Nora! Deliver it!" (p. 355).

Shari Benstock describes how women writers are always already expatriated or marginalized in a male-dominated world because "for women, the definition of patriarchy already assumes the reality of expatriate *in patria*; for women, this expatriation is internalized, experienced as an exclusion imposed from the outside and lived from the inside in such a way that the separation of outside from inside, patriarchal dicta from female decorum, cannot be easily distinguished" (Benstock, p. 20). Both Winnifred Eaton and Nora Ascough combat "the reality of expatriate *in patria*" through their writing. Nora's predicament renders her homeless both in a material and a psychological sense, but the act of carrying off a bag of her manuscripts suggests that for Nora, the act of writing will not only make her feel at home but will become home as well. As for Winnifred Eaton, inventing and rewriting her past and herself open up textual territory—an imaginary homeland, as it were—that facilitates her circumvention of the marginalization inherent in being a woman writer. The figure of Nora with her manuscripts in the snow at the end of the memoir overlaps with that of the trickster author writing with great speed amidst the white sheets of the hospital bed in Webster's introduction; it is this palimpsest effect that transforms that invalided sight into an empowered one.

It may be that it is 1990s hindsight that enables us to read Onoto Watanna's crossings, since her trickstering apparently was not as obvious to her reading public: The persona of Onoto Watanna seemed to have been accepted uncritically in their minds, and her readership over the course of several decades consumed her novels with great relish. Readers did not seem to have called her bluff: She gave them what they wanted to see, playing on the Occidental fascination for things Oriental. However, it is clear that mimicking the Other—being playful and maintaining a critical distance from what she meant to imitate—gave her the space to present overtly what the popular imagination wanted at the turn of the century.

Though she may not have been a trickster figure for her audience, she is to us now; Winnifred Eaton's "crossing" activities are what make her as a writer so compelling and intriguing to current scholars. Edith Eaton was also involved in "passing," but since her Chinese persona was "genealogically" correct, her "authenticity" somehow remains intact because hers appears to be a more straightforwardly constructed persona compared to that of her sister. Winnifred Eaton demonstrates to us a more radical version of the poetics of passing: When we view her self-construction not simply as an example of the inauthentic, we find that her tricksterlike self-fashioning is inextricably linked to her experiments in redefining conventional frontiers of ethnicity and authenticity through the contingencies of her life. In dismissing her, we choose not to interrogate the essentialism that labels her "inconsequential" and miss the revelry that she brings to "crossing." In rediscovering her, we are at least given an opportunity to explore and extend her aesthetics of "crossing" to encompass not only her persona as a writer but also her various strategies of self-representation.

Notes

1. For instance, see Amy Ling, *Between Worlds: Women Writers of Chinese Ancestry* (1990), a text I refer to repeatedly in this essay because of Ling's extensive research in the lives and writings of the Eaton sisters. See also S. E. Solberg, "Sui Sin Far/Edith Eaton: First Chinese American Fictionist," *MELUS* 8 (1981); 27–39, and Annette White-Parks' introduction to "The Wisdom of the New," *Legacy: A Journal of 19th Century American Women Writers* 6 (1989): 34–49.

2. She is featured in *The Heath Anthology of American Literature* as well as in collections of short stories such as *Imagining America: Stories from the Promised Land,* edited by Wesley Brown and Amy Ling (New York: Persea Books, 1991), and *Women's Friendships: A Collection of Short Stories,* edited with an introduction and afterword by Susan Koppelman (Norman: University of Oklahoma Press, 1991).

3. Amy Ling, in *Between Worlds: Women Writers of Chinese Ancestry,* describes the autograph in the frontispiece of Watanna's *The Wooing of Wistaria* (New York and London: Harper & Brothers, 1902) as "a reasonable imitation of cursive Japanese writing" (Ling, p. 25) but does not seem to find the imitation actually legible.

4. Even scholars such as S. E. Solberg believed part of the "Japanese" heritage of Winnifred Eaton. Solberg, in a footnote to his article "Sui Sin Far/Edith Eaton: First Chinese-American Fictionist," *MELUS* 8 (1981): 27–39, assumes Winnifred had been born in Japan "and had lived there for many years; this was her rationale for adopting the *nom de plume* of Onoto Watanna" (p. 36).

5. I wish to thank Jonathan Steinberg and Masa Sunami, two very knowledgeable and wonderful fountain pen collectors, who generously shared much information about Onoto pens with me. Neither Lorna Houseman's *The House That Thomas Built: The Story of De La Rue* (London: Chatto & Windus, 1968) nor Andreas Lambrou's *Fountain Pens: Vintage and Modern* (London: Sotheby, 1989) nor Dietmar Geyer's *Collecting Writing Implements: From the Flint Tool to the Stylus, From the Quill Pen to the Fountain Pen and Felt Tip Marker* (West Chester, Pa.: Schiffer Publishing, 1990) specifically explain why the pen acquired the name "Onoto" (as opposed to some other artificial word, for instance) other than to say that it was a word pronounced the same way around the world.

6. According to Masa Sunami's research in fountain pen histories, patents for the pen nibs that were to eventually become the Onoto pen were filed as early as 1903.

7. The photograph is found in Amy Ling, *Between Worlds: Women Writers of Chinese Ancestry* (New York: Pergamon Press, 1990), p. 50.

8. The obituary "Edith Eaton Dead: Author of Chinese Stories Under Name of Sui Sin Far" ran in the *New York Times,* April 9, 1914, p. 11, col. 4.

9. Frank Arthur Putnam, *Frank Putnam's Love Lyrics* (Chicago: The Blakely Press, 1898). This slim volume is 41 pages long and is bound in a reddish brown rough-textured handmade paper in a fashion that suggests Japanese influences in its binding.

10. She writes, "A poet wrote lovely verse to me, and the Chicago papers actually published it" (*Me, A Book of Remembrance,* p. 300). *Me* was also serialized anonymously in *The Century* (April–August 1915).

11. The cookbook collection at Radcliffe College's Schlesinger Library lists this as the earliest publication of Chinese and/or Japanese recipes published in the United States. The Culinary Institute of America's holdings include an earlier publication: Ardashes H. Keoleian's *The Oriental Cookbook: Wholesome, Dainty and Economical Dishes of the Orient, especially adapted to American Tastes and Methods of Preparation* (New York: Sully & Kleinteich, 1913). According to Professor Jacqueline M. Newman of Queens College, CUNY, there are three Chinese cookbooks in her private collection that are contemporaneous with the Bosse/Watanna cookbook: Jessie Louise Nolton's *Chinese Cookery in the Home Kitchen: Being Recipes for the Preparation of the Most Popular Chinese Dishes at Home* (Detroit: Chino-American Publishing Company, 1911), W. E. Garner's *Reliable Recipes for Making Chinese Dishes* (Long Beach, N.J.: F. M. Taylor Publishing Co., 1914), and Vernon Galster's *Chinese Cook Book in Plain English* (Morris, Ill.: Vernon Galster, Publisher, 1917). As with the Bosse/Watanna cookbook, all of these are clearly Americanized cookbooks or pamphlets with similar recipes for chop suey, chow mein, and egg foo young. I wish to thank Professor Newman for generously sharing her information with me.

12. I thank Imogene Lim for sharing her research on the evolution of Chinese American cookery through her conference papers: Imogene L. Lim and John Eng-Wong, "Chow Mein Sandwiches: Chinese-American Entrepreneurship in Rhode Island," presented at the Conference on Chinese Americans: Origins and Destinations, California State University, Los Angeles, August 1992; and Imogene L. Lim, "Fall River-Style Chow Mein: Authentic/Inventive, Chinese/American Food," presented at the Tenth Annual Meeting of the Association for Asian American Studies, Cornell University, Ithaca, N.Y., June 1993.

13. "The experiences of that year are dramatic, introspectively and retrospectively, revealing and perhaps typical of what might happen to any young girl in her position. The naïveté of her actions, the unconventional way she went to meet these thrilling experiences, could be true only of a girl with such a heritage. There is a compelling charm about the personality of the narrator." *Literary Digest* 51 (October 16, 1915): 852.

14. "While there is nothing particularly new in the book, it contains material out of which an interesting volume might be made. . . . It is a distinctly ungracious task to criticise the personality of a heroine who is asserted to be real, and in regard to Nora, no doubt opinions will differ; she certainly appears to have been a hard worker." *The New York Times Review of Books* (August 22, 1915): 302.

15. "'*Me*' is a crudely written narrative of youthful ambition and endeavor and it is filled with adventures that while possible in themselves are made preposterous by the manner of their telling." *Boston Transcript* (September 11, 1915): 8.

16. *The Dial* 59 (September 2, 1915): 157.

17. *The Nation* 101 (September 16, 1915): 359.

18. *Me, A Book of Remembrance* (New York: The Century Co., 1915), p. [i]. "Me, A Book of Remembrance" was serialized in *The Century* from April through August 1915. The April 1915 issue (pp. 803–828) is part of volume 89; the rest of the installments, May (pp. 24–47), June (pp. 275–297), July (pp. 408–432), and August (pp. 557–578), are in volume 90.

Works Cited

Benstock, Shari. "Expatriate Modernism: Writing on the Cultural Rim." In *Women's Writing in Exile,* ed. Mary Lynn Broe and Angela Ingram. Chapel Hill: University of North Carolina Press, 1989, pp. 19–40.

Bosse, Sara, and Onoto Watanna. *Chinese-Japanese Cook Book*. Chicago: Rand McNally & Company, 1914.

Brown, Wesley, and Amy Ling, eds. *Imagining America: Stories from the Promised Land*. New York: Persea Books, 1991.

[Eaton, Winnifred]. *Me, A Book of Remembrance*. New York: The Century Co., 1915.

———. "Edith Eaton Dead: Author of Chinese Stories Under Name of Sui Sin Far." *New York Times* (April 9, 1914): 11.

Goldman, Anne. "'I Yam What I Yam': Cooking, Culture, and Colonialism." In *De/Colonizing the Subject: The Politics of Gender in Women's Autobiography*, eds. Sidonie Smith and Julia Watson. Minneapolis: University of Minnesota Press, 1992, pp. 169–195.

Koppelman, Susan, ed. *Women's Friendships: A Collection of Short Stories*. Norman: University of Oklahoma Press, 1991.

Leonardi, Susan J. "Recipes for Reading: Summer Pasta, Lobster à la Riseholme, and Key Lime Pie." *PMLA* 104 (1989): 340–347.

Lim, Shirley Geok-Lin, and Amy Ling, eds. *Reading the Literatures of Asian America*. Philadelphia: Temple University Press, 1992.

Ling, Amy. *Between Worlds: Women Writers of Chinese Ancestry*. New York: Pergamon Press, 1990.

Putnam, Frank Arthur. *Frank Putnam's Love Lyrics*. Chicago: The Blakely Press, 1898.

Solberg, S. E. "Sui Sin Far/Edith Eaton: First Chinese American Fictionist." *MELUS* 8 (1981): 27–39.

Spinks, Jr., C. W. *Semiosis, Marginal Signs and Trickster: A Dagger of the Mind*. London: Macmillan, 1991.

Watanna, Onoto. *The Wooing of Wistaria*. New York and London: Harper & Brothers, 1902.

White-Parks, Annette. Introduction to "The Wisdom of the New." *Legacy* 6 (1989): 34–49. Norman: University of Oklahoma Press, 1991.

ALANNA KATHLEEN BROWN

Mourning Dove, Trickster Energy, and Assimilation-Period Native Texts

The importance of the trickster in Native American oral traditions takes a fresh turn in the assimilation period (1880s–1934), for that was when federal policies were being imposed on Native peoples to force them into Euroamerican molds. The trickster, whether Coyote, Raven, or Rabbit, has always had the power through cunning and observation to destroy, to create, and to survive. What Native peoples faced at the turn of the last century was physical and cultural genocide. If they were not to become totally absorbed into the dominant colonizing culture, they had to draw on the resources of their own traditions to turn assimilation into a survival strategy. Caught between being educated to be white and choosing to maintain an indigenous identity, some Indians intuitively incorporated their contemporary experiences into the larger frame of an ongoing Native American oral tradition. While they appeared to be assimilating, they used trickster energy to create pathways to survival.

To comprehend the need for such a strategy, it is important to have a shared understanding of some of the key historical events and federal policies that shaped the assimilation period for Native peoples. Events of critical importance include Custer's defeat by the Sioux and Cheyenne at the Battle of the Little Big Horn on June 25, 1876, an event that stunned a nation celebrating its centennial. This defeat also triggered a severe military response. Yet qualifying that movement was Chief Joseph's thwarted flight to Canada with his Nez Perce band in 1877, which stimulated some public sympathy for the American Indian's situation. The 1880s were marked by the Sioux's valiant defense of their homeland, while the Ghost Dance emerged as a powerful religious unifying force among Indian tribes. A fearful military crushed both the Sioux and the spiritual revival with the December 29, 1890, massacre at Wounded Knee, South Dakota. This terrible event ended the open hostilities between the U.S. government and indigenous peoples. But the psychosocial war had only just begun.

Even before the Wounded Knee massacre, the federal government had established a Court of Indian Offenses in 1883 that made it a crime for

Native Americans to speak their own languages, to practice traditional religious rituals, or to wear traditional dress or their hair at a male warrior length. By 1887, the General Allotment Act, or Dawes Act, had already begun to force Indians into a cash nexus while systematically opening up reservation lands for white settlement. Indian tribes lost two-thirds of their original treaty lands between 1887 and 1934. During what is now called the assimilation period, Bureau of Indian Affairs (BIA) schools and mission schools were also intensively used to eradicate Native tribal identities. Children were removed from their homes, punished for speaking indigenous languages, and drilled in English, white behavioral norms, and Christianity. Indian customs and religious beliefs were continuously ridiculed.

Because Mourning Dove's story so clearly illustrates the pressures on Native peoples at the turn of the last century, and because her choice to write was the choice to survive with an Indian identity intact, I will draw on her life and work to explore trickster energy. It is important to recognize that Mourning Dove was of the first generation of inland Salish-speaking peoples to grow up on a reservation. Born between 1882 and 1888,[1] she was sent to the Goodwin Mission School near Kettle Falls, Washington, from 1895 to 1899, at the urging of Catholic priests. When the government balked at funding Catholic education for Indians and established government schools, Mourning Dove was transferred to the newly created Fort Spokane School for Indians, which she attended from 1899 to 1900. Of her own volition, she continued a white education when she chose to become matron of the Fort Shaw Indian School in Montana in exchange for classes (1904–1907). Moreover, to pursue a writing career, she attended a secretarial school in Calgary, Alberta, from 1912 to 1914. Yet Mourning Dove ultimately rejected absorption into the dominant culture, and chose to use her education to preserve the oral traditions of her people and to record the events of her time.

Mourning Dove's final manuscripts, now published as *Mourning Dove, A Salishan Autobiography* (1990),[2] include recollections of her early childhood when the family followed traditional migration routes, her experiences of being sent off to mission and then Bureau of Indian Affairs schools, the settlement of Indians onto farm plots, and a mineral rights and then a homesteaders' run on the Colville Reservation. Her novel, *Cogewea, the Half-Blood* (1927),[3] explores the difficult situation of a young mixed-blood woman on the Montana frontier at the turn of the last century, and her collection of tribal legends, *Coyote Stories* (1933),[4] is an important act by a Native American storyteller to preserve some of her cultural heritage in the face of what then appeared to be inevitable cultural genocide.

As with many non-white women writers of the nineteenth and early twentieth centuries, Mourning Dove initially came into print through the aid of white male collaborators. Their assumptions about race relations as well as their editorial work altered the tone and substance of Mourning Dove's original manuscripts. But so did her education in mission, and then BIA, schools. That is, for Native peoples, collaboration had an internal as well as an external dynamic. The early Indian writers already incorporated to varying degrees the assumptions of the dominant culture that shaped the choice and presentation of their subject matter. How, then, did they work through such constraints to comment on their own immediate crisis?

The answer lies in their rich ongoing Native American oral tradition. In such a tradition, new stories continually come into being and old stories are altered to incorporate new circumstances. It is the contemporaneity of Mourning Dove's writing that is of particular interest in this regard, for it reveals the dynamics not only of lives in flux, but of an oral tradition in the midst of change. The most obvious complexity was that Native peoples were being coerced into speaking English. Native languages were dying out and with them entire world views. Mourning Dove believed that she had to transcribe Salish tales into English to preserve at least some of the richness and perspective of her own culture. She also chose to incorporate the stories of her people through personal recollection and by transcribing the tales others told her, which included commentary on the extraordinary period of transition. It was through that storytelling tradition that Indians found the model to recount what had been lost, what remained, and how to survive. Such stories teach one how to transcend chaos, whether they are in the Native tongue or in the language of the conquerors. It is here that trickster energy unfolds itself, for it is the role of Coyote, however bumblingly, to create a new order out of chaos, by testing the possible and learning his limits. An examination of Mourning Dove's stories reveals how the oral tradition sustained people and enabled them to outlast the assimilation pressures meant to totally subdue and eradicate them as distinct cultures.

An example of this process can be drawn from Chapter XIV of *Cogewea, the Half-Blood,* "The Dead Man's Vision," which illustrates an awkward juxtaposition of a forewarning narrative with instructions to honor Catholic priests. The speaker is oblivious to the contradictory nature of the message. He begins with a fearful picture of the encroaching Europeans:

> Then taking my hand, my guide pointed to the future—what is in store for you, my people—what the future holds for you. Listen!
>
> I saw a pale-faced nation moving from the sunrise; as many as the trees of the forest. My guide said to me: "They are coming to take your hunting grounds from you." Then knowing my thoughts, he exclaimed in pity:
>
> "No! You cannot fight them as you do the common enemies of your tribe. They

are many! Many more than your own race; many as the stars you see. When you kill the front of them, others come from the back of them; many more, double the number. This is to be! Do not attempt war with them. You would be crushed like the pine-cone by the mountain avalanche." (pp. 125–126)

Yet in the midst of this overwhelmingly negative image, an insertion appears that praises the black robes and tells the Indians to listen to their religious message:

"The first of the strangers will come to work for your good," said my guide. "Only a few of them will strive to help the tribes; not for this life's benefit, but for the Hereafter; where the warriors gather when they leave this earth. You will know them; with their white skins and hair on their faces. They will show you a new trail to the Great Spirit. You must believe them! for they, too, point to the hunting grounds of the future life which cannot be taken from you. These good men will help you from becoming lost on the night trail." (p. 126)

The narrative then returns to the holocaust of the previous paragraph, and then again to the goodness of the priests as a final instruction:

Again my guide pointed and I saw the pale faces fighting among themselves for the possession of our lands. Their feet were drowned in human blood of war which thundered everywhere.

"See!" said my guide. "When this takes place, your people will long be gone. The land will be no more as it was. Go! now, man! go back to your people with the message given you. Tell them what you have seen, and to listen to the first pale face who comes to them. He will not deceive them, but will show them a better trail to the Spirit Land." (p. 126)

Clearly the telling of this tale indicates a rupture between a cataclysmic forewarning and the need to placate or praise the Catholic fathers who first came to the tribes in the Northwest. The schism reflects the state of mind of converted Indians who must somehow make sense of disparate realities.

On the other hand, "The Story of Green-Blanket Feet," Chapter XIX of *Cogewea,* incorporates new plot elements by focusing on a mixed marriage and half-breed children, while otherwise following an older plot about surviving capture and returning to one's own people. It is not ambiguous in its message. It is a warning tale to Indian women not to trust white male wooërs. The story movingly tells of a mother who is forced to leave her own people in order to stay with her children. The white husband becomes more brutal as they travel East, and finally the mother realizes that it is better to flee with a baby and live than to remain with both children and be killed by the father near the journey's end. Her travels back to her people are filled with adventures and hardships. Her baby boy dies in a fire accident while she is a slave of the Blackfeet, and that event devastates her. But she regains heart and does eventually return to her people with her feet wrapped in the green Hudson Bay blanket her false husband gave her when she first came to him.

Obviously such a story has cultural ramifications, for Native people have been betrayed in their generosity and through their trust. Ultimately their children have been taken from them to mission and BIA schools, and Indians have faced extinction or colonization. White greed, duplicity, and violence are commonplace in their experience.

But there is another side to these evolving stories. They often grow out of individual experience. On April 28, 1916, Mourning Dove writes to her mentor and friend, L. V. McWhorter:[5]

> Green-Blanket Feet's granddaughter Susie Winegard is at the present living in Spokane. She saw my picture in the paper and hunted me up. I was sorry that I had no time to visit her, because I was just ready to leave at the time. [24–26; 366][6]

An April 30, 1916, letter refers to the granddaughter, Mrs. Winegard, once again:

> By the way. You spoke of writing to Mrs. Winegard to Republic B.C., which is a mistake in the address. It is situated in the state of Washington. And also I think I stated to you before in the last letter written that she found me the same time as I was leaving Spokane, where she now lives. On account of her husband been hurt by the railroad company of the G.N. and they are sueing for 20,000. I am sorry that I fail to know her street address. but general delivery would no doubt reach her. I intended writing her but have had no time. Your letters are the only ones that I answer promptly. I know I have to take time and write you for the sake of our little squaw "Cogeawea." [22–23; 366]

As correspondence develops among Mrs. Winegard, Mourning Dove, and McWhorter, Mourning Dove suggests changing the story in consideration of Green-Blanket Feet's descendants, for the identity of the Colville woman is too recognizable (May 3, 1916 [20–21; 366]). A story should not bring embarrassment to an individual, but rather should speak to larger issues, and Mourning Dove suggests using creative license to alter what might be problematic. However, she leaves the story as it is on the recommendation of McWhorter and his brother, with the understanding that McWhorter will not make any reference to the person who has inspired the tale:

> I am glad that your brother liked "her", and furthermore, without my personal acquaintance to him, I have a high opinion of him, because he must be a "straight tongued man" if he is your brother Big Foot. Is why I think we will leave it to his good judgment, and leave "Green Blanket-Feet" story as it is. The note is fine, with only one fault which I rather would not say to any one but you, because I am quite sure you will not say any thing in regards to it. You will understand what I mean. You understand this Injuns feelings. It is not necessary for us to expose Green-B-Feet history, if you will note. Mrs. Winegard mentioned of her several marriages,

which is hardly true and also take note of all her latter children having different names, which brings out the unfortunated Indian women of my race. It is my one objection. And I will suggest that you not mention her several marriages, because Indians that knows her true story will comment, for she was a noted character, among the Colvilles. and furthermore Big Foot do not take trouble to mention all her separate children's names unless you think best. I will leave this to your good judgment. (May 14, 1916 [27–29; 366])

Mourning Dove understands the etiquette involved in Indian storytelling, which a white editor/reader can affront by insisting on veracity and proof. What matters about Green-Blanket Feet's story is not who she is, but how the tale can be incorporated into an ongoing oral tradition that interprets the human experience for its listeners. That current experience is one of intensive exploitation and the violation of fundamental human relationships.

Legends also see change. In a letter dated February 26, 1930 [53; 269], Mourning Dove mentions: "Tomorrow—providing I have no company I shall write you a lengend [*sic*] of 'House of little Men.'"[7] What McWhorter receives is a fifteen-page story about Left Hand, an important Salish legendary warrior. It can be summarized as follows: Left Hand, the hero, was a lazy child who so shamed his father that the man dropped his son down in the deep unknown fathoms of the cotszee (caverns) where the fearless little people dwell. Those people adopted Left Hand. He learned their ways and was taught the shoomesh powers of the underground animals and given the spirit power of the frog. When Left Hand grew too big to live among the caverns of the little people, he was returned to his tribe where he quickly became recognized as an exceptional hunter who had the power to turn himself into an animal or a plant when needed. One day, enemy Shu-swaps came into his tribe's encampment while Left Hand was out hunting with his brother, and these Shu-swaps slew everyone except Left Hand's beautiful sister, whom they took with them. Left Hand intuited the slaughter, returned to find his vision had been correct, and the brothers went in pursuit of the enemy to seek their revenge and free their sister. The Shu-swaps were many, but Left Hand found them and stayed close through his ability to change shapes. Eventually the brothers attacked, freed their sister, and killed many of their enemies before fleeing themselves. In fact, the frog shoomesh song was all that saved Left Hand from his pursuers as he fled. Since the rest of his band was dead, he relocated himself and his brother and sister close to the house of the little men.

We pick up the ending now exactly as Mourning Dove transcribes it:

Many snows had past and Left Hand was the only person of the big people that ever could visit and talk with the little men in their unknown language. One day far from the rising sun (east) came word that men of the pale-face were coming in

> hordes to the hunting-grounds of Left Hand and his people. This caused the Indians many thoughts and worry of the heart. Soon Left Hand heard that the men with the pale faces were drawing nearer and nearer to his home. In the darkness of the night, he went to his adopted little people and consulted them on these men with the white skin. Then the hearts of the little men sank with chill of fear, because they foresaw that their underground home was soon to be wrecked by this strange people. Left Hand told them of a wonderful rocky hunting toward the setting of the sun (west) where he would take his adopted little people; where the mocassioned feet of the palefaces will not intrude, where new homes can be built away from all the big people, red and whit [white] faces.
>
> One dark night, Left Hand led his little men away to the rocky tops of the big mountains of the setting sun. He took them all—men women and papooses[.] That is why the little people moved their camp forever to the sinking of the sun, where they still live and enjoy the wilds of the woods and the animals to their command, where hunting-grounds are not turned into the whiteman's herbs of food, nor their berry trees chopped down, and placed with the paleface berry bush. [182–197; 1505]

The ending of this legend reveals that it is a story adapted to recent times. The palefaces, who have no reverence for the land, have come. The survival of the little people who inhabit the ground is in doubt. Left Hand moves them to less habitable lands where they will survive. This, too, mirrors the fate of Indian tribes who were pushed to the least habitable lands even on their own reservations. The key becomes surviving at all.

What must be emphasized here, in relation to the previous three examples drawn from a novel and a private letter, is that Mourning Dove is not creating the material. She is transcribing the stories into English within the context of a Native American storyteller tradition. She has chosen the very challenging route of being a mediator between two distinct cultures. A stunning example of her awareness of this role comes at the end of "The House of Little Men," when Mourning Dove feels compelled to verify the story for McWhorter in white terms:

> Note—Location of the house of Little Men is situated near Oroville Washington. Some 18 miles north in B.C. Scientists have made researches, but no one is found small enough to investigate the unknown tunnels of this legend. [182–197; 1505]

In her care to bridge two audiences, Mourning Dove has given us all an invaluable gift—an insight into chaotic times and the power of people to hold themselves together through memory and the articulation of shared experiences in an ongoing story of survival. Mourning Dove's work also represents trickster energy at a very high level. The trickster must adapt to the logic of those she or he would triumph over, and through that seeming accommodation, create the new. Mourning Dove has intuitively followed the wisdom inherent in the coyote stories of her Salish culture.

Also Mourning Dove's choice to write was courageous because English was her second language, and it was a language in which she had not mastered the spelling or the grammar. In fact, the education indigenous children received at the turn of the last century insured a third-class status. Instruction in language arts did not go much beyond the third grade expectations of the day, no matter how many years of education the Indian student received. Besides schooling, Indian children were most likely to pick up English through informal conversations and through the affordable mass media of the day, dime-store paperback novels. It was the vocabulary and the rhythms of the latter, combined with the vocabulary and rhythms of their native tongues, that shaped Indian English. Mourning Dove's first letter to L. V. McWhorter, written on February 9, 1915, best illustrates what I mean:

> My blood has called to me, I have lived the Whiteman's traits of life for years, and at last I heard the voice, which seemed but a whisper at first till it sounded so loud to me till it reached the mountaintops. Than, I could not resist. And I threw all civilized life, to the four winds, and I roamed back to my own kind, to live among the golden Race, who I would lay my life for, to endure the teepee smoke and smell the roasted Mowwich deer over the bon fire again. Than than [sic] the memory of my past childhood days, seem to all come back to me again. A life that I have cherish in my bosom, among all my travels with my "put on life." A life that no real Indian dare lead and leave his dear life of nature which God gave him, as his own.
>
> The stream and mountains that the Great White Spirit gave us as our own once, and the animals birds and even the reptiles that wears his breast crawling among the hot rocks and pebbles, in the scortching hot summer, has being taken away from us. Against our forefathers will. Than, you hear the voice of our White Brother saying Every thing, that was once ours belongs to their, (He-la me-wham,) (King) or government. And can you blame Morning Dove, for looesing confidence in human nature, especially the Silvery hue Race, who calls us brother with a forked tongue. A word that comes only from the lips, but not the bosom, where the heart throbs. [15–17; 395]

We smile at this language because it seems quaint and artificial. Yet it also is heartfelt. Mourning Dove was doing her best to impress a white man with her language skills. She had to go from Indian to English words and struggle through our demanding word order, grammar, and spelling. She also drew on the purple prose of the day to demonstrate her writing ability. It is imperative that we become sensitive to Mourning Dove's process of moving from an Indian oral tradition to the European literary tradition. Otherwise, we will misread the text as a sign of the more "primitive" skills of Native peoples, and refuse to see that their English abilities are clearly a product of our educational system for them, as well as a product of the pressure-cooker assimilation of their times.

Another problem for Native American writers, then as now, is that Indian texts often have been edited, even co-written, by members of the dominant culture. The passages from *Cogewea* that we examined earlier were edited by L. V. McWhorter, who felt compelled to correct Mourning Dove's English so that Euroamerican readers would not discount Native American insights, and editors to this day still struggle with the same issue. But rewriting sentences, selecting different words, and organizing material can alter and transform an Indian voice to the point of severe distortion. Distortion also occurs when editors add their own material in the belief that their additions will clarify or amplify the subject matter at hand.[8] McWhorter, in his need to educate and awaken the consciences of white readers, added numerous passages of ethnographic commentary and attacks on religious and government corruption. The result is that *Cogewea* is rent by two voices and two purposes. Consider the following passage in contrast to the voice and tone of the previous letter:

> Skilled in the art of white washing, brooded the girl, the Indian Bureau was an octupus, with life extracting tentacles reaching into every Indian reservation of the Union. A vampire! whose wing cools with the breeze of never-to-be-filled promises, the wound of its deadly beak, while it drains the heart's blood of its hapless "ward." Where rested the wrong? The Bureau! a branch of the Government. The Government? the dollar-marked will of the politician. The politician? the *priest,* and the *Levite,* who "pass on the other side" from the bruised, and robbed victim of systematized plunder-lust, lying naked by the trail. Should an occasional *Samaritan* stoop to minister to the sufferer's wants, he is rebuked by the Bureaucrats, and warned that such charity is ill advised; wasted where not an exigency. (Chapter XVI, pp. 140–141)

Emphatic to the point of being comical for contemporary readers, the passage condemns the Indian Bureau for betraying its moral obligations to its wards, assaults the moral weaknesses of politicians who betray democratic values for the dollar, and refers to the "Good Samaritan" parable to expose the religious hypocrisy that McWhorter believed people used to hide their selfish actions from themselves. It is also a passage of self-defense. McWhorter saw himself as the despised Samaritan, one living a truly moral and compassionate life.

In works like *Cogewea, the Half-Blood,* the key to reading is to pay attention to both voices, to ferret out what motivates both writers, and to respect what has brought them together. In *Cogewea* the two voices help us understand what it was like for an Indian woman and a white man to live in the assimilation/settlement period. We need to acknowledge the stories that they have had the courage to tell and the racist assumptions they were willing to confront, however awkwardly. But the essential story lies in Mourning Dove's narratives, which reveal what it was like to be torn between the appeals of traditional Indian life and the demands to assimilate out of Indian existence. That struggle, shared by so many, is what motivated Mourning Dove to write. An examination of her works helps us understand how Native writers incorporated English into their larger ongoing oral tradition of storytelling. That tradition has always included trickster tales of confrontation with the monstrous, and has always explored modes of psychological cunning and the right use of power for one to move forward through chaos. What at first was perceived as assimilation is truly a survival strategy.

Notes

1. Mourning Dove always refers to 1888, the Tribal Enrollment Services records indicate 1887, and the Allotment records indicate 1882, 1886, and 1887 as her birth year. This information was gleaned from Mourning Dove's probate records, which the family has generously shared with me.

2. Lincoln: University of Nebraska Press, 1990. My critiques of Jay Miller's treatment of Mourning Dove's texts are published in *The Women's Review of Books* 8, no. 2 (November 1990): 19–20, and assessed more thoroughly in *SAIL* 3, no. 2 (Summer 1991).

3. Boston: Four Seas Co., 1927; rpt. Lincoln: University of Nebraska Press, 1981. All quoted material is drawn from the 1981 reprint.

4. Idaho: Caxton Printers, Ltd., 1933; rpt. Lincoln: University of Nebraska Press, 1990.

5. Lucullus Virgil McWhorter was fifty-four years old when he met Mourning Dove, who was in her late twenties or early thirties in 1914. He was already a strong advocate for Indian concerns and had been adopted into the Yakima tribe for his work to preserve millions of dollars worth of land and water rights for that tribe. He became Mourning Dove's mentor, editor, at times co-writer, and friend over a twenty-year period. Born January 29, 1860, in what became West Virginia, he died in Yakima, Washington, on October 10, 1944. He is the author of *The Crime Against the Yakimas* (1913); *Border Settlers of Northwestern Virginia* (1915); *Adventures in Geyser Land* (1935); *Yellow Wolf: His Own Story* (1940); and *Hear Me, My Chiefs* (1952), published posthumously.

6. This letter is among the extensive twenty-year correspondence between Lucullus Virgil McWhorter and Mourning Dove, which is housed at the Manuscripts, Archives and Special Collections Division of the Washington State Universities Libraries, Pullman, Wash. 99164. The correspondence is kept in individual folders, and each sheet of paper within a folder is numbered. This April 28, 1916, letter is sheets 24–26 of file 366. All further correspondence from the L. V. McWhorter collection is indicated as shown in the brackets. The quoted material maintains the writer's original spelling and grammar with the exception that spelling or a period or comma in brackets is my insertion in order to help reader clarity. Such additions have been kept to a minimum. The letters are published with the knowledge and permission of the family elders, Mary Lemery and Charles Quintasket.

7. Jeannette Armstrong, grand-niece to Mourning Dove through marriage and Director of the En'Owkin Center, Penticton, British Columbia, is editing this text for a publication that will serve the Okanagans both of Canada and the United States. The En'Owkin Center is dedicated to preserving Okanagan culture.

8. For a discussion of the autobiographical content and inclusion of oral traditions in *Cogewea,* see Alanna Brown, "Mourning Dove's Voice in *Cogewea,*" *The Wicazo Sa Review* 4, no. 2 (Fall 1988): 2–15. Also see Brown, "The Choice

to Write: Mourning Dove's Search for Survival," in *Old West-New West: Centennial Essays,* ed. Barbara H. Meldrum (Moscow: University of Idaho Press, 1993), pp. 261–271; "The Evolution of Mourning Dove's *Coyote Stories,*" *Studies in American Indian Literatures* 4, nos. 2 and 3 (Summer/Fall 1992): 161–180; and "Looking Through the Glass Darkly: The Editorialized Mourning Dove," in *New Voices in Native American Literary Criticism,* ed. Arnold Krupat (Washington, D.C.: Smithsonian Institution Press, 1993), for an extensive discussion of collaboration and survival issues for Mourning Dove. A few passages of historical overview and discussion of the McWhorter/Mourning Dove collaboration in this essay have been drawn from the article in the Smithsonian collection.

Works Cited

Brown, Alanna. "Mourning Dove's Voice in *Cogewea.*" *The Wicazo Sa Review* 4:2 (1988): 2–15.

———. "The Evolution of Mourning Dove's Coyote Stories." *Studies in American Indian Literatures* 4:2–3 (1992): 161–180.

———. "The Choice to Write: Mourning Dove's Search for Survival." In *Old West-New West: Centennial Essays.* Ed. Barbara H. Meldrum. Moscow: University of Idaho Press, 1993, pp. 261–271.

———. "Looking Through the Glass Darkly: The Editorialized Mourning Dove." In *New Voices in Native American Literary Criticism.* Ed. Arnold Krupat. Washington, D.C.: Smithsonian Institution Press, 1993.

Mourning Dove. *Cogewea, the Half-Blood.* Boston: Four Seas Co., 1927. Rpt. Lincoln: University of Nebraska Press, 1981.

———. *Coyote Stories.* Idaho: Caxton Printers, Ltd., 1933. Rpt. Lincoln: University of Nebraska Press, 1990.

———. Letters. Washington State Universities Libraries, Pullman, Washington.

———. *Mourning Dove: A Salishan Autobiography.* Lincoln: University of Nebraska Press, 1990.

KAREN OAKES

Reading Trickster; or, Theoretical Reservations and a Seneca Tale

Unification and simplification are fantasies of domination, not understanding.[1]
BARBARA JOHNSON

In a rare moment early last winter I was watching television, and a reporter was interviewing the creators of the annual Santa's Village display at the Jordan Marsh department store in Boston. Santa's Village is a child-size recreation of a Victorian Christmas that includes shops, a home with plastic food, and "children" who are animated by a hidden array of high-tech puppet strings. The creators' aim was "to make the past real." I found myself fascinated by their Aromamatic machine, which creates the smell of baking bread. Even more fascinating was a ubiquitous feature of the Village, visible through the snow on my vintage TV. The "real name" of this feature, according to the reporter, is "real fake snow."

"Real fake snow" figures what contemporary Native American literatures, cultures, and criticisms—to make what I will argue are false divisions—face vis-à-vis the U.S. mainstream. In this vein, Gerald Vizenor cites Umberto Eco to explore the situation of tribal cultures and literatures in the context of the "hyperrealities of neocolonial consumerism," where hyperreality represents an intensification and a fabrication of "reality" in "the absolute fake," in which "the boundaries between game and illusion are blurred." One of Vizenor's more accessible passages suggests:

> Native American literatures are unstudied landscapes, wild and comic rather than tragic and representational, storied with narrative wisps and tribal discourse. Social science theories constrain tribal landscapes to institutional values, representationalism, and the politics of academic determinism. The narrow teleologies deducted from social science monologues, and the ideologies that arise from structuralism, have reduced tribal literatures to an "objective" collection of consumable cultural artifacts. ("Trickster Discourse," p. 278)

That is, according to Vizenor, a consumerist social science aims at a "monologue" of "truth" and in so doing eliminates the resonance, polyvalence, and "wildness" of Native American literatures. In contrast, he continues, "postmodernism liberates imagination and widens the audiences for tribal literatures"; and he goes on to construct his own wily and meandering discourse, asserting, "the trickster is postmodern."[2] Vizenor agrees with Andrew Wiget and Arnold Krupat that Native American tales presuppose no norm for interpretation, no need for interpretive uniformity, and he cites Vincent Leitch that there is no correct reading, only more "pleasurable misreadings."[3]

One purpose of this essay is to ask why the pleasures of reading (or "misreading") cannot be as multivalent and polymorphous as trickster's own, thief, cheat, glutton, sensualist, and scatologist that he is. Is postmodernist criticism another attempt, like those of earlier formalisms, to be "pure," to exclude the farts and belches, the contaminating dailiness of human experience? Certainly, postmodernism can be alluringly playful, as we see in Vizenor's own writing; and as such it accords with trickster impulses. But postmodernism often possesses a "monologic" quality of its own, to *steal* a word that Vizenor uses to categorize social science discourse, and it may *evacuate* trickster tales of cultural contexts that can help *engender* other "pleasurable misreadings." That is, if we elide stories' concrete cultural situations, we are not reading in a vacuum but from within another culture, namely, academic literary culture, that may be equally neocolonialist in its desires. One such desire, if we take Vizenor as emblematic of a particular strand, is to separate aesthetic complexity from cultural contexts—or to subsume the latter in the former—in order to assign higher value to the former. In spite of Vizenor's attempts to recover the power of the word, a central value for Native American societies, and hence to reenter a Native cultural context, I will argue that his postmodernist inflection disconnects the fundamental relationship between the word and the world, the symbolic and the concrete. We must ask, is the "aesthetic" ever drained of "culture"? What is "real fake snow"?

Vizenor's discussion, to which I return in part 2, has ramifications not only for Native American literature in general and for trickster stories in particular, but for literary criticism (and hence literary/cultural studies) more broadly. In the discussion that follows, Part 1, "A (Social Science) Reading of 'Twentgowa and the Mischief Maker,'" will affirm some of the insights of social science, especially for white middle-class academics like myself, by pointing out some cultural information important for a first journey through and with "Twentgowa." Part 2, "An Argument Against Postmodern Theory: Trickster in Academe," discusses the ways in which Vizenor's attempt to reinvent criticism of Native American literatures based on the figure of trickster is both promising and problematic. Part 3, "'Twentgowa' as Theory: Toward Trickster Reading" circles back "home" to "Twentgowa" to ask what it and the impulses of trickster offer to contemporary critical theory. Finally, "Coda: A Tale/Tail" attempts to set the reader on the move again. What's at stake, I will suggest throughout, is the need to refuse such artificial western dualisms as literature/criticism, theory/praxis, mind/body, academy/world, literature ("art")/life, abstraction/narration, where these terms are hierarchically inflected, with the first term the dominant or powerful one.

1. A (Social Science) Reading of "Twentgowa and the Mischief Maker"

Trickster epitomizes humor or comedy; his playfulness emerges from disjunctions, evasions, and subversions of power.[4] The trickster story that I have chosen, "Twentgowa and the Mischief Maker," emerges from the Seneca tradition and was told to Seneca ethnographer Arthur C. Parker by Edward Cornplanter early in this century.[5] Virtually irresistible to retell, "Twentgowa and the Mischief Maker" inhabits its listeners, who can see themselves in and through it.[6] A (partial) recounting seems appropriate in Seneca terms, for although I am aware of the dangers of my own appropriation of the story, the gesture of retelling confronts western norms that prohibit the "dominance" of "criticism" by the "literature" it attempts to "interpret," and it reaffirms the value of narrative.[7]

The tale plays with and subverts traditional Seneca concepts of identity and power in ways accessible to many cultural and "critical" perspectives.[8] The central character Twentgowa is, we are told at once and repeatedly, "a very lazy man," in spite of having responsibilities to "a wife and several children" (p. 208). Such laziness would most certainly have marked Twentgowa as a marginal member of the community; as anthropologist Anthony F. C. Wallace observes, "the basic ideal of [historical Seneca] manhood was that of 'the good hunter' . . . self-disciplined, autonomous, responsible. He was a patient and efficient huntsman, a generous provider to his family and nation."[9] In contrast, Twentgowa "was always giving excuses to his wife as to why he did not hunt game more often like other men," and his wife constantly "scolded him for not bringing home game." Twentgowa prefers to lie on "a mossy rock near a river and dream of the things he would like to do." He is sure, for example, of "how he would kill big game animals if he only had a chance" (p. 208); he only dreams of feats he should be performing to be a responsible Seneca man.

Twentgowa's education (and the lazy listeners') begins when he has a visit from a man who identifies himself as a "friend" and who turns out to be none other than the "Mischief Maker."[10] The Mischief Maker affirms that his relationship with Twentgowa is longstanding: "I have visited you before but this is the first time you have seen me. I have known your name for a long time" (p. 208). This announcement prefigures what will happen in the story—that while the individual named as the Mischief Maker tricks Twentgowa, Twentgowa also plays the trickster's role of the traditional overreacher.[11] In fact, many similarities link the two in a twinship foundational in Iroquois myth: For example, both are lazy, and both are ostensibly "at home" as outsiders away from the village, Twentgowa on the "mossy rock" from which he escapes his wife's chiding and the Mischief Maker in his nearby lodge. As the story progresses, we discover that Twentgowa also has in common with trickster his perpetual hunger, lecherousness, boastfulness, and foolishness—that is, his pleasurable inability to master his own desires. Like mythic trickster, Twentgowa hopes to acquire power by proxy. "Power," as he repeatedly tells his friend, is "the power to do the same as you have done, for in this manner I could feed my family" (p. 211). Four times he visits the Mischief Maker to acquire this "power" and four times he plays the fool by transgressing the limits trickster gives him to make food only twice. The most significant issue, of course, is not just Twentgowa's laziness and foolishness, but his family's (and his own) quite literal hunger. The Mischief Maker's deceptions center on food, and he repeatedly invites Twentgowa, "now is the time to eat . . . let us eat together" (p. 209).

On the first occasion, the Mischief Maker lures the gluttonous Twentgowa with a delectable pumpkin pudding that he conjures from "a loathly mess of substance that had the odor of a fish a long time dead." This transformation should be a signal to Twentgowa that he is being deceived, for such transformations are unnatural, just as is Twentgowa's lazy behavior. In some sense, then, the narrator implies that Twentgowa is self-deceived as much as deceived by trickster. To transfer this ability to Twentgowa, the Mischief Maker throws a pot through his friend's abdomen; we are told, "It vanished through magic and power was within Twentgowa" (p. 209). Excited, Twentgowa heads toward home but on the path feels it would be well to test "his newly acquired power." He easily produces "a great pile of steaming pumpkin pudding . . . on the ground," which, the narrator suggests, he wastefully leaves behind. Elated, endlessly hungry, he proclaims, "Power within me is; now I shall eat forever." Instead of using his power as instructed, which would also benefit others, Twentgowa acts apart from the community. Paula Gunn Allen remarks in another context on "the negative effect of individuality" and the need for the individual to reconnect with the community as the force behind many Native American tales.[12] We may sympathize with his desires and laugh at his antics, but Twentgowa's arrogance and foolishness are also manifest.

Those familiar with trickster's antics can anticipate and thus take even more pleasure in what will happen in "Twentgowa" as one version of the "Bungling Host" tale.[13] As Polly Pope explains:

> The Bungling Host story itself centers around the hungry trickster who visits a friend identified as a host. In the course of the visit the host prepares a more than ample supply of food in "magical" fashion. Frequently the host cuts meat from his body . . . without any ill effects. Other times he may transform wood into meat. . . . Later the trickster plans to return the hospitality. He invites the host to his house, then prepares to offer him food obtained in the same manner. However, his efforts to repeat the performance fail. (p. 276)

The failures range from his appearing mildly foolish to his actually mutilating himself, with the emphasis depending on the tribe. In "Twentgowa," we see a variation on the form in that on four occasions Twentgowa returns home to "host" not the "friend" but his own family—creating situations in which he appears both foolish and dangerously inadequate. Boasting of his "power to make [pumpkin pudding] by magic," he conjures the material the Mischief Maker has given him, but it not only remains "a loathly substance like unto a dead fish," it also overflows the dish and contaminates the house, driving out his children and his angry wife. To compound his foolishness, Twentgowa cannot see the mess he has created, for he exclaims, "Oh, it is so appetizing!" and dances around the lodge until his wife throws stones at him. Twentgowa's specious power to create pumpkin pudding, a "female" task, reflects a satire on his transgression of traditional gender roles—he "should" be hunting. The "power" within his abdomen, like his laziness, is "unnatural."

The magnitude of Twentgowa's transgression becomes abundantly clear in the community's response to this scene: "So the people saw that Twentgowa had lied and could not make food by unnatural means, but made that which was evil." Twentgowa's wife also highlights the message; this friend, she tells him, is "a mischief maker"; "if you persist in visiting him you will suffer and great calamity will befall us all" (p. 210). Power resides in responsibility to self, family, and community, not in isolation, for as trickster himself warns, "it is not good to always eat pumpkins alone" (p. 211). Hence it is significant that Twentgowa "was greatly downcast and wondered why he had failed before the people" (p. 210), for he fails to satisfy the requirements of what Allen (1989) identifies as "right relationship" or "right kinship" (p. 8).

Twentgowa's abuse of power in this instance extends also to his misuse of language. Like mythic trickster, he becomes a braggart: After "running home [from the Mischief Maker's lodge] he entered his lodge and *told his story.* He *told* of his feasting on pumpkin pudding and of the power he had to make it by magic" (p. 210, emphasis added). Brian Swann comments on the sacredness and precision of language in several Native American cultures, observing: "It is only natural that a society which carried its past in the spoken word, and incorporated its values in story and song, would invest words with reverence and power" (p. xi). Furthermore, "the only aim and intent [of linguistic creativity] is truth, not manipulation. . . . Lies destroy correct form. They destroy the real relationship between man and the natural order" (p. xii). Twentgowa's bragging, then, not only compounds his folly, error, and irreverence; it threatens a fundamental, harmonious relationship with "the natural order."

Twentgowa's second encounter with the Mischief Maker proves even more painful than his first. The Mischief Maker "shows" him how to produce pumpkins by hitting his war club with a maul. Again he wastes his two opportunities before returning home; again he brags to his wife, this time that he has been granted "new power," "good power"; he knows "the right way to proceed" to make pumpkins. But he has some "real fake snow" and succeeds only in giving his big toe "a terrible and resounding whack" with his war club, which, of course, should have been used for "proper" purposes. With this whack, he "fell off the bench like a dead man. He gave one dismal drawn-out howl and fainted." In a culture famous for the stoicism of its warriors and its testing of individuals' mettle through ritual torture, Twentgowa's behavior is even more shameful and humorous. Using this illegitimate and misapplied power, Twentgowa ironically lames himself so that he *cannot* hunt.

Twentgowa shows in this second meeting that he still fails to understand the nature of power. Questioning his "new" power as he should question his natural power to obtain food by hunting, he has to test his "magical abilities," wondering if "by some chance power was within him only so long as he was in the presence of his friend" (p. 211). Twentgowa again conceives power too individualistically, for as Swann comments, in an Indian context, "power *flowed*; it was not wielded. As often as not, power itself does the choosing, for on the highest level, power is a force for common good" (p. xii). Furthermore, "in its most meaningful sense of spiritual power, [it] is a fusion of active and passive. It links past and present in profound conservatism" (p. xvii, n. 6). Twentgowa cannot yet see his lack of power as connected to his self-centeredness and his refusal to accept a traditional role as hunter. It is not surprising, then, that when he tests his unnatural power the second time and produces a pumpkin, he does so alone and is too lazy to carry it home to share with his family; he cooks and eats it himself. In his gluttony, he forgets his responsibility to others who are hungry, as well as to himself.

Twentgowa's foolishness raises the stakes on the pain he must endure to come to himself, to return to traditional values. Echoing a common occurrence in the Bungling Host story, the next episode requires him to whittle his shins to catch fish in imitation of the Mischief Maker. As he tells his wife about his ability, he says (hilariously to the listener), "I have new power. . . my friend has given me new power. I will go now and catch fish for you but you must not mind if they have cuts in them. It is *my manner* of catching fish" (p. 213, emphasis added). Again he underscores his divergence from tribal norms. Missing him later in the day, his wife discovers him bleeding and unconscious in the stream; and the Mischief Maker must revive and heal Twentgowa with his salivary fluid, a figure of power in Seneca myth. As he does so he chides Twentgowa, "You have cheated and wasted your power" (pp. 213–214). Twentgowa's world is radically out of balance when his wife and her dog (who fetches the Mischief Maker) have to rescue the hunter-warrior in the family. Comically repeated, the wife's scolding this time concludes, "If you would get busy like a man and hunt like a man you would have food. You are no good, but a bad, lazy man. I forbid you to associate with anyone, not even the dog" (p. 214).[14]

What Twentgowa has feared, that he "may . . . be laughed at derisively" (p. 213), is precisely what has occurred because of his stubborn, foolish, self-centered inability to be a man. The final and deciding episode reiterates his mistake. The listener is given an indication, however, that Twentgowa knows the correct way to act, for when the Mischief Maker announces that he is "all ready to go hunting" Twentgowa looks around and asks, "Where are your arrows?" (p. 214). The former's reply promises more foolishness from Twentgowa and more hilarious instruction for the listeners: "Oh you will never understand my ways. I hunt underwater with strings" (p. 214). Once again, Twentgowa ignores the Mischief Maker's warning that he has the power to obtain food in this way only twice; he "tests" it for the second time on his return home alone. Significantly, when he succeeds, "he threw the ducks away and went home" (p. 215). Such selfishness in the face of his family's hunger cannot be without consequences. Twentgowa's bungling underwater attempt to tie ducks' feet together and drag them down causes the birds to fly in fear, drawing him into the sky. He ultimately falls and lands trapped in a hollow log.[15] A young woman passing by mistakes him for a bear; she calls her friends, Twentgowa sings, and they dance. In this mutual enchantment, no one can stop. As is common in Bungling Host stories, it is left to "a man"—a "new actor" (Pope, p. 282)—to "rescue" him by chopping down the dead tree, revealing him as "a man with his clothes torn off," vulnerable to the ridicule of his wife, who magically appears when "the damsels ran in fright." After a scolding by both the Mischief Maker and his wife, Twentgowa reforms and "became like other men, and hunted for his family" (p. 216).

This language reclaims traditional male identity and communal values, for "in the Indian way, singularity is antithetical to community. . . . In such a system, individualism (as distinct from autonomy or self-responsibility) becomes a negatively valued trait" (Allen, p. 9). Part of the impetus for Twentgowa's reform, interestingly, seems to be not only the "power" of his experience, but also the power of the Mischief Maker's and his wife's words. According to Wallace, Seneca men who failed to meet their responsibilities in the "proper" way would engender public ridicule, a most effective form of punishment that often followed the miscreant all through his life (pp. 25–26). The Mischief Maker reinforces the wife's scolding indirectly by such injunctions as, "I gave you power twice, but further than that I did not give you" (p. 213), suggesting that human power is limited and that such limitation must be accepted (Wiget, 1985, p. 5). Trickster's message resounds with humor, because he knows, like the community of listeners, that humans will always attempt to overreach such boundaries; the Mischief Maker's potential for subversion lingers.

As Wiget points out, "Such tales illuminate one of the highest values of comedy, its ability to instruct" (1990, p. 91). From an instrumental perspective, the ending signals Twentgowa's reintegration into the social fabric that he has torn and his acceptance of the role provided to him as a Seneca man. Finally, Twentgowa and the listener learn that power derives not from "magic" but from shouldering one's responsibilities—to self, family, and community. That is, trickster is within as well as without, and if one fails to use one's own power, both the community and the individual will suffer. The communal nature of this comedic subversion is implicated in historical and cultural context. Wiget notes, for example, that different listeners of such a story laugh at different times. Such differences may reflect disparities of status and power, with younger people responding to the middle of the tale in which social norms are disrupted and older ones more likely to laugh at the end, as those norms are confirmed. He argues that "the critical laughs are the intervening ones that sustain and implicate the audience in [trickster's] madness" (1985, p. 20).

The social/cultural/historical complexities of "Twentgowa" suggest an array of questions. Is the dual "meaning" that Wiget points toward in trickster tales generally present to contemporary non-Seneca readers of "Twentgowa and the Mischief Maker"; was it part of traditional Seneca understanding (and is it useful to separate the two)? What Allen (1989) points out in another context about Native American traditional stories may be as true for any narrative: "Stories . . . exist within the minds of the audience as much as they exist in the mind of the storyteller. Context defines significance as much as such fictional elements as characterization, plot, setting, stance, style, and language do" (p. 4). Who then is the "listener"/interpreter in this textualized version of the story? Is foolishness a cultural "universal"—even if it is differently defined? Where does power lie—in the reintegrated comic hero or in the disruptor—who, though he has "cured" Twentgowa, will inevitably find another human afflicted with gluttony, laziness, and lechery like himself? Is cultural "translation," an inevitability for most readers, appropriate or acceptable?[16]

2. *An Argument Against Postmodern Theory: Trickster in Academe*

"Twentgowa" makes more sense to western readers in the light of social science insights; without them the story could "translate" in the following way: Twentgowa, the uncommon man, the dreamer, the individualist, is hampered by his responsibilities to a nagging wife and hungry family. In an effort to escape these burdens that prevent him from discovering his true identity, he leaves the community and meets a powerful man whose abilities he emulates. This "mentor" attempts to help him escape his situation through various adventures, but Twentgowa has a fatal flaw that makes certain his ultimate failure, no matter how hard he tries. Twentgowa is finally reduced to the fate of the common man, a tragic example of the suburban drone.

Given this (potentially "pleasurable") misreading, we might well ask Vizenor, if there is no correct reading, why is the application of the social scientific perspective to literary/cultural studies so suspect? Vizenor valorizes postmodernism and tricksterism as manifestations of comic language games, performances of wildness; he criticizes social science's reductiveness in what he sees as its goal of formulating singular "truth" and its resistance to "chaos," which is a central principle of trickster performances (Vizenor, pp. 284, 286). Certainly, social science has been used to diminish Native American individuals, cultures, and literatures, as Krupat points out in his description of Louis Agassiz's championship of the "theory of polygenesis" (Krupat, *Ethnocriticism,* p. 233). However, it is not a particular method or perspective that is reductive—social science methodologies and their applications are far from monolithic in any case—but the uses to which that method or perspective is put.[17] Furthermore, as part 1 of this discussion has tried to indicate, the contextualizing insights of social science are not only necessary at times to help prevent misinterpretation, they can also help to enlarge appreciation as traditional literary studies attempts to become more interdisciplinary.[18]

In spite of this claim, Vizenor could argue, with considerable merit, that Wallace's account of the Seneca, for example, is deeply imbued with western norms and that these norms inflect his narrative, his "translation," of the Seneca. Thus, for me to "read" "Twentgowa" with Wallace's assistance is to perform precisely the kind of consumerism that Vizenor rightly criticizes. Wallace *is* inaccurate or incomplete, at least on the matter of gender roles, for he does not provide an adequate account of the power and respect accorded women in traditional Seneca culture. Without such a perspective, as I have indicated, contemporary western readers might view the wife in "Twentgowa" as a nag and Twentgowa as her henpecked husband in the mode of Rip Van Winkle—and hence more likely to gain sympathy, neglecting the possibility that Seneca listeners might also see the wife as correct in her complaints.[19] But I am not suggesting that social science should provide a single approach to "Twentgowa" or to Native American literatures, only that it can help to add a useful sociohistorical voice on the path to a more inclusive process of understanding.

Granting the problems affiliated with social science stories of culture, we need to look at the problems associated with Vizenor's rehearsal of postmodernism. We can *choose* to read "Twentgowa and the Mischief Maker" as particularly "postmodern" in the central ambiguity it creates, exemplified by the comic twinning of trickster/Twentgowa. The pleasures of (mis)reading emerge for some as much from posing questions as from answering them, but the pleasures of historically and culturally informed readings—where "readings" are verbs, not nouns, and emphasis is placed on process rather than product, as Vizenor's own work implies—must also have a part. Perhaps "tribal literatures are the world rather than a representation," to cite Vizenor (p. 278), but so are tribal people and individual Native Americans, whom we must see not as plays on hyperreality, but as "the real thing" indeed; whom "readers" must attempt to understand seriously as well as comically, individually as well as communally, and temporally as well as aesthetically.

Vizenor's trickster discourse is alluring because play, humor, and pleasure are too often absent from critical writing, although it might be appropriate here to underline again the obvious—that pleasures, especially the "pleasures of misreading," are different for different people. Nevertheless, Vizenor's essay performs a deliberate evocativeness that translates to a readerly space of creativity. In addition, as his own work indicates, "criticism" and "literature" are too often opposed rather than overlapping terms. Similarly, criticizing the traditional western "segregation" of literary genres from one another and arguing for internal, nonwestern standards for the understanding of Native American literatures, Paula Gunn Allen asserts, "Intellectual apartheid . . . helps create and maintain political apartheid; it tends to manifest itself in the practical affairs of all societies that subscribe to it" (p. 3). I would suggest that we take Allen's observations about generic purity to extend beyond poetry, drama, and prose (or fiction and nonfiction) into the critical domain. In this respect, Vizenor's trickster discourse does represent an attempt to defy western practices of "intellectual apartheid."

Yet, in spite of Vizenor's athletic playfulness, and although postmodernism may indeed create openings in Native American literature and potentially "new audiences," we must beware the possibility that it can obscure the very literatures/practices that it attempts to highlight and unfold. Vizenor argues, for example:

> The trickster, a semiotic sign in a third person narrative, is never tragic, or *hypotragic,* never the whole truth, or even part truth; social science, on the other hand, is never comic, never a chance, and never tragic in the end—causal research strains to discover the "whole truth" or the invented truth in theories and models. These "whole truth" models imposed on tribal experiences are *hypotragies* [sic], abnormal tragedies in this instance, with no comic imagination, no artistic intent, or the communal signification of mythic verism. (p. 284)

At least as much as his version of social science, Vizenor's postmodernism has inherent in it the assumption of an individualistic interpretation (a "pleasurable misreading") that seems incommensurate with the idea of collective or communal apprehension and that conflicts with Allen's statements about the "negative effect of individuality."[20] A related problem is that Vizenor speaks in an exclusive language, about which Paul Lauter, in another context, observes: "The real function of linguistic opacity is little different from that of the Latin scrawls of physicians to pharmacists: to keep the unwashed out of the game."[21] Perhaps what Lauter says of "aesthetic criticism" might well be said of Vizenor's essay: It is "a series of linguistic moves whose dominant effect [is] to sustain academic privilege" (p. 7). What Native Americans or non-Native Americans, for example, other than academics, will read Vizenor? As Krupat observes of postmodernism generally, "it's all just a 'language game' for the privileged, and, so far as I can see, no model for anyone, anywhere" (*Ethnocriticism,* 13). Swann is even more pointed: "The explication of a text, a task for the new priesthood, becomes of as much importance as the text itself. We are led into a mad mirror world where symbols refer to symbols and the concept of a real world becomes, to all intents and purposes, pointless" (p. xvii, n.4).

Vizenor's language games do help academics to understand the "principle" of trickster, but they give no assistance with individual trickster tales; he seems to be operating to confirm the current split between theory and praxis in literary studies. This split is not innocent of power relations. As Annette Kolodny has observed, theory has in recent years acquired privilege in the academy, though, of course, we need to ask "What counts as theory?"[22] Similarly, black feminist writers like Barbara Christian interrogate the motives of theoretical "purity": "Theory has become a commodity which helps determine whether we [blacks, women, third world persons] are hired or promoted in academic institutions—worse, whether we are heard at all."[23] And Lauter says: "Theory as a mode of literary discourse (or, as I would describe it, a maneuver in academic political rhetoric) has primarily succeeded in reestablishing academic privilege—ironically, not for the study of literature in the academy, but for those who practice theory within the literary profession" (p. 8). Few would disagree, I think, that postmodernist or, for Elaine Showalter, poststructuralist theory occupies the largest space in this contested domain.[24]

My goal here, as before, is not to vilify or discard a particular approach but instead to point to the uses to which it is put. To prioritize any one approach is to reenact problematic truth claims and hierarchies. Any method, discourse, or way of knowing may be a tool of patriarchy, neocolonialism, or multiculturalism, but it should always be seen as a tool.[25] To search for the tool that is inherently pure is surely "real fake snow." In any event, "purity" of criticism, like purity of race, as Gloria Anzaldúa points out, is a myth.[26] Ultimately, while Vizenor's desire to retain a space of power for Native American literatures/cultures is admirable, the space that he claims is simply a reservation within dominant Western theory.[27]

3. "Twentgowa" as Theory: Toward Trickster Reading

What happens to literature and the world—falsely separated in this sentence at the very least—if we take trickster seriously as well as comically?[28] If we accept Vizenor's criticism that social science provides an incomplete story of Native American literatures, and if his own kind of abstract approach has limitations for diverse readers journeying toward understandings of those literatures, what critical approaches can provide more signposts? Perhaps we can look to the movement of "Twentgowa" itself, via Arnold Krupat's discussion of "rootedness" and "restlessness," for guidance. Krupat cites Carter Revard's observation that for Native American persons, "the notions of cosmos, country, self, and home are inseparable" (*Ethnocriticism,* p. 210). According to Krupat, "the typical pattern of Native American fiction is what Bevis calls 'homing in' rather than—the pattern typical of Euramerican fiction—moving out, breaking away, searching, seeking, transcending, and so forth. Indians, that is to say, travel a great deal, but they don't 'go places.' The sense of rootedness seems extraordinarily persistent in Native American peoples today" (p. 114). He continues, "Criticism is a form of movement . . . criticism may be considered the product of restlessness; centered peoples don't produce it in forms recognizable to the West" (p. 115).[29]

Aside from observing that Krupat's "moving out" and "breaking away" are western masculine norms, we might also observe that like traditional trickster, Twentgowa is fundamentally restless, on the move. As Pope emphasizes in relation to the "Bungling Host" tale generally, "it is the *action* in the content [of the story] which is of major interest" (p. 276, emphasis added). Hence in our story it is essential to take note that Twentgowa is always in motion: "Twentgowa often went into the deep woods and had a mossy rock near a river where he would lie and dream of the things he would like to do" (p. 208). "The lazy man arose from his bed and went out of the house" (p. 208). "He determined to go and see his friend again" (p. 210). "When his wife scolded him for a lazy man, he sneaked away again and went to the lodge of his friend" (p. 212). "So he went away by stealth and sought his friend" (p. 214). Alternatively, we learn that "Twentgowa now said that he was about to return to his home" (p. 209). "'Now I must go home and make pumpkins. . . . Now I must go'" (p. 211). "'I must go now, I am going home'" (p. 213). "'Now I must go home. Now I go'" (p. 215). This last sequence concludes, "Twentgowa went home and was a changed man. He never went to the house of the mischief maker again" (p. 216).

Although he seems to end up rooted, the propensity for restlessness dominates the story spatially, and it erupts even in the space between his intention to return home and his actual physical return in his journeys from the Mischief Maker's lodge. In each case, this restlessness is associated with Twentgowa's desire for "illegitimate" power. For example: "He started out on his journey [home] which seemed very much longer than ever before, as if the path had stretched. He kept thinking about his newly acquired power and thought it might be well to test it" (p. 209). His imaginative restlessness, even while he is heading home, engenders Twentgowa's comic failures/successes. Nevertheless, he goes out and returns four times. According to Parker, four is a "magical number" in Seneca folklore (p. 462), and here it implies the completion of Twentgowa's "cure" (Parker, p. 217n.).

But although his going out occurs within certain limits, the story's availability for retelling suggests the continuous possibility of other, similar acts of breaking away to emerge; that is, at the same time that he does come home, Twentgowa's restlessness is available to listeners/readers at and even after the completion of the story. The effect of the story's continuing presence or overflow is to suggest that imaginative restlessness need not be separated from actual physical restlessness. To borrow Krupat's term, Twentgowa's actions, echoing the constant movement of trickster, perform a kind of "criticism": of the home and Seneca women's power within it ("More and more often he repaired to his favorite spot as his wife scolded him for not bringing home game" [p. 208]); community ("He did not want to carry the pumpkin home so he made a fire and cooked it" [p. 211]); work ("I would like to have this power of catching fish for if I possessed it I might obtain food for my family" [p. 213]); Seneca stoicism ("He gave one dismal long-drawn-out howl and fainted" [p. 212]); and restraint ("Oh it is so appetizing" [p. 210]). Regarding such narratives as criticism enables listeners—and literary critics—to be more playful, venturesome, and skeptical of social/cultural norms even as we necessarily participate in those norms. Wiget points more generally to trickster's critical function. Trickster stories, he observes, exceed their ability to instruct on social norms; finally, "trickster functions not so much to call cultural categories into question as to demonstrate the artificiality of culture itself" (1990, p. 94). Taking this view enables "critics" to resist western norms specifying the segregation of "criticism" from "narrative" or "literature" from "experience." It also reminds us that writing can be a kind of action, an idea that I will return to in a moment.

"Twentgowa" enacts some other potentially useful critical insights. We might observe, for example, how characters' actions and language in the story echo one another. Viewing the "terrible mess" of his first attempt to conjure food, Twentgowa says, "Oh, it is so appetizing" (p. 210). Moments later he visits the Mischief Maker, who urges, "Come we will now eat together. This time we will have the whole pumpkin. Oh it is most delicious" (p. 210). Similarly, the Mischief Maker's and Twentgowa's wife's language and actions often work in concert. The wife initiates the process of Twentgowa's "cure" by speaking of the "friend" who has just invited Twentgowa to his lodge: "'Oh you who are always squatting like a duck on a nest, you shall not eat but this food shall be for our children. Begone, and if you have a friend perhaps he will receive you.' So that is what she said" (p. 208). In addition, although the wife and the Mischief Maker appear to be poles of rootedness and restlessness between which Twentgowa oscillates, their repeated proximity in the action and the fact that the wife substitutes for the ostensible "host" suggest their alliance, even interchangeability. When Twentgowa has whittled his shins and fainted in the stream, "She dragged him to the lodge and then called upon her dog to go and fetch S‘hondie'o^{n}sko^{n}′, the magical friend, to come and heal the husband. The dog went and soon the friend returned" (p. 213). In the final episode, both the wife and the Mischief Maker give Twentgowa a verbal lashing, not only in close temporal but also in close verbal contiguity—Twentgowa must be "like other men." In returning home, where he indeed "became like other men and hunted for his family" (p. 216) Twentgowa accepts as integral to himself the voice(s) of his wife and the community, which are already internal but unacknowledged.

This alliance of characters' actions and words in the story implies a broader sense of "identity" and a reduced emphasis on individuality. Reading "Twentgowa" as criticism implies polyvocality, that different voices can speak together for a common purpose. How such an observation might apply to contemporary "critical" practice might include the deemphasis of the monologue (to borrow a term from Vizenor) of the individual "critic"—more spaces allotted for "the text" and for other voices, not just "critical" ones. Another move might be to do more collaborative work; a third might be to invite a "dialogue" between writer and reader. In this connection, however, we need to ask whether borrowing others' voices is ventriloquizing. What are the risks of doing so? Furthermore, how can we speak to the problems of universalizing Native American literatures/cultures and erasing the differences between historical and contemporary literatures? How might we account for differences and similarities?

"Twentgowa and the Mischief Maker" (and trickster more generally) also implies an informed and enlarged vision of what "community" means; its performance suggests that we should bridge the gap between "the academy" and "the rest of the world." A critical mode situated in a communal vision for the future—whatever that means—need not imply an obscuring of individuality but a locating of that self, or to use Krupat's term, that "person" (*Ethnocriticism,* p. 201ff.). This locating returns us to the emphasis on community in "Twentgowa." Twentgowa's laziness resonates well beyond himself, not only to his family but to the community; the problem posed by the narrative is making sure that everyone has food. To reiterate Swann, "at the highest level power is a force for the common good"; this observation suggests the moral and practical nature of such power and of the narratives that enact it as a central value. To return to Swann again, "[in traditional Native American societies] matters of the spirit were simultaneously matters of the mundane"; or, in his citation of Lame Deer, "Indians live in a world of symbols and images *where the spiritual and the commonplace are one*" (p. xii, emphasis added). What such a world view entails is a sense of "right and responsible action" (p. xvii) in narrative as in the world, which are necessarily linked. For western "criticism" to learn from this perspective implies that it should seek to be both activist and accessible. One potential route to such accessibility, at least, is humor, coupled with a sense of one's own limitations.

Regarding such limitations, it seems important here to underscore that the preceding narrative has many fleas; you will no doubt scratch for them, but I will put my finger on two. If we take trickster's wanderings as a paradigm, we find a complementarity between the experimental and the conventional, between disruption and reintegration. Many academicians love the disruptive side—it feels like home, that mossy rock. So it too becomes a norm, turning inside out like trickster himself. Perhaps the most biting concern for me is how to represent the reintegration of mind and body, intellect and movement, and hence to infuse criticism with (atypical, sometimes uncomfortable) awareness and responsibilities. Have you, for example, been aware of your embodiment as you read this narrative—of the smell of the paper, the weight of the book in your palms, the glide of the paper through your fingers, the rhythms of your own breathing, or the dog that just farted under your chair? Of the crunch of bone as a man breaks a woman's nose with his fist? Of the Native American man, dead of cirrhosis at forty-nine (Allen, p. 14)? In responding to these challenges, we must be careful not to invent a new, pure, theoretical flea spray in a shiny metal can perched high on the academic shelf.

Coda: A Tale/Tail

The theoretical reservations that I have outlined in relation to Vizenor, postmodernism, and academic culture have boundaries that are closely guarded by what we might call, improvising on Allen's terms, the purity police. "Intellectual apartheid" is a principle that continues to dominate the structures of the academy, from the kind of publications many of us are expected to produce—in which personal narrative, if it appears at all, must typically be discreet and "universal"—to the insistence that students "be objective" and not write in the first person (which, they are told, doesn't exist anyway), to the convenient segregation of departments of history from departments of sociology. Politics is not only the name of another discipline. We often convince ourselves that our "fake snow" is "real" when we haven't been through a winter in ages—though we've seen it on TV. While trickster reading and writing have an element of extravagance, of wandering outside or beyond, that extravagance is balanced by a return home. How might we most usefully define home?

In the spirit of extravagance and return, I want to close with the story that Wilma Mankiller tells of an exchange with a male student who was asked to drive her from the airport to "a major eastern educational institution" to give a speech:

> This student clearly didn't approve of me, and after an uncomfortable silence he finally had to say something. "Principal chief is a term for a man. What should I call you? Ms.?"
>
> I looked out of the window for a while. After another pause, he kept at it: "How about chiefess?"
>
> I looked out of the window a little longer that time. Finally he announced, "I know—chiefette!"

Well, I looked out of the window a very long time before I said, "You can call me Ms. Chief Mischief."[30]

Notes

1. Barbara Johnson, *A World of Difference* (Baltimore: Johns Hopkins University Press, 1987), p. 170.

2. Gerald Vizenor, "Trickster Discourse," *American Indian Quarterly* 14 (1990): 278, 279, 281.

3. Andrew Wiget, *Native American Literature* (Boston: Twayne, 1985), p. 21; Arnold Krupat, "Post-Structuralism and Oral Literature," *Recovering the Word: Essays on Native American Literature,* eds. Brian Swann and Arnold Krupat (Berkeley: University of California Press, 1987), p. 118; Vizenor, p. 278. See Wiget, "His Life in His Tail: The Native American Trickster and the Literature of Possibility," *Redefining American Literary History,* eds. A. LaVonne Brown Ruoff and Jerry W. Ward (New York: Modern Language Association of America, 1990), pp. 83–96; Arnold Krupat, *The Voice in the Margin: Native American Literature and the Canon* (Berkeley: University of California Press, 1989).

4. On comedy, humor, play, and joking in the Trickster tale, see Wiget in Ruoff and Ward (1990), pp. 91, 94, 96; Mac Linscott Ricketts, "The North American Indian Trickster," *History of Religions* 5 (1966): 347; Barbara Babcock-Abrahams, "'A Tolerated Margin of Mess': The Trickster and His Tales Reconsidered," *Critical Essays on Native American Literature,* ed. Andrew Wiget (Boston: G. K. Hall, 1985), pp. 153–185. European-Americans find more interest in Trickster's role as subverter/disruptor than in that of reintegrator; see Franchot Ballinger, "Living Sideways: Social Themes and Social Relationships in Native American Trickster Tales," *Studies in American Indian Literature* 24 (1989): 15–30.

5. William N. Fenton, "Introduction to the Bison Books Edition," "Twentgowa and the Mischief Maker," *Seneca Myths and Folk Tales,* ed. Arthur C. Parker (Lincoln: University of Nebraska Press, 1989), pp. xi, xv. All subsequent references to the narrative are in the text. For some of the reasons for my choice of this text, see Fenton's "Introduction," Parker's "Foreword" and "Introduction," and Fenton, "'This Island, The World on Turtle's Back,'" in Wiget, *Critical Essays,* pp. 134–136.

According to Fenton, among the Seneca, "trickster stories have vanished since 1930" even though "in three hundred years of continuous contact with aggressive white people in the country's most populous state, several Iroquois languages are still spoken from Brooklyn to Niagara" (p. 136).

6. Parker observes, of his own retelling, "The folklore student . . . [desires] to so present his legend that it will awaken in the mind of his reader sensations similar to those aroused in the mind of the Indian auditor hearing it from the native raconteur. The recorder of the tale seeks to assimilate its characteristics, to become imbued with spirit" (p. xxvi).

7. See Kenneth Lincoln, "Native American Literatures," *Smoothing the Ground: Essays on Native American Oral Literature,* ed. Brian Swann (Berkeley: University of California Press, 1983), p. 9ff. Some of the difficulties that Lincoln discusses in relation to translation are relevant here.

8. In spite of attempts by Native Americanists to develop pan-Indian generalizations (many of which are cited in this essay), it is not unreasonable to assume

that a Seneca perspective on such matters as gender roles and the proper relation of the individual to the community might differ significantly from, say, a Cherokee perspective. That is, my "we" in the narrative may include Native Americans who are not Seneca—as well as, indeed, those modern Seneca who are highly acculturated to western norms.

9. Anthony F. C. Wallace, *The Death and Rebirth of the Seneca* (New York: Vintage, 1972), p. 30. Except where noted otherwise, the anthropological data that follows comes from Wallace's account of the historical Seneca; see especially pp. 21–107.

10. On the participation and implication of the audience in Trickster tales, see Wiget, *Native American Literature*, pp. 16, 20; "His Life in His Tail," pp. 85, 94. Wiget cites three "recurrent formal features" of Trickster tales that "form a background of expectations even if their appearance is not necessary in each telling" (p. 88).

11. See Polly Pope, "Toward a Structural Analysis of North American Trickster Tales," *Southern Folklore Quarterly* 31 (1967): 274–86. In Pope's account, the Host is not identified as the trickster figure, but she focuses primarily on Southeastern, Western, and Southwestern tribes and does not include any Iroquois tales.

12. Paula Gunn Allen, ed., *Spider Woman's Granddaughters: Traditional Tales and Contemporary Writing by Native American Women* (Boston: Beacon Press, 1989), p. 5.

13. On another, related form see Ballinger, pp. 22–23. Ballinger's article argues far more thoroughly than I can here for the social science perspective.

14. Pope notes that the presence of this third encounter (and the fourth encounter) varies according to tribe. In the "Bungling Host" story generally, "this is the event in which the original host displays concern for trickster's almost fatal act of imitation" (p. 284); she adds that sometimes this "host goes in search of a doctor to heal the trickster." This "curer insists on being left alone with the Bungling Host, whereupon he dispatches the patient . . . leaving only the bones of the latter" (p. 282). Again, we see a variation in the tale in that the role of the "host" is assumed by the wife, the curer in episode three is the Mischief Maker himself, and Twentgowa's "cure" is not so dire. It is in the fourth scene in this story that the "new actor" appears. See my discussion of these variations below.

15. This scene may be a comic echoing of the Iroquois creation myth (in Paula Gunn Allen's version, "The Woman who Fell from the Sky"; see Allen, pp. 56–58). Parker notes the commonness of the hollow log motif in Seneca tales; see p. 29.

16. A "no" to this question implies that non-Seneca should not attempt to read stories like "Twentgowa" and gets into the politics of "ownership" and consumerism, as well as intellectual neocolonialism. While I do not have definitive answers, and while I believe that all readers of Native American literatures must be as skeptical about the latter as they are about "intellectual apartheid," I think we cannot limit ourselves to reading (or teaching) only texts in the domain of our direct experience. Taken to an extreme, this attitude would limit me to literature by white, middle-class, New England female academics who love lobster and hate liver.

17. Arnold Krupat, *Ethnocriticism: Ethnography History Literature* (Berkeley: University of California Press, 1992), p. 14.

18. A further comment on this last observation is necessary. Given (among other things) the well-mapped-out complexities of transculturation, no interpretation can claim to be "right." Nor is Cornplanter's early twentieth-century perspective likely to be uninflected by Western culture. But as Krupat observes, it is

possible to be wrong in an interpretation. See Krupat, *Ethnocriticism,* p. 182; Paul Zolbrod, Review of Seneca Myths and Folk Tales, *Studies in American Indian Literature* 3, no. 1 (1991): 90.

19. Phyllis Rogers, "The Role of Women in the Creation of the Iroquois Confederacy: A Reinterpretation," Women's Studies Colloquium, Colby College, Waterville, Maine, March 1990. Personal communications, fall 1989–present. Paula Gunn Allen points out the dangers of western misinterpretation of gender norms in *The Sacred Hoop: Recovering the Feminine in American Indian Traditions* (Boston: Beacon Press, 1986); see especially "Kochinnenako in Academe: Three Approaches to Interpreting a Keres Indian Tale," pp. 222–244.

20. Interestingly, Vizenor observes that "The tragic mode is not in structural opposition to the comic sign, but a racial burden, a postcolonial overcompensation at best; these burdens are a dubious triumph" (p. 283).

21. Paul Lauter, "The Two Criticisms: Structure, Lingo, and Power in the Discourse of Academic Humanists," *Literature, Language, and Politics,* ed. Betty Jean Craige (Athens: University of Georgia Press, 1988), pp. 8–9.

22. Annette Kolodny, "Dancing Between Left and Right: Feminism and the Academic Minefield in the 1980s," in Craige, pp. 27–38. Paul Lauter, comment, nineteenth-century American women writers study group meeting, University of Albany, Albany, N.Y., 3 October 1992.

23. Barbara Christian, "The Race for Theory," *Making Face, Making Soul, Haciendo Caras: Creative and Critical Perspectives by Women of Color,* ed. Gloria Anzaldúa (San Francisco: Aunt Lute Foundation, 1990), p. 335. Anzaldúa's title seems unfortunate to me, since the book is concerned with undoing the very oppositions that this title encodes.

24. Elaine Showalter, "Feminism and Literature," *Literary Theory Today,* eds. Peter Collier and Helga Geyer-Ryan (Ithaca: Cornell University Press, 1990), p. 189. Of course, postmodernism, like social science, is hardly monolithic.

25. Krupat, *Ethnocriticism* (1992), p. 3. Krupat defines multiculturalism in a way that moves it beyond pedagogy into critical practice.

26. Gloria Anzaldúa, "En rapport, In Opposition: Cobrando cuentas a las nuestras," *Making Face, Making Soul,* p. 146.

27. Vizenor's collection of essays, *Narrative Chance,* contains some interesting postmodernist perspectives, but as reviewer Bonnie J. Barthold observes: "Theory in *Narrative Chance* is ammunition. What is troublesome is a certain sameness of pattern in the discourse of the essays themselves. Theory, accepted at face value, is privileged by being rather unquestioningly brought into play. Its connections with Native American narrative are drawn self-consciously enough that a text sometimes emerges as something like the illustration of a theory, with Bakhtin and the others cast as ringmasters who set the narratives, who [*sic*] are mostly obedient, into motion. I looked for more occasions when the narratives might be allowed to interrogate the ringmaster." Bonnie J. Barthold, *Studies in American Indian Literature* 3, no. 2 (1991): 81. Gerald Vizenor, ed., *Narrative Chance: Postmodern Discourse on Native American Indian Literatures* (Albuquerque: University of New Mexico Press, 1989).

28. Vizenor himself remarks, "Serious attention to cultural hyperrealities is an invitation to trickster discourse, an imaginative liberation in comic narratives; the trickster is postmodern" (p. 281). I take him here to be reenacting the dualisms he is so critical of, such as "serious" and "comic."

29. See Christian and Anzaldúa, cited in note 23, on the idea of narrative as criticism.

30. Wilma Mankiller, Keynote Address, American Indian Visions Conference, Sweet Briar College, Sweet Briar, Va., 2 April 1993.

Works Cited

Allen, Paula Gunn, ed. *Spider Woman's Granddaughters: Traditional Tales and Contemporary Writing by Native American Women.* Boston: Beacon Press, 1989.

———. *The Sacred Hoop: Recovering the Feminine in American Indian Traditions.* Boston: Beacon Press, 1986.

Babcock-Abrahams, Barbara. In "'A Tolerated Margin of Mess': The Trickster and His Tales Reconsidered." *Critical Essays on American Literature,* ed. Andrew Wiget. Boston: G. K. Hall, 1985, pp. 153–185.

Ballinger, Franchot. "Living Sideways: Social Themes and Social Relationships in Native American Trickster Tales." *Studies in American Indian Literature* 24 (1989): 15–30.

Barthold, Bonnie J. Review of *Narrative Chance* by Gerald Vizenor. *Studies in American Indian Literature* 3, no. 2 (1991): 81.

Christian, Barbara. "The Race for Theory." In *Making Face, Making Soul, Haciendo Caras: Creative and Critical Perspectives by Women of Color,* ed. Gloria Anzaldúa. San Francisco: Aunt Lute Foundation, 1990, pp. 335–345.

Fenton, William N. "Introduction to the Bison Books Edition," "Twentgowa and the Mischief Maker." In *Seneca Myths and Folk Tales,* ed. Arthur C. Parker. Lincoln: University of Nebraska Press, 1989.

———. "'This Island, The World on Turtle's Back.'" In *Critical Essays on American Literature,* ed. Andrew Wiget. Boston: G. K. Hall, 1985, pp. 134–136.

Johnson, Barbara. *A World of Difference.* Baltimore: Johns Hopkins University Press, 1987.

Kolodny, Annette. "Dancing Between Left and Right: Feminism and the Academic Minefield in the 1980s." In *Literature, Language, and Politics,* ed. Betty Jean Craige. Athens: University of Georgia Press, 1988, pp. 27–38.

Krupat, Arnold. *Ethnocriticism: Ethnography History Literature.* Berkeley: University of California Press, 1992.

———. *The Voice in the Margin, Native American Literature and the Canon.* Berkeley: University of California Press, 1989.

———. "Post-Structuralism and Oral Literature." In *Recovering the Word: Essays on Native American Literature,* ed. Arnold Krupat and Brian Swann. Berkeley: University of California Press, 1987, pp. 113–128.

Lauter, Paul. "The Two Criticisms: Structure, Lingo, and Power in the Discourse of Academic Humanists." In *Literature, Language, and Politics,* ed. Betty Jean Craige. Athens: University of Georgia Press, 1988, pp. 1–19.

Lincoln, Kenneth. "Native American Literatures." In *Smoothing the Ground: Essays on Native American Oral Literature,* ed. Brian Swann. Berkeley: University of California Press, 1983, pp. 3–38.

Mankiller, Wilma. Keynote Address, American Indian Visions Conference, Sweet Briar College, Sweet Briar, Virginia, 2 April 1993.

Parker, Arthur C., ed. *Seneca Myths and Folk Tales.* Lincoln: University of Nebraska Press, 1989.

Pope, Polly. "Toward a Structural Analysis of North American Trickster Tales." *Southern Folklore Quarterly* 31 (1967): 274–286.

Ricketts, Mac Linscott. "The North American Indian Trickster." *History of Religions* 5 (1966), pp. 327–350.

Rogers, Phyllis. "The Role of Women in the Creation of the Iroquois Confederacy: A Reinterpretation." Women's Studies Colloquium, Colby College, Waterville, Maine, March 1990.

Ruoff, A. LaVonne Brown, and Jerry W. Ward. *Redefining American Literary History.* New York: Modern Language Association of America, 1990.

Showalter, Elaine. "Feminism and Literature." In *Literary Theory Today,* eds. Peter Collier and Helga Geyer-Ryan. Ithaca: Cornell University Press, 1990, pp. 179–202.

Swann, Brian, ed. *Smoothing the Ground: Essays on Native American Oral Literature.* Berkeley: University of California Press, 1983.

Vizenor, Gerald. "Trickster Discourse." *American Indian Quarterly* 14 (1990), pp. 277–288.

———. *Narrative Chance: Postmodern Discourse on Native American Indian Literatures.* Albuquerque: University of New Mexico Press, 1989.

Wallace, Anthony F. C. *The Death and Rebirth of the Seneca.* New York: Vintage, 1972.

Wiget, Andrew. "His Life in His Tail: The Native American Trickster and the Literature of Possibility." In *Redefining American Literary History,* eds. A. LaVonne Brown Ruoff and Jerry W. Ward. New York: Modern Language Association of America, 1990, pp. 83–96.

———. *Native American Literature.* Boston: Twayne, 1985.

Zolbrod, Paul. Review of Seneca Myths and Folk Tales. *Studies in American Indian Literature* 3, no. 1 (1991).

LYNDA KOOLISH

Spies in the Enemy's House: Folk Characters as Tricksters in Frances E. W. Harper's *Iola Leroy*

The American Negro slave, adopting Brer Rabbit as hero, represented him as the most frightened and helpless of creatures. No hero-animals in Africa or elsewhere were so completely lacking in strength. But the slave took pains to give Brer Rabbit other significant qualities. He became in their stories by turn a practical joker, a braggart, a wit, a glutton, a lady's man, and a trickster. But his essential characteristic was his ability to get the better of bigger and stronger animals. To the slave in his condition the theme of weakness overcoming strength through cunning proved endlessly fascinating.
ARNA BONTEMPS AND LANGSTON HUGHES

The trickster is more than a negative example or a safety valve to release unacceptable impulses. Like the bizarre behavior sanctioned during liminal periods in *rites de passage,* the trickster's antics create an anti-structure that offers a static social order the potential for change. He shakes up the elements of culture and scatters them in a kaleidoscope of novelty that projects visions of hitherto unforeseen alternatives. Traditional cultures change slowly, and marginal folly is not revolutionary. Still, when social pressures impel change, the anti-structure available in the trickster's folly offers options for rethinking culture.
ANNA K. NARDO

Frances E. W. Harper's *Iola Leroy, or Shadows Uplifted* has had no dearth of critics; until very recently (after its initial favorable response when first published in 1892), the novel has been condemned—and, I would argue, profoundly misread, especially in regard to the function of the folk characters. Various critics have referred to it as tediously ennobling, "as dull as it is pious," sentimental, assimilationist, didactic, an advocate of the concerns of the intellectual elite, a text that emphasizes the mulatto characters' "guilt and displacement," and—in perhaps the most contemptuous of current critical assessments—a book that possesses a plot that is both "creakingly mechanical and entirely predictable."[1] Barbara Christian's summation of *Iola Leroy* consolidates all of the critics' negative reactions. In *Black Women Novelists,* she describes Iola's motivations as "giv[ing] to the black race what she has learned from the white culture. And what culture means is Western Christian civilization at its best. She becomes, then, a cultural missionary to the ignorant, the loudmouthed, the coarse but essentially good-natured blacks, who need only to be shown the way" (p. 29).

Frances Smith Foster's recent appreciative introduction to the Schomburg edition of *Iola Leroy* discusses the novel's earlier reception, noting the degree to which Harper's novel, originally well-received, "had fallen from critical favor" by 1911, the time of Harper's death. She goes on to observe other critics' unflattering depictions of the novel, including W. E. B. Du Bois's perception that Harper "was not a great writer, but she wrote much worth reading. She was, above all, sincere," words damning the novel with what now reads as the same faint praise of critics, such as William Still, before him (p. xxxvi).

Certainly, like other early African American novelists discussed by Arlene Elder in *The "Hindered Hand": Cultural Implications of Early African-American Fiction,* Frances Harper experienced the tension between the desire to "educate and protest" and "the artistic need to express truthfully the complexities and ironies of being Black in America" (p. xi). The early novelists, she insists, "were not composing belle lettres; they were manufacturing literary weapons" (p. 40). Despite the pathbreaking importance of Elder's book—and the fact that she was among the few critics of early African American fiction to praise the depiction of folk characters as a wellspring of authenticity regarding the "Black experience and sensibility" (p. 54)—Elder has consistently viewed the folk characters in *Iola Leroy* as "secondary" or "minor," claiming Aunt Linda as "an amusing realistic foil for the book's idealized heroine, Iola" (pp. 9, 56). In contrast, Richard Yarborough's dissertation on early African American novels acknowledges that Harper's folk characters are complexly drawn, and cites the slaves' use of farm and produce terms to surreptitiously discuss war developments, adding that "what Harper emphasizes here is that the complexity of slave thought and motivation was to be found in that subterranean layer of interactions and coded behavior underlying the veneer of simplicity and disingenuousness which white writers could not pierce" (pp. 222–223). Yet even Yarborough claims that despite her "forthright, earthy, commonsense" opinions, Aunt Linda is "*conservative* in many of her ways" (pp. 222–223, emphasis mine). Hazel Carby, while acknowledging the folk in this novel as a somewhat autonomous community who resist and subvert attempts to control their lives, nonetheless sees Harper's representation of them as only a "marginal improvement over [William Wells] Brown's portrayal of the folk as buffoons in *Clotel*."[2]

More recent criticism, while still focused heavily on the educated octoroon characters, particularly Iola herself, has nevertheless begun the important work of rescuing Frances Harper's novel from these false critical assumptions. Elizabeth Young's brilliant 1992 *American Literature* essay, "Warring Fictions: *Iola Leroy* and the Color of Gender," is among the first genuinely new readings of the novel—one that offers no apologies for either its content or its form. In her reading of *Iola Leroy* as a war narrative, Young reveals a complexity in the novel no critic until now has ascribed to it. John Ernest, also in a 1992 issue of *American Literature,* confirms *Iola Leroy* as a "subtle and intricate novel" (p. 511), one in which Harper is alive to the subversive possibilities of language; he reveals his respect for the novel's "interracial politics and intraracial aims" (p. 502).

Henry Louis Gates, Jr., is to my knowledge the first critic to have considered *Iola Leroy*'s success as having as much to do with its folk characters as with its educated mulatto heroine. In his Introduction to *Three Classic African-American Novels,* Gates insists that

> *Iola Leroy* contains the richest and fullest representation of black dialect to be found in the nineteenth-century novel. At the same time, its characterization of the mulatto protagonist as an independent, self-conscious agent is a bold critique of the standard conventions of representing mulattos in the American novel as ambivalent, tortured, or unreliable. The female protagonist in *Iola Leroy* is the most noble and compelling black woman character in black fiction before the turn of the century. As an account of black life during Reconstruction, as an indictment of racial discrimination in the North and South, and in its technical experimentation with both dialogue and black vernacular speech as a counterpoint to standard English, *Iola Leroy* has a major place in the history of African-American fiction. (p. xiv)

If, as Gates asserts, *Iola Leroy* "is, as Sterling A. Brown has noted, a direct revision of Brown's *Clotel*" (p. xiv), it is my belief that Harper's "revision" stands in relation to *Clotel* as Jean Rhys's *Wide Sargasso Sea* stands in relationship to Charlotte Brontë's *Jane Eyre*; that is, as a radically re-visioning, re-imagining, re-vising critique of the earlier novel.

Even with recent sympathetic interpretations of the text, it is my belief that *Iola Leroy, or Shadows Uplifted* has been misread for the more than one hundred years of its existence. I will argue that a subversive subtext, specially written in encoded language, exists in the novel, and is in fact its center. Within my reading, the folk character Linda, and the other folk characters, not the putative heroine, Iola, are the central protagonists of the novel. These characters function as trickster figures whose encoded language serves as a form of communication that "simultaneously protest[s] the effects of [oppression] and maintain[s] the secrecy of that very same protest" (Hemenway, p. 51). The conscious artistic decision of Harper to use her folk characters to provide a counternovel within the novel, a play within a play, rescues the novel from allegations of woodenness, melodrama, and predictability.[3]

Iola Leroy's strongest sense of community and of racial pride stems from the folk characters Linda, her husband John Salters, Jinnie, and Uncle Daniel. The source of this novel's power lies in its withheld meanings, which reveal themselves slowly to most readers, who have been taught to believe that *Iola Leroy* reflects an essentially conservative posture. A resisting reader of the text discovers that Harper's subversive intentions and powerful awareness of her own self-worth are echoed and revealed in Aunt Linda, who insists "ef you buys me for a fool you loses your money shore" (p. 10).

Harper subversively miscasts Aunt Linda as "the embodiment of content and good humor" (p. 153) while simultaneously providing us with evidence that Aunt Linda is neither content nor good-humored but, instead, feisty, angry, righteous, politically savvy, and beholden to none. Further, Harper provides ample evidence within the novel that the apparent good humor of all her folk characters is nothing more than a necessary disguise: Marie, Iola's mother, provides the clue. In a long passage in which she defends the mask of servility and the fierce anger beneath the mask in enslaved Africans, Marie encodes Harper's racially based as well as gendered strategy of telling all the truth, but telling it slant. Rather than acquiescing in the prevailing view that "lying is said to be the vice of slaves" (p. 79), Marie, articulating Harper's views of her own characters, insists that "the more intelligent of them have so learned to veil their feelings that you do not see the undercurrent of discontent beneath their apparent good humor and jollity. The more discontented they are, the more I respect them. To me a contented slave is an abject creature" (p. 79). Other characters who resist their surface depictions include Jinny and Jake (p. 79), who appear in the novel as submissive darky caricatures, Jinny comforting her Mistress about the war news, and Jake "skylarking" about and appearing to be without "a thimbleful of sense" (p. 11). Yet each of these folk characters is a spy in the enemy's house, listening closely to white people conversing. Thus a mirror emerges throughout the book; the white characters become hapless victims of misreading the slaves' actions, just as most readers have been hapless victims of misreading the novel.[4]

At the beginning of the book, Aunt Linda is introduced to the reader by her conversation with Robert about the freshness of the butter, eggs, and fish, a device by which various black characters reveal to each other encoded news abut the events of the war.[5] Later in the text, Colonel Robinson reveals the story of an African American woman—who could be Aunt Linda, and who serves also as a double for Harriet Tubman, soldier, scout and spy—who keeps the Union troops posted as to Rebel movements via the hanging of laundry sheets in various positions.[6] Harper opens the novel not only with black folk characters who are revealed as shrewd manipulators of codes and disguises—images central to African animal trickster figures—but with what is perhaps the most characteristic trickster figure from African American slave narratives: a slave who claims himself as the consummate repossessor of his own identity. Observing that a character "was known among his acquaintances as 'Marster Anderson's Tom,'" the narrator nevertheless refers to the character with the far more dignified appellation "Thomas Anderson," thus quietly asserting the rights of slaves to a name and an identity that does not connote ownership by others.

These encoded strategies may also be seen as a direct metaphor for Harper's methodology. In providing a coded, subversive subtext, frequently revealed in dialect and addressed to a specifically black audience, Harper herself becomes a kind of trickster in this novel.[7] Through the vehicle of her educated mulatto characters, she addresses the concerns of her white audience and publishers while simultaneously providing encoded clues that signify to her black audience that the words of her folk characters are being addressed *sotto voce* to them.[8] The reasons for this encoding are revealed in passages about Robert, who frequently serves as Harper's political and methodological *doppelganger* in the novel. He echoes her acute sense of the danger of direct expression (in Robert's case, violence; in Harper's case, the violence of silencing—without caution, her words might never find their way to print). It is Robert as Harper's double for whom "in the depth of his soul the love of freedom was an all-absorbing passion; only danger had taught him caution. . . . Robert knew that he might abandon hope if he incurred the wrath of men whose overthrow was only a question of time" (p. 35). Raymond Hedin's observation that "the expression of anger at white racists has been a particularly risky emotion for black writers given their awareness that inherent savagery and lack of control have long been alleged to the black race" (p. 36) may explain Harper's sense of danger and caution, the very reason that she makes her folk characters appear foolish and ignorant at times. By so doing, she sets up a situation in which educated mulatto characters disabuse racial stereotypes allegedly held not by white racists but by ignorant blacks, thus making her white audience so comfortably dismissive of these illiterate characters that it fails to notice when the folk subsequently advocate extraordinarily radical actions or sentiments.

Folk character John Salters, while not depicted as foolish, nonetheless serves as a foil for Robert's soliloquy on comparative justice for the two races. When Salters observes of his people that they don't drink "any more dan anybody else, nor dat dere is any meanness or debilment dat a black man kin do dat a white man can't keep step wid him" (p. 170), Robert responds with an observation that reveals Harper's hidden agenda. Not only does he indict the failure of the American justice system equitably to administer punishment ("while a white man is stealing a thousand dollars, a black man is getting into trouble taking a few chickens," p. 170), but Harper uses the dialogue between educated and folk characters to raise surreptitiously the Marxist allegation of a literal theft of labor—for the "thousand dollars" a white man steals without retribution is the approximate cost of a skilled field hand at auction. The educated characters do not, however, directly challenge the racism of those who interact with them. They explore theoretical, moral issues, but when Robert's old mistress, Miss Nancy, scolds him for leaving her and ironically offers to "let by-gones be by-gones" (p. 152), he does nothing to disabuse her of the monstrous self-indulgence of a slave-owner who feels victimized by the departure of his or her slave.

Harper also undercuts the sanctimoniousness of the mulatto characters toward the folk characters. Robert, for example, offers a long and earnest sermon for Tom Anderson's benefit on the necessity of not trusting the word of a white man, insisting, " 'Tom, you must not think because a white man says a thing, it must be so, and that a colored man's word is no account 'longside of his. Tom, if ever we get our freedom, we've got to learn to trust each other and stick together if we would be a people" (p. 34). Counteracting this speech, Harper makes certain that the reader knows that Tom Anderson is at least as savvy as his more educated counterpart; when Daniel reveals his reasons for remaining on his master's plantation—Marse Robert's promise "ef he died fust he war gwine ter leave [Daniel] free"—Tom responds in no uncertain terms about the folly of trusting a white man's word: " 'Oh, Sho!' " said Tom, " 'promises, like pie crusts, is made to be broken. I don't trust none ob dem. I'se been yere dese fifteen years, an' I'se neber foun' any troof in dem' " (p. 25). Whether the antecedent to Tom's pronoun "dem" as the group of things or people not to be trusted is white men's promises, or more likely—and more subversively—simply white men, is left deliberately ambiguous by Harper. In either case, it would appear that Tom is nobody's fool, and certainly not in need of the dubious benefits of Robert's attempts to uplift the folk. Harper does not spare her educated mulatto characters' vanity, either, slyly deflating Robert's somewhat smug belief in his own worldliness. When Robert, "a little vain of his superior knowledge" (p. 16), discusses the term "contraband of war" (p. 16) with his unlettered friends Uncle Daniel and Tom Anderson, he explains that slaves who escape and reach the Union army are protected by laws that proclaim them as property. Announcing this as "the best kind of good" (p. 16), he misses completely the irony of the underlying, morally bankrupt principles of such "protection."

Through the folk characters, Harper slips the yoke and plays the joke on her white readers. While her educated octoroon heroine and other mulatto characters speak in educated white English to her white audience (including publishers) to convince them of the very basic principle that African Americans are capable, intelligent, moral human beings, her folk characters speak in code to black readers in a deliberately awkward vernacular and articulate the most important political issues in the novel. While the Reverend Carmichael, Lucille Delaney, Harry, Iola, and Robert discuss a number of social issues regarding the necessity of thrift, education, self-control, manliness, temperance and the like—issues reflecting values more of class than of race—the folk characters deftly puncture the myth of white Southern honor, courage, and fair play.

Harper provides many instances of trickster behavior among her folk characters. John W. Roberts's *From Trickster to Badman: The Black Folk Hero in Slavery and Freedom* reveals how the African animal trickster tale "offered a model of behavior for equalizing conditions between masters and slaves by breaking the rules of a system that gave the slavemasters a clear economic, political, and social advantage. It, in essence, functioned as an outlaw tradition within the value system of slavery" (p. 185). In Harper's novel, as in the traditional African trickster tales, the paradigm of the powerless overcoming a much more powerful adversary by means of subterfuge holds true. Tom, for example, pretends to be an old slug-a-bed, apparently lazily snoring away on the porch; meanwhile, he too is a spy in the enemy's house, alive to his nerve endings, straining to overhear every word when his master is conversing with Confederate generals about the war. As John W. Roberts might describe him, Tom is a "trickster who could adeptly step inside his dupe's sense of reality and manipulate it through wit, guile and deception" (p. 185). Tom's master's patronizing belief in the myth of the slave system as some kind of cooperative, benign enterprise, with each of the participants happy to remain in his or her assigned role, leaves him vulnerable to Tom's disingenuous trickster behavior.

Appearing to acquiesce while radically resisting—"overcom[ing] 'em with yeses, undermin[ing] 'em with grins" (Ellison, p. 16)—is a trickster theme more prevalent in African American folk tales than in the slave narratives, in which, as Frances Smith Foster suggests, "the dominant figure is the innocent victim, and the emphasis after freedom is upon the attainment of literacy, Christianity, and white middle-class values" (*Witnessing*, p. 141). But in feminist re-visionings of the slave narrative, as in much recent African American literature generally, the image of the trickster and the theme of lying have been preeminent, for as Henry Louis Gates, Jr., suggests, "Black people have always been masters of the figurative: saying one thing to mean something quite other has been basic to black survival in oppressive Western cultures. Misreading signs could be, and indeed often was, fatal" ("Criticism in the Jungle," p. 6).

In *Minnie's Sacrifice*, a serialized novel written by Harper and published in the *Christian Recorder* in 1869, some twenty years prior to *Iola Leroy*, Harper is explicit in revealing her folk characters as tricksters whose cunning and subterfuge triumph over the more powerful "Massa." Like Iola, Louis in *Minnie's Sacrifice* is a light-skinned character who originally believes himself to be white and subsequently claims the African American race as his own (although, unlike Iola, he has to overcome a certain repugnance toward his darker brothers). Despite an unfortunate dialect that seems almost a parody of black vernacular, Harper's folk character Sam is a trickster figure who provides crucial information to the fleeing Louis:

> "I'll get you a place to hide where nobody can't find you, and then I'll pump Massa 'bout the sojers."
>
> True to his word, he contrived to find out whether the soldiers were near.
>
> "Massa," said he, scratching his head, and looking quite sober. "Massa, hadn't I better hide the mules? Oh I's afraid the Linkum sojers will come take 'em, cause dey gobbles up ebery ting dey lays dere hans on, jis like geese. I yerd dey was coming; mus' I hide de mules?"
>
> "No, Sam, the scalawags are more than a hundred miles away; they are near Natchez."
>
> "Well, maybe, t'was our own Fedrate soldiers."
>
> "No, Sam, our nearest soldiers are at Baton Rouge."
>
> "All right Massa. I don't want to lose all dem fine mules."
>
> As soon as it was convenient Sam gave Louis the desired information. (N.Pag.)

Sam's clumsy and self-effacing dialect provides a necessary disguise, orchestrating the release of information by encouraging his dupe's patronizing sense of superiority and owed allegiance. Failing to see Sam as either an antagonist or an equal, his master sees no necessity to be wary lest he disclose information that potentially could be used against himself.

Ironically, Harper's use of dialect in *Iola Leroy* has played a major role in the repudiation of the novel by most critics, who seem unable to see that Harper employs dialect to much the same end as do her folk characters: as a conscious device by which to disseminate or gather information surreptitiously. Like her contemporary Charles Chesnutt, who "employ[ed] a tale within a tale technique [thus "framing"] black speech so that in his best stories [he] blends the literary and oral traditions without implying that the black storyteller's mode of perceiving and recreating reality is any less valid than the written word" (Wideman, p. 60), Harper also devised successful strategies for liberating black vernacular from its racist associations. John Edgar Wideman's essay on Chesnutt and the oral and literate roots of African American literature explains why contemporary readers have often felt antagonistic toward the speech patterns Harper attributes to her folk characters. He explains that through the late nineteenth century,

> Negro dialect in drama, fiction and poetry was a way of pointing to the difference between blacks and whites; the form and function of black speech as it was represented was to indicate black inferiority. Black speech, the mirror of black people's mind and character, was codified by dialect into a deviant variety of good English.

Negro dialect lacked proper grammar, its comic orthography suggested ignorance, its "dats" and "dems" and "possums" implied lazy, slovenly pronunciation if not the downright physical impossibility of getting thick lips around the King's English. (p. 60)

In my view, Harper devised a strategy for using dialect that is at least as coded, veiled, and subversive as Charles Chesnutt's or as the ingenious code employed by the folk characters at the beginning of *Iola Leroy*, who substitute produce terms for news about the victories and defeats of the Union army.

Tom Anderson's awkward dialect, for example, serves as the vehicle for Harper's acerbic observation that white Southerners imagined the slaves to be utterly incompetent whereas they had to be—and were—amazingly competent just to survive under the conditions of slavery. In relating the comments of a Rebel general conversing with his former master, Tom ridicules the foolishness of white Southerners in imagining the slaves as unable to care for themselves without the masters' "protection":

"One ob dem [generals] said, dem Yankees war talkin' of puttin' guns in our han's and settin' us all free. An' de oder said, 'Oh, sho! ef dey puts guns in dere hands dey'll soon be in our'n; and ef dey sets em free dey wouldn't know how to take keer ob demselves."

"Only let 'em try it," chorused a half dozen voices, "an' dey'll soon see who'll git de bes' ob de guns; an' as to taking keer ob ourselves, I specs we kin take keer ob ourselves as well as take keer ob dem." (p. 17)

Like Tom, the character Uncle Daniel is also duplicitous; for much of the novel, he appears to be reactionary. His deference to the lighter skinned Robert, whom he attempts to call "Mr. Robert," a title reminiscent of those given slaveowners, is repudiated by Robert, who rejects not only the title but its antebellum associations. Harper undercuts Uncle Daniel as a character worth taking seriously in other ways as well; she allows him to espouse incredibly foolish advice to Robert Johnson, whom he tells, "you've got a good owner. You don't hab to run away from bad times and wuss a comin'" (p. 17). Daniel further appears to promulgate the myth of the good slave owner by claiming that his owner, Marse Robert, loved him and deserved the loyalty that kept Daniel from seeking his own freedom. However, while refusing to claim freedom for himself, Daniel also indicts the entire system of slavery: "I'se de same Uncle Dan'el I eber war. Ef any ob you wants to go, I habben't a word to say agin it. I specs dem Yankees be all right, but I knows Marse Robert, an' I don't know dem, an' I ain't a gwine ter throw away *dirty water* 'til I gits clean" (p. 29 emphasis mine). In this passage, soft-spoken as it is, Daniel articulates the most radically subversive statement in the entire novel: that Marse Robert, whom Daniel treated as a son, whom Daniel repeatedly referred to as a good master, was, like all masters, essentially contaminated by slavery.

Daniel's apparently abject loyalty to his master also serves as a foil for Tom Anderson's trickster behavior. In the frame of a tale within a tale, Daniel becomes a storyteller, relating to Tom the incident which causes him to choose not to seek his freedom:

> "No, Tom; I can't go. When Marse Robert went to de front, he called me to him an' said: 'Uncle Daniel,' an' he was drefful pale when he said it, 'I are gwine to de war, an' I want yer to take keer of my wife an' chillen, jis' like yer used to take keer of me wen yer called me yer little boy.' Well, dat jis' got to me, an' I couldn't help crying, to save my life." (p. 25)

Fellow folk character Tom Anderson becomes in this passage the trickster wise man as opposed to the trickster fool; his profoundly ironic retort to the sentimental propaganda of the white master's expectation of loyalty demolishes Uncle Daniel's position in a single swift line: "'I specs,' said Tom, 'your tear bags must lie mighty close to your eyes'" (p. 25). In creating debates between folk characters, or having one folk character appear wise in one instance and incredibly foolish the next, Harper participates in the trickster tradition, for as Anna K. Nardo observes about the trickster, "because he prances along the margins that define society, he is radically ambiguous—smart and stupid, a menace and a hero. In one episode, he comically outwits his opponents, often with clever verbal subterfuge, but in another he is grossly gulled" (p. 2).

Uncle Daniel—also foolish at one moment, but wise the next—is the vehicle through which Harper explores the charged, tenuous connection between white women and women of color that arises out of their shared subjugation under patriarchy. While Iola is the spokesperson for Harper's less incendiary—but still remarkably forward-looking—feminist sentiments (among them, for example, that women's ability to be financially self-supporting would ensure fewer unhappy marriages), the folk characters subversively stake out far more controversial territory. Already depicted as more conservative than other folk characters for his loyalty to Marse Robert and his consequent refusal to seek his own freedom, Uncle Daniel is a trickster figure who appears to be similarly conservative—even reactionary—about issues of gender, claiming, "well, women's mighty curious kind of folks anyhow. I sometimes thinks de wuss you treats dem de better dey likes you" (p. 20). Yet by inscribing white patriarchal power as abusively directed not just at a contained and virtually defenseless population of slave women but at white women as well, Uncle Daniel's description of Marse Robert's father turning a deaf ear to his wife's entreaties against the brutality of the plantation overseer reveals the essential powerlessness of all women under patriarchy; he tells Tom, "I never thought ole Marster was good to [his wife]. I often ketched her crying, an' she'd say she had de headache, but I thought it was de heartache" (p. 20).[9]

Shedding his conservative depiction in other ways as well, Uncle Daniel plays a trickster role as the articulator of the racism of white women. As Elizabeth Ammons has pointed out, there are numerous instances in which Harper indicts the racism of white women in the novel, among them

> the white women who refuse to visit the Leroy plantation after Iola's father marries her mother, a former slave . . . the white women who run an asylum for fallen women but turn black women away; the white working girls who will not work side by side with Iola; the white Christian working girls' association that refuses a room to a black Christian working girl; and the white temperance women who set up segregated black associations for their sisters in struggle. (Ammons, p. 33)

But these incidents, repugnant as they are, are nevertheless rendered by Harper "with a light touch," as Ammons says (p. 33). When Harper wishes to unleash her most revealing denunciation of the violent and brutal abuse of power by white women corrupted by racism, she turns not to incidents involving Iola or her other educated mulatto characters, but to the folk characters, especially Uncle Daniel. Under cover of dialect and the frame of characters' storytelling within the narration of the novel, Harper confronts the complicity of her white audience while she acknowledges the anguish of her black audience. Uncle Daniel's story, as Ammons also goes on to discuss, is not of being treated ungraciously by co-workers or refused a room, but of being unable to protect his wife and himself from the gratuitous cruelty of his mistress, who refuses them the right to bury their child when the child dies suddenly of illness. His story is of living under the power of a mistress who is capable of "order[ing] a woman whipped 'cause she com'd to de field a little late when her husban war sick, an' she stopped to tend him" (p. 27). While Iola's story of being "tried but . . . never tempted" (p. 115) suggests that she successfully resists the sexual advances of her master, Daniel's comment, "I specs [Gundover's] wife would almos' turn ober in her grave ef she know'd she had ten culled grandchildren" (p. 27), refers to a far more frequently occurring scenario: that of the repeated rape of black women by slavemasters whose wives chose not to intervene—or more cruelly, who blamed the victim, not the rapist, and were especially abusive to any resulting children.[10] Children thus conceived frequently were sold by their white fathers away from their black mothers, creating a condition that Hortense Spillers has described as "enforced kinlessness" among black families (p. 74).

Finally, Harper utilizes Uncle Daniel's conservative appearance to camouflage his advocacy of some of the most subversive ideas concerning religion in the novel. As an Afrocentric preacher to the slaves, a subversive role in itself, Uncle Daniel breaks the slavemasters' unwritten law that every slave is to be dehumanized in every way possible; by preaching, he attempts to give back to black people what has been stolen from them: their humanity. Acknowledging their suffering as akin to Jesus' torment on the cross, Uncle Daniel claims not only the authority of age, but the moral authority of the folk when he angrily tells Robert, "look a yere, boy, I'se been a preachin' dese thirty years, an' you come yere a tellin' me 'bout studying yor ologies. I larn'd my 'ology at de foot ob de cross. You bin dar?" (p. 168). This retort is more than a repudiation of Robert's misguided suggestion that Daniel should formally study the Sunday Christianity of white people's theology; in his allusion here to the slave spiritual "Were You There," Daniel claims a large and serious portion of moral authority by affirming the experience of being a disciple of Christ (Barton, p. 40). Moreover, Daniel's knowledge of slave spirituals encodes to black readers evidence that Daniel, like Harper, values black culture, theology, and language, and recognizes ways of learning and teaching outside of accepted traditional white western forms and institutions of knowledge. Uncle Daniel claims spiritual kinship with Jesus not only through suffering but through knowledge, not book learning, as Robert and Iola suggest, but through life. As James H. Cone observes in *The Spirituals and the Blues: An Interpretation,* "through the blood of slavery, [slaves] transcended the limitations of space and time. Jesus' time became their time, and they encountered a new historical existence. Through the experience of being slaves, they encountered the theological significance of Jesus' death" (p. 54). Although Iola gently chastises Daniel about the necessity to "subordinate the spirit of caste to the spirit of Christ" (p. 168)—a comforting capitulation to liberal notions that no one should claim a special relationship with God and a response that, in fact, denies the validity of Daniel's own powerful spiritual connection to Christianity—it is clear that Daniel's theological vision and not Iola's is the one being offered to black readers in this novel.

The earnest conventional religious sentiments of characters like Iola are played off against the more heart-connected observations of folk characters like Mam Liza, who comforts Marie after Eugene's death from yellow fever by reminding her of the healing power of a deep and intimate faith in Jesus Christ: "'Oh, honey,'" said Mam Liza, "'yer musn't gib up. Yer knows whar to put yer trus'. Yer can't lean on de arm of flesh in dis tryin' time'" (p. 94). The religious faith of Mam Liza and other folk characters lends moral force to the trickster aspect of Aunt Linda and Tom Anderson, who, under cover of some of the thickest dialect in the novel, offer an emphatic condemnation of Christian hypocrisy. Tom Anderson's defiant comment, "I belieb in de good ole-time religion. But arter dese white folks is done fussin' and beatin' de cullud folks, I don't want 'em to come talking religion to me" (p. 22) reveals a point of view that seems directly borrowed from Frederick Douglass's *Narrative*:

> I love the pure, peaceable, and impartial Christianity of Christ; I therefore hate the corrupt, slaveholding, women-whipping, cradle-plundering partial and hypocritical Christianity of this land. Indeed, I can see no reason, but the most deceitful one, for calling the religion of this land Christianity. . . . We have men-stealers for ministers, women-whippers for missionaries, and cradle-plunderers for church members. The man who wields the blood-clotted cowskin during the week fills the pulpit on Sunday, and claims to be a minister of the meek and lowly Jesus. (pp. 117–118)

More radically, Aunt Linda's acerbic repudiation of the hypocrisy of some black ministers, "An' wen dey preaches, I want dem to practice wat dey preach. Some ob dem says dey's called, but I jis' thinks laziness called some ob dem," tackles an arena that few early African American writers of any genre were willing to take on (p. 161).

Through the voices of the folk characters, we as readers come to care about the lives that are revealed to us in this novel. Folk character Tom Anderson's voice has the power that Iola's lacks. When she piously tells him, "I should be so lonely without you," he speaks to her of God's comfort in resonant, affecting language: "Dere's a frien' dat sticks closer dan a brudder" (p. 54). Like poet Gwendolyn Brooks, Frances Harper wrote with great formality, but had she lived to see the day when Gwendolyn Brooks, in 1950, would be the first black woman poet to receive the Pulitzer Prize, she might have acknowledged more overtly the urgency that she does in fact share with Brooks, to write without constraint in black language. Brooks's poem, "a song in the front yard," seems as applicable to Harper's life and work as it does to Brooks's own:

> I've stayed in the front yard all my life.
> I want a peek at the back
> Where it's rough and untended and hungry weed grows.
> A girl gets sick of a rose. (1971, p. 10)

Aunt Linda's rough and untended speech serves to camouflage her radical political views. The constant characterization of Linda as a jolly, ignorant, dark-skinned mammy figure allows Harper's white audience to feel unthreatened by both Reconstruction and Aunt Linda. The role she plays is dual in *Iola Leroy*; within a conventional reading of the text, she provides a contrast to Iola, appearing not only unlettered but profoundly ignorant, unwilling to learn to read even after slavery is abolished. When Iola offers to teach Linda to read, she refuses, insisting, "oh, yer can't git dat book froo my head, no way you fix it. I knows nuff to git to hebben, and dats all I wants to know," and informs Robert "I think it would gib me de hysterics ef I war to try to git book larnin' froo my pore ole head" (pp. 276, 156). Since much of the novel concerns itself with issues of education and literacy, and their importance as a measure of the possibility and future toward which the race must struggle to ascend, Aunt Linda's protests about learning to read deserve some scrutiny regarding their function in the novel. The existence of Harper's "Aunt Chloe" poems, especially "Learning to Read," encourages speculation as to why Harper depicts Aunt Linda as so emphatically protesting against learning to read. These poems, published in *Sketches of Southern Life* twenty years earlier than *Iola Leroy,* provide a clue to Harper's strategy in depicting Tom Anderson as a version of Uncle Caldwell, and Aunt Linda as a version of Aunt Chloe. Aunt Chloe serves as Aunt Linda's prototype in every respect except the most crucial one: her stance toward literacy.[11] In contrast, Robert's description of Tom as someone who "never got very far with his learning" nevertheless emphasizes Tom's earnest and courageous attempts to master the ability to read. Harper's story of how Tom attempts to avoid being caught with reading material by greasing the pages of a book and hiding it in his hat is borrowed directly from "Learning to Read," in which Uncle Caldwell clearly serves as a literary double for Tom Anderson.[12] Aunt Linda's protests against learning to read seem especially curious given the existence of this poem, for it celebrates her literary precursor Aunt Chloe's triumphant and queenly acquisition of book learning:

And, I longed to read my Bible,
    For precious words it said;
But when I begun to read it,
    Folks just shook their heads.

And said there is no use trying,
    Oh! Chloe, you're too late;
But as I was rising sixty,
    I had no time to wait.

So I got a pair of glasses,
    And straight to work I went,
And never stopped till I could read
    The hymns and Testament.[13]

Given Harper's political agenda, and her hope that her fiction would inspire a determination among her people to "embrace every opportunity, develop every faculty, and use every power God has given them to rise in the scale of character and condition" (Afterword to *Iola,* p. 282), Harper must have hoped that the characterization of Aunt Linda would be at least as effective as the characterization of her earlier creation, Aunt Chloe, in promoting integrity, courage and accomplishments among African Americans. Why, then, is her most important folk character not only unable to read, but apparently unwilling?

It is my belief that Harper hoped that by denigrating Aunt Linda's obvious abilities and intelligence and utilizing a peculiarly awkward dialect for her most self-deprecating speeches, she would enable black readers to perceive that they had been cued to disregard the content of those speeches.

Through the vehicle of the folk characters, Frances Harper, with all her commitment to education, challenges the notion that the rights of human beings and their very status as human can in any way legitimately be tied to their mastery of the word. The opening of the novel, with Aunt Linda's pronouncement, "I can't read de newspaper, but ole Missus' face is newspaper nuff for me" (p. 9) reveals Harper's respect for the dignity, wisdom, and worth of the least "educated" of her characters. When Iola becomes a school teacher, her students, the members of the folk, are able to read her face long before they can read the alphabet: "Her face was a passport to their hearts. Ignorant of books, human faces were the scrolls from which they had been reading for ages" (p. 146). This unconventional folk mastery of a kind of literacy is, I believe, meant to invoke the dialogue begun by Sojourner Truth, whose much-quoted 1851 speech insists that the attainment of literacy not be the point of demarcation between those who should be accorded their rights and those who should not:

> "Den dey talks 'bout dis ting in de head—what dis dey call it?" "Intellect," whispered some one near. "Dat's it, honey. What's dat got to do with woman's rights or niggers' rights? If my cup won't hold but a pint and yours hold a quart, wouldn't you be mean not to let me have my little half-measure full?"[14]

Further, the difficulties Aunt Linda, John Salters, and Tom Anderson have with reading represent the very real obstacles facing newly freed slaves under Reconstruction. Aunt Linda's resistance to reading is revealed by Harper as a kind of post-traumatic stress disorder, for like Robert Johnson, whose mistress' cousin suggests cutting off his thumbs to keep him from writing when she discovers that he can read, write, and do accounts (p. 46), Aunt Linda associates attempting to learn to read with acts of bodily violence directed against her. In the beginning of the novel, she tells Robert: "'I allers wanted to learn how to read. I once had a book, and tried to make out what war in it, but ebery time my mistus caught me wid a book in my hand, she used to whip my fingers'" (p. 22). An embodiment of the spirit of resistance, Aunt Linda transcends the cruelty and fear associated with this memory, and quickly offers to Robert the defiant observation: "'an' I couldn't see ef [reading] war good for white folks, why it warn't good for collud folks'" (p. 22). Finally, in the very same passage in which Harper reveals that "there was one place that [Aunt Linda] drew the line and that was at reading," she signals the reader that Aunt Linda, too, values literacy for herself, by having her also announce, "I can't read myself, but I likes ter yere dem dat can" (p. 276).

In a similar fashion, Harper signals the reader to sympathize with the difficulty that folk character John Salters has with reading. Salters announces, "on Sundays I sometimes takes a book an' tries to make out de words, but my eyes is getting dim an' de letters all run togedder, an' I gits sleepy, an' ef yer wants to put me to sleep jis' put a book in my han'. But wen it comes to gettin' out a stan' ob cotton, an' plantin' corn, I'se dere all de time. But dat gran'son ob mine is smart as a steel trap. I specs he'll be a preacher" (p. 171). As this passage suggests, Salters' inability to read is revealed as a function of age and failing eyesight, not lack of intelligence. He may not be able to read, but Harper has proclaimed the importance of literacy by pinning his hopes on his grandchildren's generation. In keeping with the strategy of subversively undercutting her folk characters, Harper describes Salters' promising grandson—the one he plans to send to college—in a rather ridiculous fashion, not as poring over his books, but as a kind of grinning Stepinfetchit, a Buckwheat, munching a pear instead of the proverbial watermelon: "Salters looked admiringly at his grandson, who sat grinning in the corner, munching a pear he had brought from the table" (p. 171).[15] For Harper to provide such a buffoonlike caricature as the slender armature around which to construct a vision of the future generation of black scholars is a clear signal that she intended to reveal such a caricature as a lie, and by extension, that she condemned as false the vicious depictions of shiftless, if not monstrous and deranged, young black men made popular by Thomas Dixon and Thomas Nelson Page of the plantation tradition.

The most outrageous of Harper's denigrations of Aunt Linda is one that suggests that Linda appeared to regard slavery as something deserved, palatable even, when she conjectures as to why black people were enslaved, that "'cullud folks mus' hab done somethin'" (p. 170). This conjecture is so entirely contrary to Aunt Linda's beliefs and function in the novel as a minister, priestess, and teacher that it acts only as a decoy to lure any uncomfortable readers back to the security of imagining polite mulattos and octoroons like Iola and Robert, with their unthreatening notions of racial uplift, as the center of the novel. In other words, the trickster dynamic of the novel is at work here. Robert offers a rebuke to Aunt Linda's apparently reactionary sentiments by insisting, "O, nonsense . . . I don't think [black people] are any worse than the white people. I don't believe, if we had the power, we would do any more lynching, burning, and murdering than they do" (pp. 170–171). But in fact, it is Aunt Linda, not Robert, who acts as both witness and resister to the widespread terrorism, to the lynching and murders that dominated the lives of African Americans during Reconstruction and beyond. It is Aunt Linda, her husband John Salters, and Uncle Daniel who promise the retribution of the younger generation of black people against this violence:

> "It's ralely orful how our folks hab been murdered sence de war. But I don't think dese young folks is goin' ter take things as we's allers done."
>
> "We war cowed down from the beginnin'," said Uncle Daniel, "but dese young folks ain't comin' up dat way."
>
> "No," said Salters, "fer one night arter some ob our pore people had been killed, an' some ob our women had run'd away 'bout seventeen miles, my gran'son, looking me square in de face, said: 'Ain't you got five fingers? Can't you pull a trigger as well as a white man?' I tell yer, Cap, dat jis' got to me, an' I made up my mine dat my boy should neber call me a coward." (p. 171)

Consider the contrast to Robert's timidly wooden response: "It is not to be expected," he says, "that these young people are going to put up with things as we did, when we weren't permitted to hold a meeting by ourselves, or to own a club or learn to read" (p. 171). Clearly, Harper has decentered and deconstructed her own text in her creation of the folk characters.

The folk character Aunt Linda functions somewhat like Toni Morrison's Baby Suggs in *Beloved*. By organizing forbidden prayer meetings, Aunt Linda acts as minister, providing a subversive support system that means survival for slaves who need her affirmation. As a minister, she has covert political power, which she uses to inspire her black audience to take control over their lives by voting, not for easy money from ill-intentioned, racist candidates, but for change in the quality of their lives. Aunt Linda urges every African American to find the power in him or herself to "wote [*sic*] right an to think somethin' ob demselves," and to stand together and "be a people" (p. 179).

To make certain that her undermining of Aunt Linda is not so successful as to obscure fully her role as a griot, Harper employs several devices. One of these is to have other folk characters echo Aunt Linda's radical sentiments. Jinnie shares Linda's contempt for those who would attempt to steal black people's votes. She firmly threatens to divorce her husband, Mr. Gundover's Dick, if he capitulates to the terrorist tactics of his boss, who threatens to fire him if Dick votes the radical ticket. Jinnie defiantly announces to Dick, "now ef yer wote dat ticket ter put me back inter slavery, you take yore rags an' go" (p. 177).

When Aunt Linda or other folk characters articulate particularly reactionary sentiments, Harper makes certain that these ideas are contradicted by other characters' thoughts, speeches, or actions. Linda and Tom both reflect prevailing turn-of-the-century racist sentiment about skin color and black vernacular. In praising an educated woman's language as being pretty, Aunt Linda appears to reject her own language, black vernacular, as ugly or inferior; Tom Anderson similarly appears to repudiate his own skin color. He perceives Iola as beautiful precisely because she fits the white tradition of accepted beauty: "My! but she's putty. Beautiful long hair comes way down her back; putty blue eyes, an jis' ez white ez anybody's in dis place" (p. 38). Tom's attraction to Iola is inextricably linked to his expectation that Iola will never be drawn to him because, as Robert describes him, Tom is "just as black as black can be" (p. 44). Tom's fear of rejection by Iola ("I don't spose she would think ob an ugly chap like me," p.42) is plaintive and affecting precisely because he reveals a genuineness and a vulnerability in his (mis)perception of himself as unattractive because dark-complected.

Skin color and passing—or more particularly the decision not to pass—are among the central themes of the novel (as they are of Harper's earlier novels, *Minnie's Sacrifice* and *Trial and Triumph*), with Harry, Iola, Robert, and Dr. Latimer all light enough to pass but choosing not to out of a complex admixture of motivations that includes self-respect, claiming what is familiar and known, the greater possibility of being reunited with family, and felt obligation; Iola, for example, notes that her education came at the expense of the "unrequited toil" of the slaves on her parents' plantation. She refuses the white Dr. Gresham's offer of marriage because of their radical differences, and the dark-skinned Lucille Delaney hesitates before accepting a marriage proposal from the white-enough-to-pass Harry, yet both Iola and Lucille seem convinced that colorism is a social problem of others and not something that they themselves may have internalized. Of the educated characters, Harry comes closest to not being a plaster saint in regard to issues of colorism and passing; Harper at least raises the issue of internalized colorism by having her narrator note that Harry's love for his mother Marie enables him to overcome "all repugnance" about claiming a black racial identity (p. 203). Yet when Harper wants to explore more complex and potentially volatile issues of race and skin color—the psychological ravages of internalized colorism on the interior life of black people—it is to her folk characters once again that she turns. As tricksters, they are charged with the obligation to disguise yet contain within their stories issues that Harper wants to explore with the black component of her dual audience.

Harper makes certain that a perceptive, racially conscious reader will know that she as author does not share Tom or Linda's color-struck viewpoint because the two most dark-skinned characters in the novel—so African in appearance that "neither hair not complexion shows the least hint of blood admixture" (p. 199)—the Reverend Carmicle and Lucille Delany—are not only acknowledged to be the most intellectually accomplished characters in the novel, but are seen as physically attractive as well; it is not accidental that the dark-skinned Lucille, for example, is chosen as a wife by the very light-skinned Harry, Iola's brother. Harper also provides subtle clues that the dark-skinned folk character Aunt Linda is not as uneducated as she appears to be. On at least one occasion, Harper reverses the roles of the allegedly knowledgeable and ignorant. Upon first seeing Robert after the war, Aunt Linda tells him, "I'd a knowed yer if I had seed yer in Europe." Robert is puzzled, and asks, "In Europe, Aunt Linda? Where's that?" (p. 153). In this instance, we see that Aunt Linda might be more knowledgeable than the light-skinned Robert, possessing knowledge of geography and possibly history as well. Yet, this passage is important for another reason too. When Aunt Linda casually dismisses Europe, she is dismissing all of western, European culture, all that Robert and Iola try to teach her about white culture and about what is acceptable. Aunt Linda needs neither white English, religion, and education, nor the justice system; rather, she insists on affirmation of her vernacular language, her spirituality (a black theology learned at the foot of the cross), and the vital education derived from life experience, black family life, and black folk wisdom. Harper subversively provides this affirmation by placing upon Aunt Linda as a character the crucial responsibility of translating these experiences to her black audience.

Harper provides numerous clues that encourage the reader to question the attitudes held by her more educated characters towards the folk characters. In Iola's conversations with Aunt Linda, she is "amused" at the "quaintness" of Aunt Linda's speech (p. 175); yet a scant six pages prior to this moment in the novel, Harper reveals Iola's response to Aunt Linda as not only cliché-ridden and sentimental, but bordering on racist. Aunt Linda's appearance triggers an apparently nostalgic memory of the good old plantation days when Iola, believing herself to be white, was the young mistress of a matronly black woman named Mam Liza: "Over Iola there stole a spirit of restfulness. There was something so motherly in Aunt Linda's manner that it seemed to recall the bright, sunshiny days when she used to nestle in Mam Liza's arms, in her own happy home" (p. 169). Iola's reverie of happy plantation life profoundly belies her own understanding of the nature of the institution of slavery and its consequences not only for those who were enslaved, but also for those who assumed the power of master or mistress. In this passage, Iola's objectification of Aunt Linda as a nurturing Mammy figure whose function is to provide comfort to others serves as a warning to her readers to mistrust those who sentimentalize or objectify the folk—be they racist white Southerners or educated mulattos.

Iola's relationship to Aunt Linda regarding alcohol provides another crucial arena in which to observe Harper's subversive "re-vision" of just who is "uplifting" whom. Aunt Linda, Iola, and Robert all espouse Harper's temperance views. But it is Aunt Linda who first and most seriously warns against the mind-numbing qualities of alcohol. Like those who denounce the use of crack cocaine in the black communities as a white weapon of subjugation, Aunt Linda tells Robert,

"Well, Bobby, I beliebs we might be a people ef it warn't for dat mizzable drink. . . . I wants some libe man to come down yere an' splain things ter dese people. I don't mean a politic man, but a man who'll larn dese people how to bring up dere chillen, to keep our gals straight, an' our boys from runnin' in de saloons an' gamblin' dens." (pp. 160–161)

Aunt Linda, like Harper, is unafraid of criticizing her own people; she stands for accountability. (She is so successfully disguised, however, that Houston Baker—entirely missing Harper's emphasis on Aunt Linda's crucial and entirely sober role as spokesperson for accountability—describes Aunt Linda as someone who "spends most of her words comically condemning the tomfoolery of her people, whom she labels 'niggers,' " Baker, p. 32). When Iola sanctimoniously rebukes Linda for criticizing her own people's foolish dependence on liquor, Aunt Linda insists, "I ain't runnin' down my people. But a fool's a fool wether he's white or black" (p. 16). Because Linda's temperance statement, "it does rile me ter see dese mean white men comin' down yere an' settin up dere grog-shops, tryin' to fedder dere nests sellin' licker to pore culled people. . . . An its a shame how dey do sling de licker 'bout election times" (pp. 159–160), is also a fierce denunciation of disenfranchisement, of the racist postbellum intention to use alcohol to have black people, for all intents and purposes, voting themselves back into slavery, Harper must have felt obliged to disguise and soften her radical statements, which she does by consistently undermining Aunt Linda, while simultaneously allowing her to articulate the viewpoint closest to Harper's own (p. 159). It is for this reason that, some pages after Aunt Linda speaks against alcohol and its role in disenfranchisement in the black community, Harper has her offer Iola and Robert some wine, thus setting the stage for Iola and Robert to rebuke Aunt Linda while professing their own temperance views. Iola condescendingly lectures, "Aunt Linda, the Bible says that wine at last will bite like a serpent and sting like an adder," a sanctimonious metaphor that Robert subsequently echoes (p. 185). Ironically, the young people here, of course, simply reiterate what Aunt Linda—with far more effectiveness and moral authority—has been saying about alcohol all along.[16]

Aunt Linda, not Iola, becomes the spokesperson for the most Afrocentric viewpoints in the novel. While Iola's Uncle Robert and her brother

Harry fight with courage for the Union Army, and Iola's tender ministrations as nurse to wounded Union soldiers likewise represent individual acts of involvement in the war effort, it is Aunt Linda who reveals as myth the idea that the Civil War was fought by whites over states' rights and slavery; it is she who ultimately stakes out the claim that blacks were central participants in the war and in the political and moral issues around which the war was fought, telling Robert, "somehow, Robby, I raley b'lieves dat we cullud folks is mixed up in dis fight. I seed it all in a vision" (p. 12). In this brief speech, Aunt Linda serves as Harper's double, echoing the language of one of Harper's most fiery speeches. "We Are All Bound Up Together" (quoted in Foster, ed., *A Brighter*, p. 217). That Harper entrusted this incendiary point of view to folk character Aunt Linda—with its attendant implication that the wisdom of the folk was a more appropriate vehicle for the assertion of this idea than the polite if ardent speech-making of her more educated characters—is not a literary accident, but something that had clearly been germinating for a considerable length of time in Harper's mind. Her earlier novel, *Minnie's Sacrifice,* foreshadows Aunt Linda's declaration that "we cullud folks is mixed up in this fight" in the words of folk character Miriam, who warns her educated and white-appearing mulatto son Louis, a double in some sense for *Iola Leroy*'s Harry, not to trust the secret of his racial identity to any white person, adding, "but if you meet any of the colored people, just tell them that you is for the Linkum soldiers, and it will be all right; we don't know all about this war, but we feels somehow we's all mixed up in it."[17]

The Civil War itself becomes the backdrop for a far more intimate struggle that takes place in the consciousness of the folk characters, one that follows an important convention of the slave narratives: what Frances Smith Foster describes as "an account of the manner by which the slave developed a concept of freedom" (*Witnessing Slavery,* p. 132). Like Aunt Linda's twentieth-century spokesperson, Baby Suggs, the folk characters in *Iola Leroy* discover that "freeing yourself was one thing; claiming ownership of that freed self was another" (Morrison, p. 95). Harper embodies the spiritual legacy of freedom in the folk character John Salters, Aunt Linda's husband, for it is through him that Harper elucidates not only the concept of resistance but the power of naming: what it means, as someone else's property, to be made to wear one's owner's name as an overt label of forced servitude, and finally, what it means to name oneself as an act of reclaiming oneself as one's own person. In casting off his slave name, John Andrews, Harper's character Salters seems an early source for Sherley Anne Williams's poems about the power of naming.[18] He explains, "got 'nuff ob my ole Marster in slave times, widout wearin' his name in freedom. Wen I got done wid him, I got done wid his name. . . . Now Salters is my name, an' I likes it better" (p. 167). Harper uses the folk character Tom Anderson as well for parables about naming. It is Tom who explains the self-empowerment that comes from naming oneself, as he tells Robert and Aunt Linda of a slave who insisted on keeping his place as a man with an historical past: "old Marse war trying to break him in, but dat fellow war spunk to de backbone. . . . He allers kep' his ole Guinea name . . . Potombra" (pp. 22–23). Through Tom, Harper reveals to the reader the importance of claiming the right to one's individuality, an African ancestry as represented by an African name, an identity that slavemasters and mistresses tried and failed to extinguish. Finally, parables about naming in this novel emerge in the names of the folk protagonists and in the title of the book itself. By naming the two most powerful folk characters, Linda and Daniel, "Aunt Linda" and "Uncle Daniel," titles suggesting servility, powerlessness, and humility, Harper provides them with a camouflage so effective it almost—but not quite—stops the reader from considering at last why, instead of *Iola Leroy,* this novel shouldn't have been titled *Linda Salters,* in honor of a fierce uneducated old ex-slave, in whose folk wisdom the meanings of the novel lie.[19]

Notes

A preliminary version of this essay was presented at the December 1992 Modern Language Association convention in New York. Some of the ideas contained in that version of the essay emerged out of a collaborative paper I wrote with the research assistance of two of my students, Jennifer Cost and Dhana Marie Branton; the paper, "Subversive Subtext in Frances Harper's *Iola Leroy,*" was presented at the 1990 Philological Association of the Pacific Coast. I would like to add that my reading of *Iola Leroy* has been deeply enriched by intellectually rigorous and emotionally inspiriting dialogues with a number of students, especially those from my Black Women Writers seminar in the fall of 1990, among them Victoria Featherstone, Beth Sherman, Regina Meister, Jill Holslin, Sue Reilly, and Sharen Rosenfeld, whose perceptive responses to the text have clearly informed and enlarged my own. I would also like to thank Henry Louis Gates, Jr., and Frances Smith Foster for their generosity in reading the earliest draft of this essay and offering suggestions and encouragement. I am also deeply indebted to Frances Smith Foster for her extraordinary generosity in making available to me her original research; she provided me with xeroxes of the microfiches of chapters of two early Harper novels, *Minnie's Sacrifice* (1869) and *Trial and Triumph* (1888), both serially published in the *Christian Recorder.* Finally, I would like to thank Elizabeth Ammons, whose painstaking editing of this essay enabled it to be a more graceful finished work than it otherwise would have been.

1. Sondra O'Neale's *MELUS* essay, "Race, Sex and Self: Aspects of *Bildung* in Select Novels by Black American Women Novelists," insists that "Iola, with her family and friends, builds an upper middle class island of nearly white pariahs who are devoted to uplifting the unfortunate 'shadows.'" She goes on to suggest that Harry's choice of a wife in whom "neither hair nor complexion show the least hint

of blood admixture" (*Iola Leroy,* p. 199) emphasizes the mulatto characters' "guilt and displacement" (p. 28). Sterling Brown refers to the character Iola as "another of the octoroon heroines too angelic for acceptance" (*The Negro in American Fiction,* pp. 76–77). Robert Bone falsely claims that the novel "lacked the urgency of other protest novels of the 1890's" (*The Negro Novel in America,* p. 32). Bone goes on to laud the 1894 novel *Appointed,* written by Walter Stowers and William H. Anderson, as "the first novel to treat peonage, convict labor, lynching, disenfranchisement and segregation as aspects of a systematic repression" (p. 32), yet all of these issues, with the exception of convict labor, are directly or indirectly referred to in Harper's novel, which was published two years earlier. William Still, Harper's contemporary, called *Iola Leroy* "an interesting, moral story-book," a comment meant to praise the book at the time, but one that certainly seems lukewarm at best today (rpt. in Harper, *Iola Leroy,* Beacon Press edition, 1987, p. 3). Houston Baker's 1991 critical study, *Workings of the Spirit* (p. 31), is the source for the comment about *Iola Leroy*'s allegedly "creakingly mechanical plot"; his assessment of the folk characters in the novel is no less dismissive, referring to one character as "poor self-sacrificial dialect-speaking Tom" (p. 31). Indeed, of all the critics from William Still (1871) to Hazel Carby (1987), only Nellie McKay suggests that if Harper "had published nothing else, *Iola Leroy* would have been sufficient for her to claim a place among the intellectuals of her time" (jacket blurb of the 1987 Beacon Press edition of *Iola Leroy*).

2. Introduction, *Iola Leroy,* Beacon Press, p. xix.

3. In a discussion with me following the presentation of an earlier version of this paper at the 1992 Modern Language Association trickster panel, Arlene Elder raised the possibility that my attribution of subversive or trickster qualities to the folk characters or my belief that Harper on some level intended to foreground them to a black audience was perhaps a bit of wish fulfillment, a casting of a 1990s spin on an 1890s text. Given my own research on the folk characters, and the new and rather elegant readings of Iola as a character by Elizabeth Young and P. Gabrielle Foreman ("Looking Back from Zora, or Talking Out Both Sides My Mouth for Those Who Have Two Ears") I feel on somewhat safer ground offering this new reading of the folk characters as considerably more complexly rendered than has been previously thought.

4. I would like to thank my student, Sue Reilly, for her thoughtful comments on Harper's use of mirroring in *Iola Leroy.*

5. This coded language is also discussed in Elizabeth Ammons, *Conflicting Stories,* chapter two, as well as by a number of other critics, among them Richard Yarborough, in his dissertation, and Hazel Carby, both in her introduction to the Beacon Press edition of *Iola Leroy* and in *Reconstructing Womanhood.* It is important to note that the use of folk characters as embodying a kind of folk literacy and as the bearers of codes and disguises appears not only in this novel, but also earlier in Harper's work. *Sketches of Southern Life* contains lines that are clearly a precursor to this scene in *Iola Leroy* ("The Deliverance," rpt. in Foster, ed., *A Brighter Coming Day,* pp. 198–204):

I used to watch old Mistus' face,
    And when it looked quite long
I would say to Cousin Milly,
    The battle's going wrong;
Not for us, but for the Rebels.—
    My heart would fairly skip,

When Uncle Jacob used to say,
"The North is bound to whip."

6. My thanks to Frances Smith Foster, who in her written response to the first draft of this essay first suggested to me the possibility that the woman hanging laundry sheets might be Aunt Linda (personal communication, 1990).

7. My meaning here is more metaphorical than literal. While clearly Harper has borrowed appropriate strategies from the trickster tradition to cloak but not disguise completely her radical intent, it is her characters, not Harper herself, who can most accurately be said to be tricksters. The complexity of Harper's narrative choices and expressive strategies (in contrast to the actions of their trickster characters, whose very following of the conventions of trickster behavior make them somewhat predictable) rules out the literal confounding of author with trickster.

8. That Harper felt an urgency to address her fiction not only to a white audience but also to a specifically black audience can scarcely be questioned. In her earlier novel, *Trial and Triumph,* she risked the censure of potential allies, black and white, for eschewing the rhetoric of uplift to expose and criticize a less than heroic aspect to life within the black community and the black family. In *Trial and Triumph,* the heroine, Annette, may share some of Iola's sublimation of individual self-interest for the common good, but Annette's black classmates are revealed as snobbish and unkind to the plain-featured young woman. Even her grandmother—more than a little cold-hearted—reveals a contempt for education, believing that Annette's interest in poetry is something that will cause her to "go crazy one of these days," and describing the time Annette devotes to such intellectual pursuits as literature as "a sin" (chapter 10, n.p.). In *Iola Leroy,* Harper appears to foreground both her educated mulatto characters and a sympathetic white audience, yet as in *Trial and Triumph,* her confrontation of such black-centered issues as alcoholism, the selling of votes, and internalized colorism leads us as readers again and again to the moments in the novel when the folk characters are foregrounded and taboo subjects are raised.

9. Daniel also reveals that Miss Anna, "Ole Marster's" wife, feels anguish at other aspects of her own powerlessness in relationship to her husband. Despite her wish to, she is unable to manumit Daniel; he quotes her telling him, "'Uncle Dan'el, I wish you war free. Ef I had my way you shouldn't serve any one when I'm gone; but Mr. Thurston had eberything in his power when he made his will. I war tied hand and foot, and I couldn't help it'" (p. 21). Behind the strained, often stilted diction of Harper's heroines and narrators lies a feminism that is startlingly contemporary. In a comment whose content if not style might have come from Ntozake Shange's pen, or Audre Lorde's, or Alice Walker's, Mrs. Harcourt, a character in Harper's earlier novel *Trial and Triumph,* posits, "I don't believe there would be so many trifling men if the boys were trained to be more helpful at home and to feel more for their mothers and sisters" (chapter 3, n.p.). In *Iola Leroy,* Harper's feminism appears in subtle as well as more overt statements. Aunt Linda's playful dialogue with her husband, John Salters, for example, has a purposeful feminist agenda:

"Ain't you men powerful 'ceitful?"

"Oh, Aunt Linda, don't put me in with the rest!"

"I don't know 'bout dat. Put you all in de bag for 'ceitfulness, an' I don't know which would git out fust." (p. 155)

10. Elizabeth Ammons's *Conflicting Stories* cites this same constellation of incidents in *Iola Leroy* as evidence of the racism of white women. My point in citing

the same material is to suggest that there is a qualitative difference between the relatively petty cruelties inflicted by white women and endured by Iola, and the brutally savage consequences of white women's racism as endured by Uncle Daniel, whose story, in my opinion, is *not* rendered "with a light touch" (p. 33).

11. Aunt Chloe's courage, her outspoken denunciation of vote selling, and her belief—one shared with Aunt Linda—that African Americans are "mixed up in dis fight" (*Iola Leroy,* p. 12) are all clues that link Aunt Chloe to Aunt Linda.

12. *Sketches of Southern Life,* rpt. in Foster, ed., *A Brighter Coming Day,* pp. 205–206; see also *Iola Leroy,* pp. 44–45.

13. *Sketches of Southern Life,* rpt. in Foster, ed., *A Brighter Coming Day,* pp. 205–206.

14. Quoted in Davis and Gates, *The Slave's Narrative,* p. xxviii. Harper's respect for a slave community in which traditional literacy may be absent but kindness and strategies of mutual support take its place is evocatively reported in the narratives themselves. See, for example, the interview with former slave Susan Davis in George P. Rawick, ed., *The American Slave: A Composite Autobiography,* vol. XI (Missouri Narratives), p. 284, quoted in Roberts (p. 93): "'People in my day,' reported Susan Davis, who had been enslaved in Missouri, 'didn't know book learning but dey studied how to protect each other, and save 'em from such misery as they could.'"

15. My thanks to Dhana Marie Branton for her description of Salters' grandson as a kind of Buckwheat figure (personal communication, 1990).

16. Aunt Linda's sense of outrage regarding the abusive use of alcohol as a form of domination and control is surely intended to allude to the misuse of alcohol as a device of social control not only during Reconstruction, but during slavery as well. John W. Roberts, citing both Genovese (pp. 642–643) and Blassingame (p. 209), points out that "while the practice of some slaveholders to provide enslaved Africans with opportunities to vent their frustrations and hostilities supported their interests in maintaining a contented work force, it did little for the maintenance of the moral and spiritual values that Africans had traditionally recognized or came to view as definitive of their identity" (p. 143). He goes on to cite Blassingame's observation that "many slaves tried to drown their anger in the whisky bottle, and if not drowned, the anger welling up was translated into many other forms. Sometimes the slave projected his aggression onto his fellow slaves: he might beat up, stab, or kill one of his fellow sufferers" (Blassingame, p. 209).

17. Harper's poem "The Deliverance" (1865–1875), also expresses this idea, one clearly of great importance to Harper, given its appearance in a speech, two novels and a poem:

> Though the house was very lonesome,
> I thought 'twould all come right,
> For I felt somehow or other
> We was mixed up
> in this fight.

(From *Sketches of Southern Life,* rpt. in Foster, ed., *A Brighter Coming Day,* pp. 198–204.)

18. Forced to live in a world in which speech and naming is forbidden, even the right to name her own children, Odessa (the character who becomes Dessa in *Dessa Rose*), who is also the speaker in Williams's poem "I Sing This Song for Our Mothers," paradoxically claims the power of naming:

I say yo name
now and that be love. I say
yo daddy name and that be
how I know free. I say Harker
name and that be how I
keep loved and keep free . . . (Williams, pp. 79–82)

19. Joanne Braxton's observations of Harriet Jacobs' character Linda Brent as a trickster figure who "employs warfare and defensive verbal postures as tools of liberation" (*Black Women Writing Autobiography,* pp. 30–31) should encourage us to speculate whether Harper had the Linda Brent character—and the idea of the trickster—in mind when she provided her most important folk character with the name "Linda," especially as more than one critic has noted the possible historical origin of names of other characters, including Lucille Delaney, Frank Latimer, Dr. Latrobe, and Iola herself (Ernest, p. 509). Even Jacobs's title *Incidents in the Life of a Slave Girl* suggests a trickster at work, for it employs in the word "incidents" a classic device of both tricksters and slave narratives: understatement.

Works Cited

Ammons, Elizabeth. *Conflicting Stories: American Women Writers at the Turn into the Twentieth Century.* New York: Oxford University Press, 1991.

Baker, Houston A., Jr. *Workings of the Spirit: The Poetics of Afro-American Women's Writings.* Chicago: University of Chicago Press, 1991.

Barton, William Eleazar. *Old Plantation Hymns.* New York: Lamson, Wolffe and Co., AMS Press, 1972.

Blassingame, John W. *The Slave Community: Plantation Life in the Antebellum South,* 2nd ed. New York: Oxford University Press, 1979.

Bone, Robert. *The Negro Novel in America.* New Haven: Yale University Press, 1965.

Bontemps, Arna, and Langston Hughes. *The Book of Negro Folklore.* New York: Dodd, 1958.

Braxton, Joanne M. *Black Women Writing Autobiography.* Philadelphia: Temple University Press, 1989.

Brooks, Gwendolyn. *A Street in Bronzeville.* New York: Harper, 1945. Rpt. in *The World of Gwendolyn Brooks.* New York: Harper, 1971.

Brown, Sterling A., Arthur P. Davis, and Ulysses Lee. *The Negro Caravan: Writings by American Negroes.* New York: Dryden, 1941.

Brown, Sterling A. *The Negro in American Fiction.* 1937. Rpt. New York: Atheneum, 1969.

Brown, William Wells. *Clotel: or the President's Daughter, A Narrative of Slave Life in the United States.* London, 1853. Rpt. New York: Arno, 1969.

Carby, Hazel V. *Reconstructing Womanhood: The Emergence of the Afro-American Woman Novelist.* New York: Oxford University Press, 1987.

———. "Introduction." In Frances E. W. Harper. *Iola Leroy, or Shadows Uplifted.* Boston: Beacon Press, 1987.

Christian, Barbara. *Black Women Novelists: The Development of a Tradition 1892–1976.* Westport, Conn.: Greenwood Press, 1980.

Cone, James H. *The Spirituals and the Blues: An Interpretation.* New York: Seabury Press, 1972.

Davis, Charles T., and Henry Louis Gates, Jr. *The Slave's Narrative.* New York: Oxford University Press, 1985.

Douglass, Frederick. *Narrative of the Life of Frederick Douglass: An American Slave.* Boston: Boston Anti-Slavery Society, 1845. Rpt. Garden City: Doubleday and Co., Dolphin Books, 1963.

Elder, Arlene A. *The "Hindered Hand": Cultural Implications of Early African-American Fiction.* Westport, Conn.: Greenwood Press, 1978.

Ellison, Ralph. *Invisible Man.* 1952. Rpt. New York: Vintage, 1980.

Ernest, John. "From Mysteries to Histories: Cultural Pedagogy in Frances E. W. Harper's *Iola Leroy.*" *American Literature* 64 (1992): 497–518.

Foreman, P. Gabrielle. "Looking Back from Zora, or Talking Out Both Sides My Mouth for Those Who Have Two Ears." *Black American Literature Forum* 24 (1990): 649–666.

Foster, Frances Smith, ed. *A Brighter Coming Day: A Frances Ellen Watkins Harper Reader.* New York: Feminist Press, 1990.

———, ed. *Iola Leroy, or Shadows Uplifted.* By Frances E. W. Harper. The Schomburg Library of Nineteenth Century Black Women Writers. New York: Oxford University Press, 1988.

———. *Witnessing Slavery: The Development of the Ante-Bellum Slave Narrative.* Westport, Conn.: Greenwood Press, 1979.

Gates, Henry Louis, Jr., ed. *Black Literature and Literary Theory.* New York: Methuen, 1984.

———. "Criticism in the Jungle." In *Black Literature and Literary Theory,* ed. Gates. New York: Methuen, 1984.

———, ed. *Three Classic African-American Novels.* New York: Vintage Press, 1990.

Genovese, Eugene D. *Roll, Jordan, Roll: The World the Slaves Made.* New York: Vintage Books, 1976.

Gloster, Hugh M. *Negro Voice in American Fiction.* New York: Russell and Russell, 1948.

Harper, Frances E. W. *Iola Leroy, or Shadows Uplifted.* Philadelphia: Garrigues Brothers, 1892. Rpt. Boston: Beacon Press, 1987.

———. *Minnie's Sacrifice. The Christian Recorder.* N. vol. Philadelphia: 1869.

———. *Sketches of Southern Life.* Philadelphia: Merrihew, 1872. Rpt. in Frances Smith Foster, ed. *A Brighter Coming Day: A Frances Ellen Watkins Harper Reader.* New York: Feminist Press, 1990.

———. *Trial and Triumph. The Christian Recorder.* N. vol. Philadelphia: 1888.

Hedin, Raymond. "The Structuring of Emotion in Black American Fiction." *Novel* (Fall 1982): 35–54.

Hemenway, Robert. *Zora Neale Hurston: A Literary Biography.* Chicago: University of Illinois Press, 1977.

Jacobs, Harriet. *Incidents in the Life of a Slave Girl,* ed. Jean Fagin Yellin. Cambridge: Harvard University Press, 1987.

Morrison, Toni. *Beloved.* New York: Knopf, 1987.

Nardo, Anna K. "'Sung and Proverb'd for a Fool': Samson as Fool and Trickster." *Mosaic* 11, no. 1 (1989): 1–16.

Nichols, Charles H. "The Slave Narrators and the Picaresque Mode: Archetypes for Modern Black Personae." In Charles T. Davis and Henry Louis Gates, Jr. *The Slave's Narrative.* New York: Oxford University Press, 1985.

Northrup, Solomon. *Twelve Years a Slave*. 1853. Rpt. New York: Dover Publications, 1970.

O'Neale, Sondra. "Race, Sex and Self: Aspects of *Bildung* in Select Novels by Black American Women Novelists." *MELUS* 9 (1982): 25–37.

Rawick, George P., ed. *The American Slave: A Composite Autobiography*. Westport, Conn.: Greenwood Press, 1977.

Rhys, Jean. *Wide Sargasso Sea*. 1966. Rpt. New York: W. W. Norton, 1982.

Roberts, John W. *From Trickster to Badman: The Black Folk Hero in Slavery and Freedom*. Philadelphia: University of Pennsylvania Press, 1989.

Spillers, Hortense. "Mama's Baby, Papa's Maybe: An American Grammar Book." *Diacritics* 17 (1987): 65–81.

Stowe, Harriet Beecher. *Uncle Tom's Cabin: or, Life among the Lowly*. Boston: John P. Jewett and Co., 1852.

Wideman, John Edgar. "Charles Chesnutt and the WPA Narratives: The Oral and Literate Roots of Afro-American Literature." In Charles T. Davis and Henry Louis Gates, Jr. *The Slave's Narrative*. New York: Oxford University Press, 1985.

Williams, Sherley Anne. *The Peacock Poems*. Middletown, Conn.: Wesleyan University Press, 1975.

Yarborough, Richard Alan. *The Depiction of Blacks in the Early Afro-American Novel*. Ph.D. diss., Stanford University, 1980.

Young, Elizabeth. "Warring Fictions: *Iola Leroy* and the Color of Gender." *American Literature* 64 (1992): 273–297.

Contributors

ELIZABETH AMMONS is Professor of English and of American Studies at Tufts University. She is the author of *Conflicting Stories: American Women Writers at the Turn into the Twentieth Century* (1991) and *Edith Wharton's Argument With America* (1980). She is the author of numerous essays on U.S. women writers, and the editor of several volumes, including *Short Fiction by Black Women, 1900–1920* (1991).

ERIC ANDERSON is a doctoral candidate in English and American literature at Rutgers University, where he is completing a dissertation titled "Southwestern Dispositions: American Literature on the Borderlands, 1880–1990."

ALANNA KATHLEEN BROWN is Associate Professor of English at Montana State University. She has published articles on Mourning Dove in *Plainswoman, The Wicazo Sa Review, Legacy, Canadian Literature, Studies in American Indian Literatures,* and *The Women's Review of Books,* as well as in essay collections: *Native Writers and Canadian Writing, Old West–New West: Centennial Essays,* and *New Voices in Native American Literary Criticism.*

JULIA FARWELL is a doctoral candidate at Tufts University, where she is working on a dissertation on the literary representation of American national borders.

LYNDA KOOLISH is Associate Professor of English at San Diego State University, where she teaches African American, Ethnic American, and Feminist literature. Her work has appeared in *Signs, Feminist Studies, Mosaic, MELUS,* and elsewhere; she is now completing a book on Toni Morrison and the feminist re-visioning of the slave narrative, which will be published in 1995.

ALEXIA KOSMIDER has master's degrees from Brown University and the University of New Mexico, and a Ph.D. from the University of Rhode Island. Her dissertation, "Tricky Tribal Discourses: The Poetry, Fables, and Short Story Writing of Alex Posey," is under consideration for publication as a book.

TIFFANY ANA LÓPEZ is editor of *Growing up Chicana/o* (1993). She is a doctoral candidate at the University of California at Santa Barbara in the departments of English and Women's Studies, and an affiliate of Chicana/o Studies. Her dissertation explores the relationship between Latina drama and coalition building.

YUKO MATSUKAWA is Visiting Assistant Professor of English at Tufts University. She has completed a long study on turn-of-the-century transatlantic writing and representations of American women in Europe. Her essay in this volume on Onoto Watanna is part of her current work, which explores how early twentieth-century American women artists imagined the Orient.

KAREN OAKES is Assistant Professor at the University of Hull in England. She has taught American literature, Women's Studies, and American Studies at Brandeis University, Colby College, Tufts University, and the State University of New York at Albany, and she has published essays in feminist theory and cross-cultural studies.

JEANNE SMITH teaches at the University of Texas at Arlington. She has published an essay on Louise Erdrich in *SAIL* and is completing a book on tricksters in the works of three contemporary American women writers: Erdrich, Maxine Hong Kingston, and Toni Morrison.

ANNETTE WHITE-PARKS is Associate Professor of English at the University of Wisconsin–La Crosse. She is the author of a book-length study, *Sui Sin Far: The Beginnings of Chinese North American Literature* (1995) and editor, with Amy Ling, of *Selected Works of Sui Sin Far* (1995).

Index

UNIVERSITY PRESS OF NEW ENGLAND publishes books under its own imprint and is the publisher for Brandeis University Press, Brown University Press, Dartmouth College, Middlebury College Press, University of New Hampshire, University of Rhode Island, Tufts University, University of Vermont, Wesleyan University Press, and Salzburg Seminar.

Library of Congress Cataloging-in-Publication Data
Tricksterism in turn-of-the-century American literature : a multicultural perspective / edited by Elizabeth Ammons and Annette White-Parks.
p. cm.
Includes bibliographical references (p.) and index.
ISBN 0-87451-680-3
1. American literature—19th century—History and criticism.
2. American literature—20th century—History and criticism.
3. American literature—Minority authors—History and criticism.
4. American literature—Women authors—History and criticism.
5. Trickster in literature. 6. Individualism in literature.
7. Ethnic groups in literature. 8. Folklore in literature.
I. Ammons, Elizabeth. II. White-Parks, Annette.
PS217.T79T75 1994
810.9'920693—dc20 94-20520
∞